IS FANATIC ISLAM A GLOBAL THREAT?

by
Victor Mordecai

December 1997
Fifth Printing
Revised and Expanded Edition

Direct inquiries to:

Victor Mordecai
P.O. Box 18209
Jerusalem, Israel 91181
Fax: 011 972 2 629 0574 Ext. 7157

For reordering this book in the U.S.
1-800-540-0828

www.vicmord.com
email: vicmord2001@yahoo

ISBN 1-931600-12-0

Table Of Contents

Preface 5

Introduction 9

1. The Biblical Basis of Judeo-Christian Civilization: A Similarity and a Difference Between Christians and Jews 19

2. A Short History of Islam 37

3. The Role of the Media 43

4. One World Government Allied with Islam 55

5. Is Islam un-American 71

6. Israel's Striving for Peace in the Middle East vs. Fanatic Islam 77

7. Israel's Dilemma in Returning Territories 81

8. Iran's Nuclear Capability, Subversive Activities in Europe and Persecution of Christians 95

9. Iranian Persecution Of Its Own Christian Citizens .. 111

10. Islamic Persecution of Christians in the Holy Land . 123

11. Palestinian Authority: Realities 143

12. Israel's Moral Duty Towards Christian South Lebanon 153

13. Massacre Victims Mourned 157

14. Algeria: Islamic Fratricide — Islamic Self-Destruction 165

15. Afghanistan: Another Islamic Hell Bordering On The Ridiculous 173

16. Global Conflicts With Ishmael — Islam 177

17. The Islamic Genocide In Africa 195

18. Farrakhan's Swamp Of Hatred 221

19. Testimony Of A Martyr — Rashad Khalifa 233

Conclusions 257

Addenda 269

Appendix 277

First printing: January, 1995
Merrick, New York
1,000 copies / 63 pages

Second printing: May, 1995
Merrick, New York
1,000 copies / 93 pages

Third printing: February, 1996
Springfield, Missouri
1,000 copies / 170 pages

Fourth printing A: May, 1996
Springfield, Missouri
5,000 copies / 200 pages

Fourth printing B: July, 1996
Springfield, Missouri
5,000 copies / 200 pages

Fifth printing A: December, 1997
Taylors, South Carolina
10,000 copies / 280 pages

Fifth printing B: September, 1998
Taylors, South Carolina
10,000 copies / 280 pages

Fifth printing C: October, 2001
Taylors, South Carolina
10,000 copies / 280 pages

Fifth printing D: November, 2002
Taylors, South Carolina
10,000 copies / 280 pages

Preface

The Islamic Threat to Judeo-Christian Western Civilization

Any student of World War II and the Holocaust interested in acquiring hindsight must read the book "Mein Kampf" written by Adolf Hitler while in a Munich jail in 1923. Scoffed at by critics, Hitler was considered a buffoon and a guttersnipe. No one took him seriously.

Hitler may have been crazy, or may have suffered from different megalomanic complexes, but Hitler was honest when he wrote "Mein Kampf." Everything he wrote in this book he meant and later carried out. Hitler had no hidden agenda. The fact that few read his book, or did not take him seriously, was not Adolf Hitler's fault.

Today, with the power of oil and the petrodollar, radical fanatic Islam has been able, after hundreds of years of submission to the more powerful world of Christendom, to again raise its head and to entertain dreams of conquering or converting the entire world to the Islamic religion. It is Ayatollah Janati, a leading Moslem cleric in the Iranian government, who has said again and again: "The 21st century will be the century of Islam."

It is Bosnian Prime Minister Alija Izetbegovitch who wrote his doctoral thesis on how he would take Bosnia, break away from the Yugoslav Republic and turn Bosnia into an Islamic fundamentalist state.

It is the Koran which serves as a guide, as a "Mein Kampf" to these two gentlemen. The Koran is the "infallible and divine revelation of Allah to Mohammed His prophet" which cannot be amended or interpreted in any other than a literal meaning and says:

"Believers, take neither Jews nor Christians for your friends. They are friends with one another. Whoever of you seeks their friendship shall become one of their number. God does not guide the wrongdoers."
Chapter V "The Table" (page 116 of the Arabic and English Penguin Classics Version).

Just as reading Hitler's "Mein Kampf" was a sure giveaway to understanding the Nazi system, so, too, is the Koran a book which must be read by all, Jew, Christian and Moslem alike, in order to understand the aims and goals of the radical Islamic powers.

Similarly, just as Josef Goebbels was the Nazi master of propaganda and disinformation for foreign needs, the Nazi press for local domestic needs told the Germans exactly what the Nazi regime intended to do. So, too, is the Islamic press a clear guideline in Arabic or Persian to the Moslem believers as to what to do to the corrupt West, the Great Satan - America, or America's agent in the Middle East - Israel.

The questions again arise: Are America's Christians and Jews aware they are the target? Is the democracy of America and the world endangered? Is there a danger that the State of Israel will be destroyed by its radical Islamic enemies? All one must do is read the Koran, Hadith and the Islamic press. Unfortunately, the vast majority of people in America and in the world have not read any of these.

There are those who scoff at the Islamic threat to America and to Israel and the entire world. There are those who think that this is just a passing phenomenon. I pray I am wrong, but my fear is that radical Islam will be around for the next 70 years, or at least, as long as the world runs on petroleum energy. As long as radical Islam is around, America, Israel and all other non-Islamic entities are at risk, possibly, ABC risk (atomic, biological and chemical weaponries).

It is, therefore, with great appreciation that I thank my wife of 25 years who was born in Cairo, Egypt, and lived the first 20 years of her life there; the Government Press Office which is part of the Prime Minister's Office in Jerusalem, Israel; and finally, the Jerusalem Institute for Western Defense which deals with providing America and the world with up-to- date translations from the

Islamic press, the three major sources of information for giving me insights into the Koran and the Islamic press, which reveal clearly what are the Islamic global designs for world domination.

Unfortunately, most Americans are fed on a diet of "trash-news," an insult to the intelligence of the average American. Since 1994, I have witnessed the inordinate amount of news dedicated to Lorena Bobbitt, Tanya Harding, Whitewater, O.J. Simpson, Mrs. Smith killing her two sons, other various heinous crimes in the streets, and, of course, sports.

Not mentioned is the genocidal slaughter by Moslems of at least two million Christians in Sudan over the last few years, the continuing genocide over the last two decades by Moslems of Catholics and Protestants on the Indonesian archipelago island of East Timor, as well as a long list of other modern day atrocities against all religious groups by Moslem fundamentalists.

For some reason, there is an agenda by the media to squelch any negative news item involving Moslems. The attempted blowing up of the twin towers of the World Trade Center in New York City by Moslems was at first attributed by CNN to Serbian nationalists! When a bomb went off in a Paris subway station in July 1995 causing the deaths of several innocent commuters, again the Serbians were blamed, when later it was proved to be an Islamic Algerian bomb. Why are Americans not better informed about why US airports and aircrafts are under ever increasing security alerts? Why was the Islamic involvement in the Oklahoma City bombing ignored by the press? Why is the thought of TWA800 being shot down by an Islamic missile too terrible even to consider?

The question must be asked, why? The answer must be given: there is an agenda to block American eyes and minds from what really is going on in the world. Eyes must be opened to sensitive questions which may be considered politically incorrect by the powers that be and, therefore, are censored at the major media centers.

I hope this book will serve as an eye-opener and wake-up call.

Introduction

I feel it is incumbent upon me to make a confession about two sins I have committed, sins of ignorance and prejudice.

Having been born four years after the end of the Holocaust at the same time that the newly nascent State of Israel was fighting for its survival in its war of independence against seven invading Arab armies, I was a product of an environment and society greatly influenced by these two events. Having lived the first 19 years of my life in the New York area alone, I was also shaped by a mentality typical of only one area in the U.S. — the "liberal" northeast.

I made my move to Israel, my "aliyah" to Israel in 1968, partly because I felt and still feel that Israel is where the future of the Jewish people lies, but mainly, secondly, and this is my first confession, because it had been inculcated in me by my teachers, neighbors, and peers, that all the gentiles "hated" us as was the experience taught to us so painfully by the Holocaust. On the other hand, many people, including my sister who still lives in the midwest, told me that I had not given the U.S. a chance — that my experience in New York did not typify all of the American people. But still, my mind was made up, and so I moved to Israel. And thank God that I did.

In 1986, about 18 years after having moved to Israel, I read an advertisement placed by Ray and Sharon Sanders of CFI (Christian Friends of Israel) in the Israeli English language daily, "The Jerusalem Post". The advertisement was seeking English language Israeli penpals for Christian Zionists all over the world. Since my children were at that time studying in middle school, or junior high, I thought that for them, writing to young American penpals would really whip their English into shape. So my kids agreed, and this was the beginning of a relationship which was to change my life forever. Because of numerous excuses, my kids never really got into the letter-writing and I began corresponding with the mother of the two American Christian teenagers.

Four years of correspondence and friendship with this dear Christian woman in San Antonio, Texas, brought an unexpected dividend. After leaving Prime Minister Yitzhak Shamir's Government Press Office in October 1990, I found myself, all of a sudden, invited by this Christian woman to speak in numerous churches, synagogues, radio, TV shows, and other civic groups.

Her church in New Braunfels, Texas, the first church I ever spoke in or attended in my life, was an experience never to be forgotten. It was a beautiful cross-section of America. There were blacks, "Tex-Mex" hispanics, and of course, white Americans, all holding hands and praying to God together as one body. The pastor gave an impassioned sermon of support for Israel, and why Christians must love Israel.

When my turn came to speak, I noticed that many of the white congregants looked really quite "aryan". Indeed, New Braunfels, Texas is the heart of "New Bavaria", an area settled by German immigrants about 170 years ago. I was baffled because there in front of me sat hundreds of blond and blue-eyed Americans of German extraction praying for the peace of Jerusalem. How strange it seemed to me. All my life I had been told that all Germans genealogically hated all us Jews genealogically, no matter where they were. All of a sudden, here they were — the descendants of immigrants from over a century ago praising Israel and the Lord with their hands raised in the air and tears streaming down their faces. How could I hate these people? How could I not love them? Did these Americans of German descent kill a single Jew in America? No, of course not. So there was no collective guilt here. Did the Jews as a nation collectively kill Jesus? No. Jesus according to the New Testament was a miracle worker, a rabbi, and revolutionary social reformer. He was a threat to the Roman one-world government establishment of that time. He overturned the moneychangers' tables and was crucified by a few corrupt scared people who ruled Rome and Herodian Palestine at that time. By the way, our very own Hasmonean King Alexander Yannai crucified 800 Pharisee rabbis in one day in the year 100 BCE simply because he was a Sadducee and had a disagreement with the Pharisees. There was nothing personal about it. It was just the way in those days, accounts were settled. If you believed in something, you just had to be ready to pick up your cross to pay for your beliefs. This is a well known literary genre throughout Midrashic literature. So it suddenly dawned on me that just as the Jews as a people did not kill Jesus, so, neither did these "diaspora" American Germans kill the Jews in the Holocaust. I sinned against them for the first 40 years of my life.

Indeed ever since November 1990, when I began speaking in churches around America and visiting all the different Christian denominations in the US, I have come to realize how wrong and prejudiced I was that indeed I did not give the US a chance, and that there are many, maybe most, Christians who do love Israel. Never have the Jews been murdered in America for being Jews. There were never crusades, inquisitioins, expulsions, pogroms or a Holocaust or any other form of persecution inflicted upon the Jews as elsewhere in the world. So, it was wrong for me to categorize America's Christians as hating the Jews or hating Israel. And this applies to all the Christian denominations in America. This was my first sin. As I travelled around the US "old-timers" explained to me about how their forefathers fled the persecutions of the mainline churches in Europe. Groups such as the Pilgrims, Puritans, Quakers, Huguenots, and many more came to America to be free to worship as they wished, and these founding fathers and mothers created an America which was "one nation under God, indivisible with liberty and justice for all" including the Jews and any other religion.

The second was a sin of ignorance. At age 40, after 21 years of living in Israel, I was humbled before the Lord by this Christian woman from the hill country of Texas who showed me just how ignorant I was of my own books, let alone the book of the Christians - The New Testament. Every letter I would receive from her would have quotes from Isaiah, Psalms, Ezekiel, etc., and I was just totally inadequate in dealing with this. It is to this woman that I am indebted for convincing me to go, at age 41, to study for three years for a Masters program at the Masorti Movement's Seminary for Judaic Studies (affiliated with the conservative movement's Jewish Theological Seminary of America) in Jerusalem, Israel.

Today, at age 48, I feel just a little bit more adequate, though most of the black holes in my knowledge still remain. It is in this spirit that I hope to devote the rest of my life to studying God's word, and to sharing with both Jews and Christians all that I have learned. I am guided by something that Rabbi Abraham Joshua Heschel, former dean of the Jewish Theological Seminary once said: "When you pray to God, you speak to God, but when you study God's word (The Bible) God speaks to you."

One last observation I would like to make to both Jew and Christian is that just as this Texan friend of mine taught me that a Christian had to learn the Jewish texts to better understand Christianity, so I have concluded that Jews must also (after they have studied Jewish texts) read The New Testament because this book sheds much light on the period of the oral tradition — the Mishna and Talmud which were the crucibles of rabbinic thought which formed modern day Judaism, and helps to shed light on many rabbinical issues of that period and many of which are even being addressed today.

After 2,000 years of Judeo-Christian polemics, the time has come to dialogue and to study together, not only because Jews and Christians pray to the same God, the God of Abraham, Isaac and Jacob, but that the two main commandments of The New Testament are Jewish commandments: Love the Lord *thy God with all thy heart, with all thy soul, and with all thy might; and secondly, love thy neighbor as thyself.* (Mark 12:28-31), and (Deuteronomy 6:4-9 and Leviticus 19:18).

But above and beyond that which unites in theology, there is indeed another reason for us to put our minds and hearts together: the mutual enemy which seeks the destruction of what it calls the Great Satan: Judeo-Christian America, and any and all religions other than itself: radical, fundamentalist Islam.

Just as I have come to realize my sins of prejudice and ignorance towards Christians in general and America's Christians in particular, so have I come to realize how much Jews and Christians must now work together not only to glorify and sanctify God's name, but very frankly, in order to survive the Islamic tidal wave which threatens to sweep both our biblical religions into the sea of destruction.

It is for this reason that I write this book: to help foster this Judeo-Christian alliance in order to save Israel, which cannot stand alone, to save America and its democracy from the new evil empire based in Iran and certain other Islamic countries, but also save the entire world which is radical Islam's target. This includes Buddhists and Hindus, half the world's population, who are slated for destruction at the hands of Islam since they are considered pagans to be put to the sword. Last, but not least, it is the billion or more Moslems in the world who will be the first to suffer the fundamentalist radical brand of Khomeini Islam should it rise to power — especially 50% of the Moslems, the women who are downtrodden and in status lower than slaves. Indeed, the Bangladeshi lawyer, Taslima Nasreen, a good Moslem who wants to improve the status of women in Moslem countries, is now on the death list of the religious radicals in her country — merely because she wanted to amend the Moslem holy book — the Koran — in order to improve the status of women in the Islamic world.

In verse 34 of chapter IV of the Koran, entitled: "Women" it says:

"Men have authority over women because God has made the one superior to the other, and because they spend their wealth to maintain them. Good women are obedient. They guard their unseen parts because God has guarded them. As for those from whom you fear disobedience, admonish them and send them to beds apart and beat them."

And indeed, since the Koran must be taken literally, and is by devout Moslem men, women are routinely beaten for disobedience or even disagreeing with their husbands because it is commanded so in the Koran. This is what Taslima Nasreen wanted amended. This is what got her the death sentence from Islamic radicals.

Because, as it says in the Koran: "When our clear revelations are recited to them, those who entertain no hope of meeting us say to you: 'Give us a different Koran, or make some changes in it.'

"Say: It is not for me to change it. I follow only what is revealed to me. I cannot disobey my Lord, for I fear the punishment of a fateful day.'"

(From the Koran's chapter "Jonah" verse 15, page 209 in the Penguin Classics Koran).

A final point embedded somewhere in the back of my childhood memories: My grandfather told me about the hunger and misery of his life in Warsaw, Poland under the Russian Czarist administration. When the German army marched into Poland in World War I, the Jews greeted the German invaders as liberators. Indeed, the German officers and soldiers were perfect gentlemen. They fed the starving Jews, provided them with livelihoods and removed the Czarist yoke of suffering from the necks of the Polish Jews. Up until 1933, Germany was one of the most advanced, civilized and progressive countries in the world. It blessed its Jews.

From January 1933, with Hitler's rise to power, there was a change in Germany. Satan took over, and the Jews were now slated for destruction. It was impossible for the Polish Jews of 1939 to believe that such a transformation or metamorphosis could have taken place in the psyche of the German nation that this time the Wehrmacht would come as mass murderers.

With the allied victory in Europe in May 1945, "western Judeo-Christian civilization and democracy" were imposed on West Germany by the Americans, the British and the French. Again, Germany behaved well with the Jews and so it was again a blessed country, one of the most desirable in the world in which to live.

Indeed, I wanted to conclude this preface by saying that just as I have learned from my experience in New Braunfels, Texas not to hate the German people for what they did to the Jewish people during the holocaust — merely the Satanic Hitlerian system — so, too, do I not hate the Moslem people — but only the Satanic system as propagated by the Teheran regime of the ayatollahs, and their satellites.

A brief look at history shows the positive role of Persia in the history of the Jewish people. In 516 BCE, seventy years after the Babylonian destruction of the 1st Temple in Jerusalem and the exile of the Judeans, it was the Persian King Cyrus, described as "messiah" in the Bible who allowed the Jews to return to Jerusalem, permitted, encouraged and even supported the building of the Second Temple.

The famous Persian story of a near holocaust followed by the salvation of the Jewish people in the kingdom of Ahasuerus ends with a Jewish Queen Esther and Prime Minister Mordecai ensuring Jewish life in Persia-Iran down to this very day.

Finally, it was the Persians in 614 AD (CE) who conquered the Holy Land from the Byzantines and delivered the Jews from Orthodox Christian persecution, at least until the invading Moslem Arab armies arrived in Jerusalem in 638.

Indeed, the Iranian people until 1979, were Israel's allies and friends under Shah Reza Pahlevi's Peacock Throne. Ayatollah Khomeini deposed the Shah together with a coalition of democratic, socialist, and women's groups, but like Hitler, immediately turned upon his coalition partners and usurped power. Today's Iranian leadership seeks the total extermination of Israel just as the Nazis did. But hopefully, a way will be found to return a non-Satanic and hopefully democratic system to the Persian people, with whom Israel has never ever had a quarrel.

I also wanted to stress that many of the Moslems living today in America are Iranian Moslems who fled the tyranny of Ayatollah Khomeini and came to America because they had been allies of the west and were slated for destruction by the Islamic fanatics. Most Moslems are wonderful people just like people anywhere, it is only the satanic system seeking the total destruction of the Jews and Christians which must be checked.

It is now time for all good people of all religions, including moderate and open-minded Moslems, to come together to preserve the greatness of America's traditions and democracy; the budding and emerging democracies, in Latin America, the former Soviet bloc as well as the rest of the world, which are now threatened by radical fanatic Islam.

I would like to dedicate this book to America, to its people of all religions, races and creeds who follow Voltaire's credo: "I may not agree with what you have to say, but I will defend with my life your right to say it"; and finally, to those abstract terms, democracy and freedom, which one does not appreciate until they are lost.

Having lived in the Middle East for these last 28 years, I think I can say that I love America and its people more today than ever before, even if it is from afar, or maybe, especially, because of this geographic and physical distance, but seeing how tenuous human rights and democracy are in the Middle East, it is all the more reason to appreciate that which I took for granted in my youth in America, that which cannot be taken for granted any longer either in this mean part of the world or even in the democratic west in which I was nurtured.

My conclusions, at age 48, after experiencing what America is all about, what the Middle East is all about, and what the new "evil empire" of fanatic Islam threatening us is all about, force me to put into print that which is in my heart, my soul, and my mind — to share with you, my readers, that fear, that warning of things to come which religious people say was prophesied in all monotheistic texts — the war between good and evil — the end of days — Armageddon.

IS FANATIC ISLAM A GLOBAL THREAT?

Chapter One

The Biblical Basis
of Judeo-Christian Civilization:
A Similarity and a Difference Between
Christians and Jews

It is a prophecy of both Judaism and Christianity that the Messiah will come (or return a second time) at the end of days. The difference between Judaism and Christianity rests almost entirely on whether it is the first or second coming. But the Messiah, when He comes, will, of course, be the same Messiah for all. Then, presumably, arguments and rhetoric between Jews and Christians will at last end.

To illustrate this point, there is a popular joke told by many Israeli emissaries to Christian audiences in America:

The Messiah is reported by the press to be standing on the Mount of Olives awaiting his triumphal entry onto Mount Moriah in Jerusalem. The Israeli government, of course, is now in a dilemma. Is it the Messiah of the first or second coming? So it is decided in Jerusalem to phone up the police chief at Ben Gurion International Airport in charge of passport control to shine his shoes, button up his shirt, and drive immediately up to the Mount of Olives and ask the Messiah: "Excuse me, Sir, but is this your first visit to Israel?"

Again, the bottom line here is that Judaism and Christianity are essentially the same religion, with the emphasis being on charity, righteousness, prayer, and belief in the precepts of the Bible, the coming of the Messiah, and the afterlife.

The coming of the Messiah will be preceded by tribulations, wars, and just generally, difficult times. But the Messiah, both for Jews and Christians, is a man of love. The religions are religions of love.

Compare Old and New Testaments:

In Deuteronomy VI: 4-9, it says:

4. *Hear, O Israel: The Lord is our God, The Lord is One.*
5. *You shall love the Lord your God with all your heart and with all your soul and with all your might.*
6. *Take to heart these instructions with which I charge you this day.*
7. *Impress them upon your children. Recite them when you stay at home and when you are away, when you lie down and when you get up.*
8. *Bind them as a sign on your hand and let them serve as a symbol on your forehead.*
9. *Inscribe them on the doorposts of your house and on your gates.*

In Mark 12:28-30, it says:

28. *And one of the scribes came, and having heard them reasoning together, and perceiving that he had answered them well, asked him, which is the first commandment of all?*
29. *And Jesus answered him, The first of all the commandments is, "Hear, O Israel; The Lord our God is one Lord";*
30. *And thou shalt love the Lord thy God with all thy heart, and with all thy soul, and with all thy mind, and with all thy strength: this is the first commandment.*

The above two quotes deal with the commandment that man love God Almighty.

In Mark 12:31, it says:

31. And the second is like, namely this, Thou shalt love thy neighbor as thyself. There is none other commandment greater than these.

Compare this to Leviticus 19:17-18, 33-34:

17. You shall not hate your kinsfolk in your heart. Reprove your kinsman but incur no guilt because of him.
18. You shall not take vengeance or bear a grudge against your countrymen. Love your fellow as yourself: I am the Lord.
33. When a stranger resides with you in your land, you shall not wrong him.
34. The stranger who resides with you shall be to you as one of your citizens; you shall love him as yourself, for you were strangers in the land of Egypt: I the Lord am your God.

The above two quotes deal with man's love of one's fellow man.

And so, it is clear that both Judaism and Christianity teach man to love God, as well as his fellow man.

Jesus, in Matthew 5:43-44, takes this even one step further:

43. Ye have heard that it hath been said, Thou shalt love thy neighbor, and hate thine enemy.
44. But I say unto you, Love your enemies, bless them that curse you, do good to them that hate you, and pray for them which despitefully use you and persecute you.

One may conclude from all the above quotes that both Judaism and Christianity teach love, love of God, love of man. The coming of the Messiah, whether it be the first or second, will usher in a period of love for this will be the messianic era. How could it be anything other than a period of love?

Similarities and Differences Between
Judeo-Christianity and Islamic Tradition

It is interesting to compare the Judeo-Christian tradition regarding the coming of the Messiah to the Islamic tradition.

"The second coming of Jesus is only mentioned once in the Koran, in a place where both the reading and the meaning of the text are very doubtful. However, this did not prevent Jesus from assuming a central messianic role in Islam. Tradition tells us that, at the end of days, he will appear, spear in hand, on the mountains to the east of the Sea of Galilee. At that time, the false Messiah, ad-dajjal, will be ruling the earth and Jesus will meet him at the gates of the city of Lydda and kill him. Having killed the dajjal, Jesus will proceed to Jerusalem at the time of the morning prayer and will pray among the rest of the Moslems according to the Islamic law. Thereafter, he will break all the crosses and lay the synagogues and churches in ruins. According to one tradition, by that time, all the Jews and Christians (The People of the Book) will believe in him and become part of the great Islamic community." (pp. 149-150 "Judaism, Christianity and Islam," by Professor Moshe Sharon, 1989).

So much for the messiah of love. Neither Jew nor Christian can imagine the Messiah with a spear in His hand killing anyone. For Jews and Christians alike, the Messiah will be a messiah of love and mercy. It is God, not man, who will judge and decide retribution at the end of days.

A second similarity between Judaism and Christianity is the belief often-times repeated in the Bible that God will gather the Jewish people from all corners of the earth and return them to the Land of Israel. Jews believe this will happen on the eve of the coming of the Messiah, while Christians believe this will happen in preparation for the return of the Messiah. Again, the polemics between Jews and Christians refer to whether it is the first or second comings. But the agreement is that it is a Messiah of love and a God of love. The messianic era therefore will be an era of love and peace for all God's children. Jews and gentiles will serve the Lord together in Jerusalem.

As it says in the Book of Isaiah, chapter 60:

1. *Arise, shine, for thy light is come,*
   And the glory of the Lord is risen upon thee.
2. *For, behold, darkness shall cover the earth,*
   And gross darkness the peoples;
   But upon thee the Lord will arise,
   And His glory shall be seen upon thee.
3. *And nations shall walk at thy light,*
   And kings at the brightness of thy rising.
4. *Lift up thine eyes round about, and see:*
   They all are gathered together, and come to thee;
   Thy sons come from far,
   And thy daughters are borne on the side.
5. *Then thou shalt see and be radiant,*
   And thy heart shall throb and be enlarged;
   Because the abundance of the sea shall be turned unto thee,
   The wealth of the nations shall come unto thee.
6. *The caravan of camels shall cover thee,*
   And of the young camels of Midian and Ephah,
   All coming from Sheba;
   They shall bring gold and frankincense,
   And shall proclaim the praises of the Lord.
7. *All the flocks of Kedar shall be gathered together unto thee;*
   They shall come up with acceptance on Mine altar,
   And I will glorify My glorious house.
8. *Who are these that fly as a cloud,*
   And as the doves to their cotes?
9. *Surely the isles wait for me,*
   And the ships of Tarshish first,
   To bring thy sons from far,
   Their silver and their gold with them,
   For the name of the Lord thy God,
   And for the Holy One of Israel,
   Because He hath glorified thee.
10. *And foreigners shall build up thy walls,*
    And their kings shall minister unto thee;
    For in My wrath I smote thee,

But in My favour have I had compassion on thee.

11. *Thy gates also shall be open continually,*
    Day and night, they shall not be shut;
    That men may bring unto thee the wealth of the nations,
    And their kings in procession.
12. *For that nation and kingdom that will not serve thee shall*
    perish; Yea, those nations shall be utterly wasted.

Compare this to the glaring opposite and conflicting Islamic prophecy: According to Sheikh Abdul Aziz Oudeh, a leading figure in the Islamic Jihad movement, speaking at an ICP (Islamic Committee for Palestine) conference in Chicago, Illinois on December 28-31, 1990: "Now Allah is bringing the Jews back to Palestine in large groups from all over the world to their big graveyard where the promise will be realized upon them, and what was destined will be carried out." (From PBS-Heritage Foundation TV documentary "Jihad in America" by Steven Emerson screened in the US for the first time on November 22nd, 1994.)

It is clear that this Islamic prophecy is totally contrary to the Judeo-Christian viewpoint and totally unacceptable.

Further to this quote of Sheikh Abdul Aziz Oudeh is a quote from an Egyptian Sheikh Yousef al-Kirdawi who also appeared in Emerson's film: "On the Hour of Judgement, Moslems will fight the Jews and kill them." (Speaking at a rally in 1989 in Kansas City, Missouri.)

The same message appears in the Islamic oral tradition known as the Hadith, which has also come to be canonized much like the Koran, itself, and accepted as holy over the years, and just as fervently by fanatic Moslems.

Professor Moshe Sharon, who, as advisor on Arab and Islamic affairs to Israel's Prime Minister Menachem Begin from 1977-1982, provides us with another quote from the Hadith in his book: Page 103 deals with the "Islamic tradition describing the conditions for the 'Final Hour,' for the Day of Judgment and for the establishment of the ideal (Islamic) divine order. According to this tradition, attributed to the Prophet Mohammed, himself, the 'Hour' will not come before the Muslims fight a final battle with the Jews and annihilates them. In the course of the war, the Jews will hide from their Muslim pursuers behind rocks and trees. On that Day, Allah will give mouths to the rocks and to the trees and they will call out: 'O Muslim, there is a Jew behind me, come and kill him.'" This same quote also appears frequently on handbills issued by the Hamas terrorist organization in territories administered by Israel as a rallying cry to kill the Jews.

Again, to Jews and Christians, the Islamic apocalyptic prophecy is genocidal, hideous and totally objectionable. How can the Messiah stand on the Mount of Olives if the end time scenario for Moslems is the eradication of all the Jews? Whether it be the first or second comings of the Messiah, we know that the Messiah will be Jewish and speak Hebrew. So, clearly, the fanatic Moslems have declared Jihad, or holy war against the Jews and the Christians. For Palestine to become the mass graveyard of the Jews, this would include murdering the Messiah as well.

Another insight into Islamic plans for Jerusalem can be seen in the following commentary by an announcer on the Palestinian Authority TV of September 24th, 1996: (With permission from Sonya Baevsky — Middle East Television News Archive, Jerusalem, Israel)

"Yes, Jerusalem is awaiting those who will liberate it and return it to the times when it was the city of peace under the guardianship of Omra (Omar el-Khattab) agreed upon by all churches in Christianity which recognized Islamic sovereignty over Jerusalem and that the Moslems would be the guardians of the Christian holy places.

According to the Omariya Agreement (Sophronios — 638 AD (CE) there was one stipulation made by all the Christians to the Moslems: Absolutely no Jews in Jerusalem. This agreement was in effect from the time of Khalifa Omar ibn el-Khattab until the British Mandate in 1917. Britain then allowed the Jews not only to enter the city, but even brought them in and planted them throughout Palestine and gave them a state. And this is the truth (sic) of the problem."

Now I have a few problems with this text.

First, the Christians recognized Islamic sovereignty over Jerusalem in 638 because they had the sword of Islam over their necks replacing the sword of Persia.

Secondly, the Jews were the majority in Jerusalem from the early 1800's, so it is not true that the Omar el-Khattab agreement was in effect until 1917.

Thirdly, the British never "brought" us in. We had to fight the British and their White Papers banning Jewish immigration. We lost six million Jews in the Nazi Holocaust due to the British White Papers.

Fourthly, the British did not give Israel a state. The UN did after the Jewish people lost a third of its people in the Holocaust.

But most important of all is not the lies in this PLO TV diatribe, but the truth. The truth of the Palestinian viewpoint is that Jerusalem must be Judenrein or Jew-free. This is the true intention of Yasser Arafat, the Palestinian Authority and the Moslems who are 95% of the Palestinian people. It is over this issue that war or peace will be decided.

I think the answer to the Islamic end-time scenario nightmare is as follows: We know from Ezekiel 38-39 and Zechariah 12 that the armies of many nations will rise up to wage war on Jewish Jerusalem. In Zechariah 12 it says:

1. The burden of the word of the Lord for Israel, saith the Lord, which stretcheth from the heavens and layeth the foundation of the earth, and formeth the spirit of man within him.

2. Behold, I will make Jerusalem a cup of trembling unto all the people round about, when they shall be in the siege both against Judah and against Jerusalem.

3. And in that day will I make Jerusalem a burdensome stone for all people: all that burden themselves with it shall be cut in pieces, though all the people of the earth be gather together against it.

4. In that day, saith the Lord, I will smite every horse with astonishment, and his rider with madness: and I will open mine eyes upon the house of Judah, and will smite every horse of the people with blindness.

5. And the governors of Judah shall say in their heart, the inhabitants of Jerusalem shall be my strength in the Lord of hosts their God.

6. In that day will I make the governors of Judah like an hearth of fire among the wood, and like a torch of fire in a sheaf; and they shall devour all the people round about, on

*the right hand and on the left: and Jerusalem shall be inhab-
ited again in her own place, even in Jerusalem.*

*7. The Lord also shall save the tents of Judah first, that the
glory of the house of David and the glory of the inhabitants of
Jerusalem do not magnify themselves against Judah.*

*8. In that day shall the Lord defend the inhabitants of Jerusa-
lem; and he that is feeble among them at that day shall be as
David; and the house of David shall be as God, as the angel of
the Lord before them.*

*9. And it shall come to pass in that day, that I will seek to
destroy all the nations that come against Jerusalem.*

And in Ezekiel 39:

*1. Therefore, thou son of man, prophesy against God, and
say, Thus saith the Lord God; Behold, I am against thee, O
Gog, the chief prince of Meshech and Tubal.*

*2. And I will turn thee back, and leave but the sixth part of
thee, and will cause thee to come up from the north parts, and
will bring thee upon the mountains of Israel.*

*3. And I will smite thy bow out of thy left hand, and will
cause thine arrows to fall out of thy right hand.*

*4. Thou shalt fall upon the mountains of Israel, thou, and all
thy bands, and the people that is with thee: I will give thee
unto the ravenous birds of every sort, and to the beasts of the
field to be devoured.*

*5. Thou shalt fall upon the open field: for I have spoken it,
said the Lord God.*

In both Zechariah 12 and Ezekiel 39, the Lord God Himself
intervenes on behalf of Israel and Jerusalem. It must be remembered that Jerusalem is mentioned 619 times in the Old Testament
and over 195 times in the New Testament. (Strong's Exhaustive
Concordance of the Bible) It is never once mentioned in the Koran. Jerusalem is not a holy city for Islam. But it is a target for
Islam to usurp it from the Jews and Christians or destroy it all
together. The fanatic Islamic program would brook at nothing including the use of atomic, biological or chemical weapons at turning the Holy Land into the mass graveyard of the Jews. Fanatic

Islam's final objective is no less than Hitler's: world domination and the extermination of the Jews. God will not allow this.

But there is an interesting epilogue to what will happen after this great war between those Islamic nations which rise up against Judeo-Christian Jerusalem and the war's aftermath.

In Zechariah 14 it says:

1. *Behold, the day of the Lord cometh, and thy spoil shall be divided in the midst of thee.*
2. *For I will gather all nations against Jerusalem to battle; and the city shall be taken, and the houses rifled, and the women ravished; and half of the city shall go forth into captivity, and the residue of the people shall not be cut off from the city.*
3. *Then shall the Lord go forth, and fight against those nations, as when he fought in the day of battle...*
12. *And this shall be the plague wherewith the Lord will smite all the people that have fought against Jerusalem; Their flesh shall consume away while they stand upon their feet, and their eyes shall consume away in their holes, and their tongue shall consume away in their mouth,*
13. *And it shall come to pass in that day, that a great tumult from the Lord shall be among them; and they shall lay hold every one on the hand of his neighbor, and his hand shall rise up against the hand of his neighbor.*
14. *And Judah also shall fight at Jerusalem; and the wealth of all the heathen round about shall be gathered together, gold, and silver, and apparel, in great abundance.*
15. *And so shall be the plague of the horse, of the mule, of the camel, and of the ass, and of all the beasts that shall be in these tents, as this plague.*
16. *And it shall come to pass that every one that is left of all the nations which came against Jerusalem shall even go up from year to year to worship the King, the Lord of hosts, and to keep the feast of Tabernacles.*
17. *And it shall be, that whoso will not come of all the families of the earth unto Jerusalem to worship the King, the Lord of hosts, even upon them shall be no rain.*

18. And if the family of Egypt go not up, and come not, that have no rain; there shall be the plague, wherewith the Lord will smite the heathen that come not up to keep the feast of tabernacles.
19. This shall be the punishment of Egypt, and punishment of all nations that come not up to keep the feast of tabernacles.
20. In that day shall there be upon the bells of the horses, HOLINESS UNTO THE LORD; and the pots in the Lord's house shall be like the bowls before the altar.
21. Yea, every pot in Jerusalem and in Judah shall be holiness unto the Lord of hosts: and all they that sacrifice shall come and take of them and seethe therein: and in that day there shall be no more the Canaanite in the house of the Lord of hosts.

From the above texts, it is clear that the Lord will intervene on behalf of Israel and Jerusalem; that five-sixths of the enemy that comes up against Jerusalem will be smitten directly by the Lord; but that a remnant will be spared and then that remnant will be called upon to repent, accept the Lord and join those gentiles and Jews in serving the Lord in Jerusalem.

This is why it is so important for the Jews and Christians to witness to the Moslems and to try to "save" their souls. The following is a testimony I want to share with my readers.

Now, being a rabbinic Jew, I am criticized often by Jewish communities for going to meet with "messianic" congregations which are actually Christian prayer groups. One of the "messianic" group leaders in the mid-western US invited me to speak several times to his group, and we really "clicked". There was something special about him, and I love him as my brother. Then, one day, he invited me to meet with someone very special. He said, this is a "born-again" Christian who originally was a Palestinian Moslem terrorist.

I said to him: "Are you crazy? I should meet with a Palestinian Moslem terrorist? He said to me: "Don't worry — he's a Christian now. He's "kosher". I reminded him that in the Koran, it says: "Thou shalt not kill any man whom Allah has not deemed that you should kill, except for a just cause." (Koran, Chapter XVII "The Night Journey": verse 33)

It seems logical to me that if you can kill for a just cause, so, too, can you lie, cheat, steal, rape, pillage enslave and burn for a just cause. This Palestinian terrorist could say he is a Christian, but if you can kill for a just cause, so, too, can you lie.

So this "messianic" leader said to me: "Listen, he's married to a Christian woman. He's OK, but forget it." But now, my curiosity was aroused, so I agreed to meet with him.

His testimony was most unusual. He was born in Gaza as a Moslem. All his life, he was taught to hate and kill the Jews. At a certain stage, he decided to go to a terrorist training camp somewhere in the Persian Gulf to put theory into practice. He could kill a Jew with firearms, knives, dynamite, poison, firearms. Anyway one could kill a Jew, he knew how to do.

One day, he had a falling out with his comrade terrorists and had to flee for his life. He arrived in the US surreptitiously, got a job as a head waiter in a most exclusive French restaurant and "disappeared" into the anonymity of the mid-west.

This Moslem terrorist hated the Jews, but was astounded to see that the Jews all loved him. They tipped him generously, the reform rabbi being the most generous of the tippers. One Jewish tailor even made this Moslem waiter a suit for free just because he loved him! But the waiter was confused. He said to himself: "Here I hate these Jews, want to kill them, and all they can do is love me. I don't understand them."

One day, this Moslem became depressed and could find no solace in the mosque. The depression got worse, and so, this waiter approached the reform rabbi and asked him to counsel him, to advise him, to "witness" to him. But the rabbi retorted that Passover was only a few weeks away, and he, the rabbi was busy preparing his community for the Passover. He recommended to the Moslem waiter that he come back in a month. Now, when one has a headache, one does not wait a month to take an aspirin. So this Moslem approached a Christian believer and asked for help. To make a long story short, the Moslem became a Christian, and all of a sudden, he no longer hated the Jews. "I had only love in my heart now for the Jews, Christians, Moslems and everybody else!"

After the Passover holidays, the reform rabbi came to the exclusive French restaurant to dine. This now Christian a former Palestinian Moslem terrorist came up to the rabbi and said to him:

"You know, I used to be a Moslem. I hated you. I wanted to kill you because you were a Jew. Now that I am Christian, I no longer hate you. I love you brother."

The ironic end of the story is that now, the reform rabbi will not talk to the formerly Moslem waiter because he became a born-again Christian! In the eyes of many Jews in America, the Moslems are the good guys and the Christians are the bad guys. Such a pity. It just shows that Jews have their fair share of ignorance, bigotry and hatred.

It also shows what happens when a Moslem abandons the Koran. He loses his hatred of the Jews and Christians. Therefore, does it not behoove Jews and Christians to witness to the Moslems. And if we Jews do not witness, proselytize, or mission to others, should not the Christians be encouraged by the Jews to reach out with love to the Moslems to cause the Moslems to come over to the religion of love, to the God of Abraham, Isaac and Jacob?

I must go on record as saying that I, as a Jew, do support Christian missionary work among the Moslems. The Judeo-Christian message is a message of love. Nowhere in our common belief is there a call for a total annihilation of the enemies of God. On the contrary, we seek repentance from and mercy for those on the wrong path. God does not delight in seeing the destruction of those created in His image. But it cannot be that the Islamic tradition calls for the annihilation of the Jews and Christians. Every Moslem that can be delivered from Islam and brought over to our side is a new ally and one less enemy.

I suppose the proper scripture for those who believe in the Bible can be taken from Zechariah 8:23 where it says: "Thus saith the Lord of hosts: In those days it shall come to pass, that ten men shall take hold, out of all the languages of the nations, shall even take hold of the skirt of him that is a Jew, saying: We will go with you, for we heard that God is with you."

The Patriarchs - A Common Link Between Christians and Jews and a Point of Contention with Islam

In both the Old and New Testaments, it is specifically written that Isaac was the chosen son of Abraham, and not Ishmael, the son of Hagar. The Old Testament was written some time in the middle of the second millennia before the common era (BCE or BC). The New Testament was written sometime during the 1st century of the common era (CE or AD).

The New Testament begins with the genealogy of Jesus according to the Gospel of Matthew 1:1:

> *"The book of the generation of Jesus Christ , the son of David, the son of Abraham. Abraham begat Isaac; and Isaac begat Jacob; and Jacob begat Judas and his brethren."*

In Matthew 8:11, it says:

> *"And I say unto you, that many shall come from the east and west, and shall sit down with Abraham, Isaac and Jacob, in the kingdom of heaven."*

In Mark 12:26, it says:

> *"Have ye not read in the book of Moses, how in the bush God spake unto him, saying, I am the God of Abraham, and the God of Isaac, and the God of Jacob?" (also in Exodus 3:6).*

In Luke 3:33-34, another genealogical tree shows:

> *33. Juda,*
> *34. which was the son of Jacob, which was the son of Isaac, which was the son of Abraham, which was the son of Thara, which was the son of Nahor."*

In Acts 3:13, Peter says:

> *"The God of Abraham, and son of Isaac, and of Jacob, the God of our fathers, hath glorified his Son Jesus."*

Again, in Acts 7:8:

> *"And he gave him the covenant of circumcision: and so Abraham begat Isaac, and circumcised him the eighth day; and Isaac begat Jacob; and Jacob begat the twelve patriarchs."*

Finally, in Romans 9:7-13 it says:

7. Neither, because they are the seed of Abraham, are they all children; but, in Isaac shall thy seed be called. (Genesis 21:12)
8. That is, They which are the children of the flesh, these are not the children of God: but the children of the promise are counted for the seed.
9. For this is the word of promise, at this time will I come, and Sara shall have a son. (Genesis 18:10-14)
10. And not only this; but when Rebecca also had conceived by one, even by our father Isaac;
11. (For the children being not yet born, neither having done any good or evil, that the purpose of God according to election might stand, not of work, but of him that calleth;)
12. It was said unto her, The elder shall serve the younger. (Genesis 25:23)
13. As it was written, Jacob have I loved, but Esau have I hated. (Malachi 1:2,3)

It is surprising, therefore, that sometime between the middle and the end of the 7th century CE (AD), the Koran, according to Islam, was divinely revealed to Mohammed by Allah, 2,000 years after the Five Books of Moses, and 600 years after the writing of The New Testament. And in the Koran, now, all of a sudden Ishmael is the son who was to be sacrificed on Mt. Moriah by Abraham and not Isaac. So, the New and Old Testaments are supposedly invalidated and replaced by the Koran and by Islam, and the genealogy of Jesus is thereby refuted, something obviously unacceptable to Christians.

The Common Bond of Islam - Ishmael and Esau

As we know later on in the book of Genesis, the elder son, Esau, despised his birthright and sold it to his younger brother, Jacob. With guile, therefore, Jacob acted to obtain Isaac's first blessing of the elder brother while Esau had to settle for a lesser blessing from his father.

In Genesis 27:39-40, Isaac blesses Esau as follows:

39. And Isaac his father answered him (Esau) and said unto him:
Behold, of the fat places of the earth shall be thy dwelling (fat places in Hebrew literally means "of the oils of the land!")
And of the dew of heaven from above (meaning the desert);
40. And by thy sword shalt thou live and thou shalt serve thy brother; and it shall come to pass when thou shalt break loose, That thou shalt shake his yoke from off thy neck.

It is also important to note that Abraham, Isaac and Jacob insisted that their progeny marry only Aramean women from their place of origin because Canaanite women were hateful due to their idolatry. *"Thou shalt not take a wife of the daughters of Canaan."* (Genesis 28:6)

In spite of Isaac's command, *"When Esau was forty years old, he took to wife Judith the daughter of Beeri, the Hittite, and Basemath the daughter of Elon the Hittite. And they were a bitterness of spirit unto Isaac and to Rebekah."* (Genesis 26:34-35)

Then, in Genesis 28:7-9 it reads:

7. And that Jacob hearkened to his father and his mother, and was gone to Paddan-aram;
8. And Esau saw that the daughters of Canaan pleased not Isaac his father;
9. So Esau went unto Ishmael, and took unto the wives that he had Mahalath the daughter of Ishmael Abraham's son, the sister of Nebaioth, to be his wife."
Esau lived thereafter with his uncle Ishmael. It is also interesting to read the angel's blessing Hagar and her still unyet born son Ishmael in Genesis 16:9-12:
9. And the angel of the Lord said unto her: "Return to thy mistress (Sarah) and submit thyself under her hands."
10. And the angel of the Lord said unto her: "I will greatly multiply thy seed, that it shall not be numbered for multitude."

11. And the angel of the Lord said unto her: "Behold, thou art with child, and shalt bear a son; and thou shalt call his name Ishmael, because the Lord hath heard thy affliction." 12. And he shall be a wild ass of a man: his hand shall be against every man, and every man's hand against him; and he shall dwell in the face of all his brethren.

Therefore, we have thus seen how the Old and New Testaments refer to the genealogy of the patriarchs Abraham, Isaac and Jacob and their descendants, and how the Old Testament alone refers to Ishmael and Esau, who were to lead the lives of brigands in the desert — Ishmael, not even mentioned once in the New Testament and Esau mentioned only once. Ishmael and Esau are the forefathers of the Ishmaelites, and later the peoples of the deserts, the Arabs and the Moslems. This book will try to show the fulfillment of biblical prophecy — that to this very day Ishmael's hand is against every man's hand and that he shall dwell in the face of all his brethren. It will be fanatic Islam against the world.

Chapter Two

A Short History of Islam

The descendants of Ishmael and Esau, today known as the Arabs, though mentioned scantily in the Bible as well as in Greek and Roman historical texts, played a minor role in world history until the prophet Mohammed and the Koran galvanized the Arab peoples into a fighting and conquering force.

The origins of Islam, the third great monotheistic religion in the world, stem from Judeo-Christianity, but the Koran and Allah have very little to do with the Bible and the God of Abraham, Isaac, and Jacob.

At the outset, the prophet Mohammed had two major groups to convert to his cause: The Judeo-Christians on the one hand and the pagans of Mecca and Medina on the other. When the Judeo-Christians rejected Mohammed and his teachings, all the emphasis was then placed on the pagans of Mecca and Medina as well as the whole Arabian peninsula. The Judeo-Christian origins of Mohammed's beliefs were then put on the back burner, and the pagan Arabian origins of Islam were emphasized.

According to world-renowned scholar and theologian Dr. Robert Morey, Mohammed decided to build his new religion, Islam, on the foundations of Arabian paganism in order for it to be more palatable to the pagans who were his target audience. According to Arabian paganism, there were 360 pagan gods, one for each day of the lunar year. The greatest of these gods was Allah, originally known as al-Ilahi, the Moon God. This pagan Allah, the greatest in the pagan pantheon, was the war god, just as Zeus was the war god for the ancient Greeks and Romans.

In order to build his new religion, Islam, on a monotheistic basis, Mohammed abolished the other 359 lesser gods, leaving Allah as the only god. But Allah still remains a war god, and bears no resemblance to the God of Abraham, Isaac and Jacob, which is the God of love, as I explained in Chapter I. Allah, the moon god, the war god, is a god of the bow, the arrow, the spear and the sword. Islam is a war religion, a warrior religion and merciless religion in which beheading, crucifixion and severing of arms and limbs is common practice even today and a religion in which no "Protestant reformation" can ever be countenanced which would allow modernization as happened in the Jewish and Christian religions. This is why the 7th century is so glorified in Islam and is the direction in which the pan-global Islamic conquest is headed. It is locked into and fossilized in a mindset totally contrary to the 21st century which we are rapidly approaching. It opposes the progress and development of the renaissance and enlightenment following the dark medieval ages of Europe and dreams of the distant past.

Dr. Morey also disagrees with the Islamic claims of descendance from Ishmael and Esau. He claims, possibly correctly that the original Moslems genealogically had no relation to the descendants of Abraham, but were strictly desert tribes of the Arabian peninsula whereas the Ishmaelites were more to the north in Syria and perhaps in Jordan of today.

But, in my opinion, it matters little whether there was a direct genealogical link to Ishmael or Esau. What matters is the spiritual inheritance of Abraham, Isaac and Jacob which is love, for all those who embrace Judeo-Christianity, while the spiritual inheritance of Ishmael and Esau is the arrow, the sword, and perpetual warfare. Genealogy here matters little. What matters is the spirit.

As for who wrote the Koran, there are theories that it was written up to five hundred years after the death of Mohammed, but the accepted notion is that a few decades after his death the verbally handed down Koran was committed to writing. There is also a theory which I have heard in Israel from a rabbi of Iranian (Persian) extraction and corroborated by many rabbis of middle eastern extraction (of Jewish communities under the yoke of Islamic rule) that the early followers of Mohammed were illiterate desert nomad warriors and therefore needed a "black-belt" in holy scripture writing, so with the conquest of Babylonia by the Arab armies, a leading rabbi was kidnapped from the seat of Talmudic learning and sequestered until he wrote the "holy" book of the Moslems.

After studying Talmudic and Midrashic literature for three years at the Jerusalem branch of the Jewish Theological Seminary, I must say that whoever wrote the Koran put in a lot of Talmudic and Midrashic texts. I personally don't believe that a desert warrior from Arabia could have known these texts. Unfortunately, learned Jewish and Christian scholars don't take time today to read the Koran in order to see the inconsistencies in light of the original writings Jewish and Christian. God is not confused. I will elaborate more fully on how the Koran was fabricated by the Babylonian rabbi in chapter 19 at the end of the book.

Within a hundred years of the death of Mohammed in 732 AD (CE), the Arab Moslems had succeeded in conquering North Africa and Spain, the entire Arabian peninsula and most of the Middle East. Christendom from that period and until Columbus discovered America was limited to a relatively tiny plot of land known as western Europe. In fact, the Islamic pincers reached even to Poitiers in France in the west and the gates of Vienna in the east. Christianity was in a very real danger of being vanquished by the Islamic hordes.

Even the Crusades to the Holy Land starting in 1096 barely made a dent in the Islamic armor. The crusader presence in the Holy Land lasted merely 200 years until the Battle of the Horns of Hittim in which Saladin put an end to the Christian expeditionary force.

However, Islam started to fall due to internal rivalries as well as Christendom's emergence from the Middle Ages, the Renaissance. Strides were made in science, commerce and industry, while the Islamic world fell into backwardness.

With Columbus's discovery of the New World, two new continents were opened up to Christian settlement, thus overcoming the Islamic stranglehold on Europe. It is never emphasized enough in American schools how critical the gold and silver as well as other riches sent back to Europe by the settlers and conquistadores in the new world were to the building of fleets and fielding of armies to fight Islamic armies be they Arab, Turkish or Persian.

Russia also adopted Christianity in 995 AD greatly due to the Islamic invasions from the east. Therefore it was to the east that Russia turned in order to defend itself, and later to subdue its Moslem inhabitants as well as Turkish and Persian tribes, and Russia finally reached the Pacific Ocean in a "manifest destiny" quite similar to that of the Americans.

Following the rise of Christian Europe came a period known as colonialism, in which the new European powers established footholds in the Islamic world and later carved up Africa, as well as Asia.

It was not until the advent of Communism in Soviet Russia and the period of the world wars, as well as the discovery of petroleum, that new forces of militant Islam were unleashed, leading to the rise of renascent Islam. Today, the communist east is gone and Islam considers the west as the only remaining great "Satan" whose days are numbered. The Iranian Ayatollah Janati has boldly proclaimed, "The 21st century will be the century of Islam."

According to Islam, there is an eternal war between the house of peace of Islam and the house of war of the infidel non-Moslem. Islam, in its early stages, adopted a strident ideology of war between "good and evil," i.e., Islam against the infidels. All who embraced Islam were of the House of Peace or, in Arabic, "Dar es Salaam" while all the infidels were grouped together in the "Dar el-Harb," or House of War, a war which could not end until the entire world became Moslem. Since it was impossible in so short a period to impose such a rigorous new religion on so many peoples, it was necessary to show moderation in light of the reality that perhaps the Moslem hordes were biting off more than they could chew.

Therefore, a policy of compromise was established between the Moslems on the one hand and the enemies of Islam on the other hand; at least until Islam was strong enough to resume the battle of conquest.

During the early period of Islam, many Jews and Christians saw Islam as a force saving them from the harsh regimes of Orthodox Byzantium in the east and Catholicism in the west both of which persecuted Jews and those Christians who were considered to be heretic. (A striking example of this is the conversion to Islam of the entire Bosnian nation which had been considered as a heretical form of Christianity and persecuted by the eastern orthodox church.) It was decided that the Moslems would utilize these Jews and Christians to establish a firm financial and administrative organization that would allow the Moslems to consolidate power. Hundreds of years later, most of these Jews and Christians were "absorbed" by conversion into Islam.

In this manner, the Moslems established themselves finally as firm majorities in each country from Morocco on the Atlantic to Indonesia on the Pacific. The infidels were divided into two categories: Jews and Christians, known as the "People of the Book," were considered as "dhimmis" to be protected but subjugated. The other infidels, such as Hindus, Buddhists and other eastern sects, were to be put immediately to the sword, whenever possible because Moslems considered them pagans.

Between 1492 and 1992, Islam came under the dominion of Christian leaders with the rise of European and Russian Christendom. By 1492, the Moors were completely expelled from the Iberian peninsula (Spain and Portugal). In addition to colonizing the Americas, the two Iberian powers colonized the islands off the west coast of Africa, the Azores and Cabo Verde, as well as numerous African and Asian areas.

In Europe, though Ottoman Turkey marched northward from Anatolia, subdued Greece, the Balkans, Hungary, Romania and virtually conquered Vienna, Austria, by the end of the 1500's, Turkey was also, now, on the retreat. After a series of wars with Russia and other European powers, Turkey was forced to withdraw from the Crimea, southern Russia, the Caucasus mountains, Ukraine, Hungary, Romania, Bulgaria and what are now the constituent former republics of Yugoslavia. Greece achieved its independence in 1821 and grew in size after the Balkan campaigns in the early 1900's. Except for Albania and a small piece of Europe across the Bosphorus Straits, Turkey was now almost entirely an Asiatic power. And so, the Islamic pincers from North Africa and Turkey were now retreating in defeat.

Again, Islam was forced to moderate and compromise with forces stronger than itself. More and more Islamic lands fell under European Christian dominion and administration. Missionaries were brought in and there was little Islam could do about it.

Then, in the early 1900's, the world entered its modern era with the various nationalisms, world wars, and most of all, the discovery of large deposits of petroleum. Moslem leaders in Africa and Asia were suddenly influenced by western education and western power struggles, and they learned to develope the world's thirst for oil. Since the Moslem leaders controlled the areas where the oil was located, these western powers in turn played up to the sheikhs who learned ably to play one Christian power off against the other. As the years went by, these Moslem oil sheikhs became richer and richer, and eventually took over more and more control of the oil resources until, finally, as in the case of the sheikhs of Saudi Arabia they took over full ownership of what was rightfully theirs.

At the same time, the United Nations brought about the decolonialization of Africa and Asia in which the European powers were forced out leaving a power vacuum which the U.S. and the USSR vied to fill. In most cases, the Moslem world was considered "Third World," i.e., neither pro-U.S. nor pro-USSR. But one thing was sure, the Moslem oil countries became very adept and skilled at manipulating the world powers to get what they wanted. Most important, the petrodollar and vast oil reserves made the leaders of the oil rich countries virtually omnipotent.

Now, ironically, instead of Columbus sending back gold bullion and silver to Europe to build armies and fleets it is the Moslem "black-gold" or oil which is building the Islamic armies and fleets. It is this black gold which leads the Moslems to believe that Allah has given them the wherewithal to finally vanquish Christianity and conquer the world.

Today, with the fall of Communism after nearly seventy-five years of confrontation between the west, led by the U.S. and the east, led by the USSR, many Americans believe that all is now good and well; that the U.S. is world power number one alone; that the evil empire is vanquished; that it is time for Americans to return to the fold of isolationism and self-induced hypnotic sleep of pre-WWI and pre-WWII. Well, this is wrong.

There is a new menace threatening world peace and stability with its plans of establishing an all- embracing Islamic empire, especially with the flaunting of this new found oil wealth.

Chapter Three

The Role of the Media

Indeed, during my visit to the U.S. in January-February, 1994, all I could find on American TV networks news programs was coverage of such earth-shattering issues as Tanya Harding, Lorena Bobbitt and the Lillehammer games. To give a slight hint of what was not mentioned on the tube was: that over 1.5 million south Sudanese, mostly Christians, were being genocidally starved or tortured to death by the Arab Moslem government of Northern Sudan in Khartoum. At the time of the fifth printing of this book in the fall of 1997, at least another half a million black Sudanese Christians are expected to die in the coming months because of this continuing purge by the fanatic Iranian-backed Moslem government of President Omar Hassan Ahmed Bashir and the leader of the National Islamic Front, Hassan Turabi (a soft-spoken, erudite, Sorbonne-educated Sheikh, who is widely seen as an architect of the Islamic revival that has spread from Algeria to Afghanistan.)

It is estimated that somewhere between 6 to 8 million black Sudanese will die during the coming two years from this Islamic policy imposed on non-Moslems of either converting to Islam or starving.

A reason for this is that the south of Sudan sits astride the last, greatest, unknown and unexploited oil reserves in the world. But first, the non-Moslem Sudanese must be exterminated and replaced with Moslems from the north before the oil can be exploited. Unbelievably, slavery has also been reimposed in the Sudan according to the precepts of the Koran. Just when we all thought that slavery was finally abolished, we see it back with a vengeance, and with the blessing and official sanction of Islam. According to reports from Radio Monte Carlo at the end of November, 1995, the Islamic government of Sudan is now using poison gas to kill the Christians of southern Sudan.

It is even stated explicitly in the Koran that Moslem men may not marry married women because this is adultery, that is, unless they are the wives of slaves. (Chapter IV verse 24 entitled "Women", p.81) From this, therefore, one may infer that it is possible to enslave the non-Moslem man — and then take his wife into one's harem, or sell her as a slave. Slave trading is so endemic now from the Sudan, that women and children are being sold as chatel slaves for as low as fifteen dollars each and are being exported to Libya and other Islamic countries. Also, slavery, which was never really abolished in Senegal and Mauritania, both Moslem countries, is increasing in spite of UN condemnations.

President John F. Kennedy once said: "As long as one man is not free, none of us are." I would also like to add, that just as we Jews lost six million of our people in the Holocaust during WWII, now the black people are having a Holocaust in Sudan, and the world again is silent. We will all be judged by God for this.

Media Bias In The Balkans

For some reason, the conspiracy of silence of the media is aimed at lulling Americans, most of whom are Christians, into a false sense of security and of American omnipotence. It is an insidious and self-serving silence. The petrodollar of the Middle East, which pays for so much of the media's advertising and therefore the lifeblood of such organizations as CNN, causes a tilting toward those who do the paying, as opposed to those who are in the way of the "new world order" such as Israel or America's evangelical Christians. This is why there is no reporting of the genocide and slavery of millions in Sudan, but the "poor" Bosnian Moslems have exclusive coverage of CNN and the media. The UN has even sent an army to protect, train and arm the Moslems of Bosnia.

On Friday, October 25th, 1996, Israel's English language daily newspaper "The Jerusalem Post" carried an article by Steve Rodan about the Iranian arming and training of the Bosnian Islamic Army. Here are some excerpts:

"Croatia Watches As Iran Arms Bosnia"

Croatia, worried about inroads made by Islamic fundamentalism, is seeking assistance from Israel.

Nika Cipci looks out the window of his fourth-floor office at police headquarters, toward the busy docks of this Croatian port city.

Many of the arriving shipments are marked as containing food and medicine. But Cipci, police commander of the Split region since 1993, knows better. He acknowledges that many of these shipments might contain weapons heading for neighboring Bosnia. "The humanitarian convoys that come through this city are very difficult to control," he says in an interview in his office in Split. "It would be very stupid to believe that all the convoys are humanitarian."

Croatian officials say Iran is sending large supplies of weapons to Bosnia for what both they and regional diplomats assess will be an offensive by Sarajevo, backed up by thousands of members of Teheran's Revolutionary Guard, to capture territory now held by the Serbian minority. They say the Iranian deliveries usually arrive by boat to Split, and then are driven through Croatia to landlocked Bosnia.

"This has been a meeting point between East and West," Cipci said. "Everything has gone through Split, including all of the armies."

But even as they worry about Teheran, Croatian officials acknowledge that they are allowing the Iranian arms supply to Bosnia, in an arrangement in which Zagreb obtains badly needed oil as well as a selection of the thousands of light arms, mortars and other weapons headed for Sarajevo. "Iran is moving into the region on a big scale," a European diplomat based in Zagreb says. "It is investing and influencing events, not only in Bosnia, but in Croatia as well."

Publicly, Iranian officials play down the Iranian connection, saying arms supplies are no longer a factor. But privately, a senior Croatian official says Teheran sells oil to Zagreb in return for Croat ships, built in Split. "The Europeans don't seem to want us, and we had to live during the embargo," the official says. "So, Iran was the option. This is a commercial relationship, not a military one."

Croatia, with 4.8 million people and with the lowest debt of all the former Yugoslav republics, hopes to widen its military relationship with the US, despite what diplomats say is Washington's concern over Zagreb's ties with Iran.

US military trainers are in Croatia organizing its military of 40,000 regular troops. They are augmented by a reservist force of 400,000.

Officials say they are concerned that renewed fighting could torpedo the US-sponsored Dayton agreement reached earlier this year and ruin Croat efforts to rebuild the economy, particularly in attracting tourism.

NATO's Implementation Force now has 52,000 troops in Bosnia. But US President Bill Clinton has promised to withdraw American troops by the end of the year, and NATO military planners say that could affect their plans to keep a follow-on force that would be about half of the current international military presence.

Officials regard Israel as a key to the Croat defense strategy. They point to what they say are the similarities of the two countries: beleaguered pro-western democracies with Moslems as their neighbors...

Croat officials are hopeful that Israel will help Zagreb, if only to decrease Iranian influence in the region. "Croatia does not see Iran as its first choice but it needs friends and help badly," a Croat diplomat says. "Croatians are also working in Iraq and Libya, also because of the lack of other options."

But some Croat officials suggest that even if Israel agrees, Zagreb's relations with the Jewish state will be low-key, particularly in the military field. They point to the Moslem-Croat federation in Bosnia as a factor in determining the intensity of future ties between Jerusalem and Zagreb.

"Israel is always there. But we don't want to be seen as enemy of the Arabs because of Bosnia," Tourism Minister Nico Bulic said earlier this month.

Vesna Girardi Jurkic, Croatia's ambassador to UNESCO, in Paris, suggests that her country's ties to Iran will continue regardless of any new friends it makes. We must exchange goods," she said. "We can't stop developing. But we must not be linked by any contract."

Croat officials say they might soon be faced with the question of how costly their Iranian relationship will end up being. One concern is that Serbia will see the entry of Iran in the region together with Croat cooperation as being directed against Belgrade; with Teheran's weapons being delivered and stored in preparation for an eventual offensive to capture more territory from the heavily-armed Serbian minority.

"I think we will have similar problems with Islamic fundamentalism," Zovko, the deputy science minister, says, "They will try to assert influence here. On the other hand, this country has to stay democratic."

We have a lot of Moslem refugees from Bosnia and if you see their schoolbooks, it is pretty problematic in that they're fundamentalist. Before the war, Bosnia was pro-Europe. Now it's fundamentalist. I'm afraid there will be problems for Croatia."

It is indeed strange how much the western media and in particular American media pander to the petrodollar advertisers, and therefore have been so taken up with the plight of the Bosnian Moslems, and have so stacked the cards against the Serbs.

A very abridged and brief history of the Balkans teaches one that the Balkans as well as Greece and Byzantium in Anatolia were the main components of the Eastern Roman Empire, and Constantinople was the home of the Eastern Orthodox Churches, until only a few centuries ago.

Then came the various Turkish tribes and powers, last of which were the Ottomans who from the 1300's until the 1500's literally wiped out whatever there ever was of eastern Christian orthodoxy and reached the gates of the Catholic countries more to the west.

(The first 20th century genocide was of 1.5 million Christian Armenians by the Ottoman Turks in 1915.)

Those who are today Bosnia's Moslems were Christians only four centuries ago, but considered heretic by the Orthodox churches and persecuted. The Turks were received by these "heretic" Christians as liberating heroes, and finally, the Bosnians converted to Islam in gratitude.

With the final expulsion of Ottoman Turkey from mainland Europe, a new federation of south slavic peoples was created after WWI and was known as Yugoslavia and was dominated primarily by Serbia. The six federated republics comprising Yugoslavia were Slovenia and Croatia, which were Catholic; Bosnia and Herzegovina as well as Montenegro which were Moslem; and Serbia and Macedonia which were Eastern Orthodox. But all the peoples of Yugoslavia whether they be Orthodox, Catholic or Moslem were slavic peoples by race, culture and language.

If one thinks that the civil strife in Northern Ireland is ridiculous because the inhabitants there are white and Christian, then how much more confusing and complicated is the situation in Yugoslavia were there are three religious groups — all of the same race, culture and language. But the hatred and fratricide go back hundreds of years.

Americans should be very careful when calling upon the United States to intervene in Bosnia. Even the most uninitiated in European history remember the spark that ignited WWI, the assassination of Austrian Arch-Duke Ferdinand by a Serbian militant in Sarajevo. Germany and Austria backed the Croats and Slovenes. Russia backed the Serbs. Hence World War I. (Since the Russians still firmly back the Serbs, the world must be careful not to ignite World War III.)

With World War II, Hitler and the Nazis marched into the Balkans. There were Slovenians and Croats who identified with the axis powers because of co-religionist Catholic Austria and broke away from the Yugoslav federation to form pro-Nazi puppet states. The Republic of Bosnia and Herzegovina also broke away, being Moslem, and distanced itself from Serb hegemony.

During WWII, over 100,000 Jews and 500,000 Serbs were slaughtered by the Nazi German-Croation-Bosnian allies. Obviously, the surviving Jews and the Serbs as well as Communists of the Croat and Slovenian peoples served in the forests of Yugoslavia as partisans and fought the Nazis bravely until liberation in 1945 as part of the victorious allied armies. But Serbs and Jews will never forget the genocide carried out against them.

I picked up an interesting anecdote in June 1994 while in Russia. During an interview I gave on Radio Moscow, my host,

Oleg Gribkov, told me about the battle of Stalingrad which lasted for nearly two years.

The Nazis had an array of multi-national forces on their side: Spanish, Italian, Hungarian, Romanian, Croatian and Bosnian units. When "general winter" and the Red Army finally cracked the axis armies on that front, everyone raced to surrender, all that is, except with the exception of one, the Bosnian Moslem fighters who, Gribkov said, were the most ferocious of the Nazi warriors. "They would charge at us with their bayonets drawn and daggers clenched between their teeth. The Russian people will never forget the Bosnians for this."

For those of us from the Holy Land, neither will we forget the antics of the Mufti of Jerusalem, the pro-Nazi Haj Amin el-Husseini who helped to organize and was photographed in Nazi uniform reviewing Bosnian Moslem Nazi units. This is a matter of record. It is also a matter of record that there were Palestinian Moslem volunteers in the Bosnian units; that Haj Amin el-Husseini had agreed with Adolf Hitler to extend the "Final Solution of the Jewish Problem" to the Jews of Palestine as well; and finally that Adolf Hitler planned to abolish all religions other than Islam and Nazism after the Nazi victory. (From 1943 speech made by Hitler)

With the allied victory and the Nazi defeat, the federation of Socialist Yugoslavia was established by Josip Broz Tito with Soviet and allied assistance.

What simply happened was that Tito, with his iron hand, decided there would be no more fratricidal hatred between the different Yugoslav peoples, and in essence, everything was covered over with the cement of Communism, at least until the downfall of Communism in 1990.

At one stage, in order to mollify the Bosnian people, Tito the Great took away lands from what was formerly the Serbian part of Yugoslavia and handed it over to Bosnia. But since it was all still part and parcel of the same country, it really didn't matter. That is until the breakup of Yugoslavia in the early 1990's.

When Bosnia decided to break away from the Yugoslav Federation, Serbia in essence said: "You want to break away, that's all right, but give us back the traditional Serbian lands given over to Bosnia by Tito in the 1950's" as above mentioned. But now, Bosnia said, no, this is now all of Bosnia. So is it any wonder the Serbs are

fighting for lands given away under a different Communist political system and whose population which has always been Serbian
now anxiously seeks to rejoin Serbia?

All this is especially true in light of the plans I mentioned at
the beginning of this book by Prime Minister Alija Izetbegovitch
to convert Bosnia into another Iran or Gaza. This was the subject
of his doctoral thesis. The Serbs are basically saying: Do whatever
you want with traditional Bosnian land. But give back to the Serbs
the traditional Serbian lands Tito gave away as a present to the
Bosnians under different circumstances. This in essence is what
the war in Bosnia is all about today.

The Greek Awakening

One more "small" detail, that Westerners in general, and
Americans in particular are glaringly unaware of is that both the
Serbs as well as the Greeks, feel very surrounded and threatened
by Islamic enemies: Albania, sizeable Islamic groups in Kosovo,
Macedonia, Greece, Cyprus and Bulgaria. These could also become flashpoints in the future, flashpoints in which Moslem Turkey with its burgeoning population of 60 million could quickly
become militarily involved.

This reminds me of a military experience I had during the
summer of 1993 in the Israel Defense Forces reserves where I serve
as an army spokesman.

I was escorting a group of Greek-American lobbyists from
Washington, DC to the Golan. It was at this time that Constantine
Mitsotakis was Prime Minister of Greece and Glafkos Clerides was
President of Cyprus. Diplomatic relations had just been established
between these two Greek countries and Israel, and this group of
American VIP's was in Israel to strengthen relations between the
pro-Greek and pro-Israel lobbies in Washington.

Basically, they said to me: "Our Greek governments in Ath-
ens and Nicosia were wrong to bash Israel for all the years preced-
ing the establishment of diplomatic relations. Even our Greek
Orthodox Church realizes that it is not the Jew but the Moslem
who threatens the Greeks. We have come to realize that we are in
the same boat as the Jews and Israel, and we really should be allies." They concluded: "We must correct the mistakes of the past

and mend our fences with Israel. Your situation with the Arabs is exactly like our predicament with the Turks and Balkan Moslems."

People are astounded when I tell them the background to Balkan wars and history. I never fail to be amazed at either the shallowness of western news reporting, or the tendentiousness of those sold out to the Islamic petrodollar of the advertisers.

With all the tragedy involved in the Balkans, over a 200,000 people of all three ethnic groups have been killed, and with the horrors of ethnic cleansing of which all sides are guilty, I still feel it outrageous that over 200,000 East Timorese were slaughtered by the Indonesian army in 1976; over half a million ethnic Chinese were branded as Communists in the 1960's and also slaughtered in Indonesia, although they weren't Communists; millions have died and millions more will die in Sudan over the coming years; and countless other inter-ethnic and inter-religious struggles have caused Moslems to kill and persecute minorities throughout the Middle East including the Copts of Egypt and the Christians of Lebanon: and the media ignores these tragedies because the perpetrators are Moslems and oil rich. It just does not pay for the media. Besides, which reporter seeks to be put on an Islamic hit-list?

In 1914, long before the Islamic petrodollar's control of the media became a well established fact, John Swinton, then editor of "The New York Times" was quoted as saying at a dinner of the American press:

"There is no such thing as an independent press in America... it is the duty of the New York journalist to lie... and to sell his country and his race for his daily bread... his salary. We are tools and the servants of the rich behind the scenes... Our time, our talents, our lives, and our capacities are all the property of these men, we are intellectual prostitutes." (Salen Kirban's "Analysis of World-wide News")

Saudi Arabian Control Of The Media

Saudi Arabia presently bankrolls its interest groups such as the Bechtel Corporation, but also the media in the Christian west — Europe and America. Former Italian President Berlusconi was quoted in the Jerusalem Post (Israeli English language daily) of

July 21st, 1995 as saying "He recently sold a twenty percent stake in his vast television and advertising empire to an international consortium...comprised of German media magnate Leo Kirch, Saudi Prince Waleed bin Talal and the Dutch Nethold/Richemont group controlled by South African businessman Johann Rupert. Kirch will take ten percent and Waleed and Rupert the other ten percent."

The Saudis also own innumerable newspapers, radio and TV networks throughout Europe as well as world wide. UPI (United Press International) was recently acquired by Islamic petrodollars.

The following is an article by AP's Anthony Shadid out of Nicosia, Cyprus which was picked up by the "The Jerusalem Post" which appeared in its July 26th, 1995 edition.

"The Arab world's most prestigious newspapers and magazines cover the Middle East from London. Its most ambitious satellite broadcast network has set up shop outside Rome.

"All have one thing in common — Saudi control.

"In a trend that has accelerated in the 1990's, Saudi Arabian investors and princes have set up or purchased leading Arab media, most of which are based in Europe, particularly London.

"With wealthy owners, large staffs and modern communications, the media are free of the rigid censorship that exists in much of the Middle East and have outclassed their poorer competitors in Arab countries. But there's growing criticism that the Saudis have too much influence over the information that circulates in the Arab world.

"'There is one political umbrella, which covers all the Arab press, and that is the Saudi umbrella,' said Abdel-Barri Atwan, editor of London-based 'al-Quds', a struggling Palestinian newspaper often critical of Saudi Arabia and other Gulf states.

"'How can you have freedom of expression if one country dominates the scene completely?' he asked.

"Press freedom is notoriously limited by most Middle East governments, which impose explicit controls or rely on self-censorship to keep journalists in line.

"For years, Beirut was the exception. But Lebanon's civil war drove journalists abroad in the 1970's and 1980's, many of them in fear for their lives. Saudi Arabia, flush with its tremendous oil wealth, began stepping in.

"Today, dozens of publications and radio and television stations, many under Saudi tutelage, have opened or relocated in London and Paris, including 'al-Hayat', recognized across the Middle East as the leading Arab newspaper.

"Controlled by Prince Khalid Bin Sultan, the Saudi military commander during the Gulf War, 'al-Hayat' is read by the Arab elite and regularly breaks stories ahead of Western newspapers. Its circulation is far smaller than Egypt's venerable 'al-Ahram' newspaper, but 'al-Hayat's' strength is its ability to reach across national boundaries.

"With more than twenty bureaus, and correspondents in most Arab capitals, 'al-Hayat's' editors consider the newspaper an international publication and its coverage Pan-Arab.

"They say from the vantage point of London, they can take a broad view of the region, unfettered by national sentiments or arbitrary restrictions placed on Arab journalists at home.

"'There's a merit in looking at things from a distance, You can put it into a global perspective,' said Maher Othman, editor of Arab news and Arab affairs at 'al-Hayat'. 'We know we reach the decision-makers, the elite, the people who matter.'"

"Its in-depth reporting on the unrest in Algeria, the Arab-Israeli peace process and Islamic militants has been widely praised. But stories on Saudi Arabia and other Gulf states are rarer and hardly ever critical, the newspaper's opinion columns and editorial even less so.

"A recent flap — the Saudi decision to bar Egyptian workers from entering the country — was not mentioned in 'al-Hayat'. The paper has regular stories quoting Iraqi dissidents, but Saudi opposition figures receive scant attention.

"'Al-Hayat's' managing editor, Khairallah Khairallah, acknowledged self-censorship occurs. He defends it as necessary because the newspaper relies on Saudi advertising.

"'Our main concern is not to be banned in Saudi Arabia because most of the advertising comes from the Saudi market,' Khairallah said in a telephone interview from London. 'From time to time we have to take into consideration Saudi censorship.'"

"Atwan, who formerly worked at the Saudi-owned newspaper 'Asharq al-Awsat', also based in London, said the pressure extends to other Gulf states as well.

"'The only country we were allowed to criticize was Israel,' said Atwan, now the editor of 'al-Quds'.

"In a similar development, Pan-Arab satellite television channels and networks have emerged in recent years, including the Middle East Broadcasting Centre, Orbit and Arab Radio and Television. All three are controlled by Saudi investors, and only ART is based in the Arab world — Cairo, Egypt.

"Although all have struggled financially, they carry tremendous influence in reaching the burgeoning satellite dish audience in the Middle East, which has swollen to 2.5 million viewers by some estimates.

"The oldest, the Middle East Broadcasting Centre, was set up in London four years ago and is owned by Sheikh Walid al-Ibrahim, a businessman whose sister is the wife of Saudi King Fahd.

"Its fast-paced, Western-style news broadcasts and roundtable discussions on topics like Arab nationalism and Islam have won it devoted viewers.

"But as with newspapers, Saudi ownership means diminishing diversity of opinion in the Arab world, critics say.

"'A decade ago, there were many parties to the Arab media — the Iraqis, the Libyans, the Palestinians, independent businessmen,' said Riad al-Rayyes, a respected publisher who has written a column syndicated in several Arab newspapers.

"'In those days, you had different voices, rightly or wrongly. Now there is only a monolith, one media state,' he said. 'Diversity has ended.'"

Chapter Four

One World Government Allied With Islam

Today in the United States and worldwide as well, there is, I believe, an agenda by the media for uniformity and an end to diversity. Though CNN has not yet merged with CBS, it has merged with Time-Warner. There seems to be a monopolistic cartel forming, all in league with the One World Government, New World Order, New Age ideology, or one-world media agenda or whatever one wants to call it. One thing is sure, this one world government mind control agenda will be inimical to the interests of the individual, be that person an American, an Israeli, an Arab, or a citizen of any country in the world for that matter as we see in Chapter III.

The infamous Trilateral Commission seeks precisely such a new world order and it knows that its interests lie with Saudi Arabia and the petrodollar. The basic understanding between the two is that world stability is based on stable oil prices and oil supplies.

This fact is underscored by the reported meeting in mid-summer 1990 between United States Ambassador to Iraq April Gillespie just six days before Saddam Hussein's invasion of Kuwait. Reports have it that Saddam queried Ms. Gillespie about what the U.S. reaction would be to his invading Kuwait. April Gillespie denies reports she answered, "Well, as long as the U.S. gets its oil, and its interests are not harmed, the U.S. would basically look the other way."

Whatever Gillespie said, a startled Saudi Arabia immediately cried SOS when Iraq occupied Kuwait in merely six hours, and the United States dutifully did what its Saudi overlords told it to do, namely, stop Saddam from invading Saudi Arabia, and get him out of Kuwait, though Saudi Arabia put in a veto, when the U.S. was in a position to have Saddam Hussein deposed. The administration in Washington in 1991 has sometimes been described as the Bush-Baker-Bandar administration. (The last of the three names is that of Prince Bandar Ibn-Sultan, Saudi Ambassador to Washington).

A cynical viewpoint is that April Gillespie was specifically instructed by President Bush to wink at an Iraqi invasion of Kuwait because he knew that such an invasion would mean big bucks for the United States. Firstly, oil prices would go up, meaning bigger profits for the oil industry i.e., the one world government businessmen. Secondly, U.S. intervention would cost the Arab world dearly both in direct payment for U.S. military services rendered in expunging Saddam Hussein from Kuwait, and indirectly for the mass weapons purchases from the United States expected from the oil-rich Arab regimes in deep gratitude for the Americans saving the hides of the oil rich sheikhs. In any event, it is a cynical, commonly known fact that war is good for business, good for the One World Order because commissions increase on oil imports from the Middle East as well as arms exports to the Middle East. So what if millions of innocent people die in the process? So long as the select rich few in control of the world line their pockets.

An interesting experience in my life highlighting the role of petrodollar one world government interests in America happened to me on April 14th, 1991, just weeks after the end of Desert Storm. This was later to play a crucial formative role in my mission to the Christians and in the writing of this book.

I was invited to speak before the Dallas Council on World Affairs, headed at that time by a General (ret.) Latham. Now, I had not realized it at the time, but the Dallas Council was a local branch of an organization affiliated with the Council on Foreign Relations based in New York City.

Whereas in the past, I spoke usually only in churches and synagogues, this was my first secular forum. It was a petrodollar-banker's forum. It was the monied people of Dallas who were hosting me this time, not Bible people.

Since this speaking appearance took place while the Likud administration of Yitzchak Shamir was still in office, I had to take the brunt of some heavy criticism by the Dallas Council people who were very unhappy with Shamir and the Likud party's "intransigent" position.

It must be remembered that Israel was the unsung hero of Desert Storm. In spite of being hit with a barrage of 43 Iraqi scud missiles, Israel held its fire and did not counterattack against Iraq, exactly as the U.S.-Arab coalition of allies instructed Israel. Yet Israel has always "been there" for the U.S. if so needed as a land-based "aircraft carrier", a logistical prepositioning station, or a second line of defense for the U.S. and the West throughout the Cold War period as well as after. I was not prepared for the rough "broadside" with which I was about to be bombarded by the Dallas Council people.

The main thrust of my message that night was very politically correct from a quasi-Israeli government spokesman. It should be remembered that it was the administration of Prime Minister Yitzhak Shamir which initiated the Madrid Peace Talks of 1990.

I explained in my lecture that Israel had already complied 93% with United Nations' Resolutions 242 and 338 calling for Israeli withdrawal from territories taken during the 1967 and 1973 wars by returning all of Sinai to Egypt (91%) and half of the Golan (2%) to Syria. The remaining 7% of the territories (Judea, Samaria, Gaza and the other half of the Golan Heights) should remain with Israel, because Israel had already compromised 93%, and these few remaining territories were vital to Israel's defense.

In addition, it should be remembered that the two U.N. resolutions do not call for a full withdrawal from all territories taken by Israel in a war of self-defense in 1967. On the contrary, it calls for negotiations between Israel and its neighbors for secure, defensible and recognized new boundaries, because even former Israeli foreign minister Abba Eban had called the 1967 armistice lines "Auschwitz Lines" because they were indefensible. Had the U.N. meant total withdrawal, it would have said so. Had the U.N. meant total withdrawal, there would not have been any room for the words "negotiations for secure, defensible and recognized borders."

After I finished speaking, we adjourned to dinner, to be followed later by a closed businessmen's meeting, during which questions would be asked of me.

During that question and answer period, I was dealt one of the harshest experiences of my life. I was basically told that in spite of my being born and educated as an American, and as a result was an eloquent spokesman for Israel, I had to be "taught" the "realities" of life or realpolitik.

The first reality was as follows: "America is tired of paying for Israel's wars. Israel will pay whatever price it has to make peace with its Arab neighbors. In other words, Israel must fully capitulate to the Arabs and return all the territories it was forced to take in 1967 and 1973, including East Jerusalem, disregarding U.N. resolutions 242 and 338, because the United States would no longer stand by Israel. Israel was all alone, and the U.S. was no longer to be considered an ally.

The second reality was as follows: "The only thing that made America great was the barrel of oil, the steady price of oil and the steady supply of oil, and we (the United States) will not let Israel stand as an obstacle to steady oil prices and supplies."

Now, before I could answer them, two Christian evangelical couples which had invited me to appear on Marlin Maddoux's radio program as well as Zola Levitt's "Holy Land Program" both out of Dallas, and who were now my guests at this dinner and lecture I gave, asked permission to address the Dallas Council people.

One of them, a Mr. Eric Gustavson got up, shaking with fury, and said: "You should all be ashamed of yourselves. You call yourselves Christians? What made America great was not the barrel of oil, but Jesus Christ!" and he sat down. Then his daughter arose, and added: "Besides, it says in the Book of Genesis: 'Whoever blesses Israel is blessed, and whoever curses Israel is cursed!'". (Genesis 27:29 and Numbers 24:9)

Then, it was my turn. My reply to the Dallas Council on World Affairs was as follows:

"We Jews have been around 4,000 years. We don't deserve to have been around. We are a stiffnecked, rambunctious and rebellious people. God punished us again and again for our failing to fulfill God's commandments as we had agreed to do in Exodus 19:5. Only a remnant of the Jewish people remains today. But we do remain because God made a promise to us. Also, Israel was resurrected from the ash heap of history after 2,000 years of Jewish

Diaspora. Whether we deserved it or not is a moot point. What matters is that God and biblical prophecy called for the return of the Jews to the Holy Land and for the recreation of the Jewish State a third time. This is scriptural.

Now oil reserves will run out some time during the coming century, perhaps in 60 to 70 years. God in His divine wisdom will provide man with the wisdom to discover or develop an alternative energy source. Until that time happens, we Jews will not sacrifice ourselves and 4,000 years of our existence for sixty more years of steady oil prices and oil supplies. It is enough that we paid six million Jews as a price for the petrodollar-Arab pressure on England to slam shut the doors of emigration to the Jews of Europe by not allowing them to go to Palestine in the 20's and 30's, thus leaving them prey to the Nazi satanic Holocaust. So the Jews have already paid the price for steady oil prices and supplies. We will not pay with yet another five million Jews from Israel so that the oil corporations will be pleased. Sorry!

But the importance of that night in my life was not in what I said, but what I heard and learned: That the Jews were the sacrifice on the altar of oil. That the Jews had no friends, except perhaps for Bible Christians. Mr. Gustavson and his daughter were my allies that night, but we were the minority.

I saw a battlefield in front of me. My four evangelical Christian friends represented Christian America and the other twenty or so people in the room of the Dallas Council on Foreign Affairs represented the anti-Christ or anti-Christian America. The battlefield at this stage was being controlled by the victorious armies of mammon (money) while the Christians were weak, ineffectual and disorganized.

To quote from the Gospel of Luke 16:13: "No servant can serve two masters: for either he will hate the one and love the other; or else he will hold to the one and despise the other. Ye cannot serve God and mammon."

It was that night, on the 14th of April, 1991, that I, an Israeli, a Jew, and an officer in the Israel Defense Forces reserves, came to the conclusion that for God's sake, for the sake of Israel, for the sake of all Jews, I would devote my future efforts to promoting the cause of the Christian side as opposed to the anti-Christ side that would acquiesce to and maybe even support another Jewish Ho-locaust for the sake of oil and money. After all, the anti-Christ side has a proven track record from World War II. President Roosevelt would not even bomb the railroad tracks to the concentration camps. At least one million Jews could have been saved. The British did everything in their power to lock the Jews into the Nazi inferno of occupied Europe behind Wehrmacht lines. Since the British and Americans would not let the Jews out, due to Arab oil pressure, Hitler was stuck with them, and so the decision regarding the "Final Solution of the Jewish Problem" was taken. Now, I am not defending Hitler at all. But Hitler was not a alone. Churchill and Roosevelt were accomplices. They belonged to the "One World Government."

The inescapable conclusions of that evening on my life were that Christians who love God, the Bible, Israel and the Jewish people must be organized and supported by us so that they, too, can support Israel and a pro-Israel administration in Washington. Otherwise, Washington will be pro-oil, pro-Arab (as it has always been), and will sacrifice Israel with all its population, five million Jews and Christians plus three million Moslems, and "look the other way", as April Gillespie reportedly put it, while the corporation, big-business, petro-dollar backed Moslems close in on the kill of the expendable relatively poorer Israel.

Another conclusion from that evening which became more and more evident after the bomb attack on the World Trade Center in New York City in February 1993 and the showing of Steven Emerson's famous "Jihad in America" documentary movie on American TV in November 1994 was that America and the West, whether they realize it or not are really in the same boat as Israel.

It is now the Arabian petrodollar which has Christendom by the jugular. However, since oil reserves are expected to be depleted by seventy years from now and replaced by alternative energy sources, it is the coming seventy years which will be critical for Islam to impose its will on the world and convert the world to Islam. Or, as Iranian Ayatollah Janati was quoted as saying in Teheran: "The 21st century will be the century of Islam."

Is Time Running Out for Islam and its Petroleum?

My contention is that time is running short for Islam to take over the world. In seventy years, there will be no more oil. Therefore, mutant fanatical Islam must act now while it still has the petrodollar and petroleum reserves and those Christians who do the bidding for them.

There is a Christian prophecy in Chapter twelve of the Book of the Revelation about a dragon, Satan, attacking a woman and her child. According to this tradition, the woman is Israel, her child Jesus.

Verse one reads: "And there appeared a great wonder in heaven; a woman clothed with the sun, and the moon under her feet, and upon her head a crown of twelve stars:"

(In my opinion, the moon under her feet is the netherworld of darkness. Since the moon is holy to Moslems, and Allah, the moon-god is a war god — so the moon is rising up out of the netherworld to attack the woman and child.)

Verse twelve reads: "*Therefore, rejoice, ye heavens, and ye that dwell in them. Woe to the inhabiters of the earth and of the sea! For the devil is come down unto you, having great wrath, because he knoweth that he hath but a short time.*"

Could this not be an accurate allegory for the end-time scenario we now face?

For what has the Islamic system done with all the blessings and riches God bestowed on them with their petroleum? What major industries have they developed in their countries? Why is illiteracy growing and the birthrate exploding? Why are they creating desolation instead of rolling back the deserts? Why is it that when the military dictatorships of Latin America have all gone democratic; when the former communist and socialist world is striving to become democratic; it is only the Moslem and Arab world, with the exception of a shaky Turkey that precludes any possibility of democracy and freedom of worship, and marches backward to the 7th century and the brutality of the middle ages?

The wealth has gone to profligate spending on weapons of mass destruction, building war machines, the few amassing great wealth while the overwhelming majority suffer in poverty. Gold-plated faucets, expensive cars and debauchery in casinos outside of their home countries are the order of the day for oil-rich Islamic leaders while the masses starve. And, of course, America and Israel are to blame for that.

During and after Israel's War of Independence in 1948-9, an exchange of populations took place. One million Jews were expelled from Islamic countries (including my wife and her family) and one million Arabs left Israel. Israel cared for its fellow Jews, while the Palestinian refugees were holed up in camps to serve as political pawns. The oil-rich Moslems could have easily settled them and healed this festering wound. Now the Islamic side wants Israel to take back the four million Arab refugees and resettle them within Israel meaning — the end of Israel. Obviously, Israel will never take them back just as Greece and Turkey, India and Pakistan, and other nations had population exchanges and took back fellow nationals or co-religionists and were not forced to take back those hostile populations which left.

Why is it that when one thinks of fanatic Islam, one cannot help but think of Somalia, where there are no longer any Christians or Jews to cast the blame upon, but where rival clans fight it out for control of a totally devastated country. In Islamic Somalia, there is no democracy.

What about Afghanistan? There are no Christians or Jews there either. Yet there are four rival factions with the fanatic Taliban having the upper hand. Women can no longer leave their homes to go out to work. They must now remain at home and be paid for staying at home. Since there is no money in the exchequer, so they probably will starve. Afghanistan's male population suffered heavily during decades of civil war and Soviet intervention. Women were trained to be doctors, nurses, teachers and administrators, because there were simply no men around or left. Now that is over. The women must remain home and starve. This is fanatic Islam.

Another charming example of fanatic Islam is Libya and Muammar Gaddafi. There are no Jews or Christians there, either, that can be blamed. There have been numerous bloody attempted coups against Gaddafi, all ruthlessly suppressed. And yes, Gaddafi is the biggest importer of black children slaves from the slave markets of Khartoum, Sudan. Gaddafi is also the big financial backer of another great lover of Jews and Christians — Louis Farrakhan. I will deal with him later.

Algeria, though not officially a fanatic Islamic state, had a majority of its people vote for a fanatic Islamic party. The results of the elections were annulled and a bloody civil war is now taking place with over 65,000 deaths at the time of the writing of this book. Many were blown up by bombs, many were hacked to death with knives and axes. Some were just dismembered by chain saws. It is still not clear what the outcome will be. By the way, this war has nothing to do with the Jews or Christians.

So, here, one has some of the above examples of the pure Islamic utopias one can expect when the Islamic system takes over. Those who suffer first and foremost from fanatic Islam are the Moslems themselves. Again, as I said at the beginning of this book, my message is not against Moslems as human beings, but rather, at the fanatic Islamic system which dooms all the Moslems living under this system to starvation, deprivation, misery and tyranny. My heart goes out to the Moslems. What will happen to these retrogressive radical Islamic regimes when the oil money runs out?

The Islamic Demographic Invasions Of America And Europe

I believe there is a "push-pull" tendency of Islamic emigration which will play a major role in the futures of all western countries. As I said in the last few paragraphs, the tyranny of the fanatic Islamic regimes is so oppressive that millions of Moslems have fled for better lives in the west. This is the "pull" effect of the west for better living conditions.

Most Americans do not realize that there is an insidious demographic invasion of Christian America and Europe taking place right now by Moslems who are now the third religion in America (14 million) after Protestants and Catholics, leaving the Jews as a diminishing fourth (5 million)? The 14 million Moslems are more than 5% of the American population. In France, for example, the Moslems comprise close to 10% of the population.

These same Moslems quietly move into their new adopted homes, at first, quietly accepting and respecting the laws of the land in which they live. However, as their birthrate far surpasses that of their Christian or Jewish neighbors, and as the flood of Moslem refugees swells their ranks, they become a sizeable minority with a great voting constituency, a fact which cannot go ignored by politicians who need their votes to be elected.

The second effect of the "push" is the bribing of United States and European universities by oil-rich benefactors from the Middle East. Once money has been accepted by the universities, they are powerless to refuse granting visas or green cards to the thousands of new Moslems students entering the new western countries every year.

Whether or not this is an insidious plan by the Islamic leaders over a period of a few decades to create sizeable Islamic populations to influence and perhaps takeover formerly Christian countries, is a moot point. The point is that these sizeable Moslem communities are in place and are now threatening , and will increase their threat as time goes on, to the former traditions of the pre-Islamic invasion times.

After these students arrive in American and European universities, many decide to stay in their new host countries upon completion of their studies, receive citizenship, marry local Christian women, and join the vanguard of the Islamic invasion of America and Europe.

This reminds me of an experience I had in a church in Brownsville, Texas in January 1995. During the question and answer period, a woman asked me, "Why do Moslem men seek to marry American Christian women?"

I answered that I was not going to "knock" romance. That indeed, opposites attract, and the Rudolf Valentino image of the romantic Arab sheikh was a familiar flashback to the movies of that era. But I did say that it is common for many men and women immigrants or tourists to seek the "Green Card", which is the gateway to U.S. citizenship, but that after this green card has been attained, many of these marriages end in divorce. I added that unfortunately, though, Moslem men do live by different rules than Christian women, and it is unfortunate that the latter are unaware of the differences between Christian western and Moslem eastern cultures and behaviors.

I also related the story about Nizar Hindawi, a Palestinian who went to seek his fortunes in London, England, befriended an

Irish cleaning girl, got her pregnant, and in the eighth month of pregnancy made her the following proposition:

"The time has come for us to marry. You must go to Palestine to meet my family and get their approval so that we may marry." The young Irishwoman, carrying this gentleman's baby was anxious for the marriage, so she was glad to agree to go to Israel to meet the prospective in-laws.

Upon arrival at Heathrow Airport in London, EL AL Airlines security went through the routine security check and asked the woman, bulging in her eighth month of pregnancy where her husband was. She answered that she was not yet married and that she was going to "Palestine" to meet the prospective groom's parents.

At this point, the alert EL AL security agents became suspicious, thoroughly checked the lady's luggage and found an altitude bomb set to go off as the plane reached an altitude of 20,000 feet, thus averting perhaps one of the worst aviation terrorist acts in history. Perhaps Nizar Hindawi's guide was the Koran. In verse thirty-three of Sura 17 "The Night Journey" we read the Islamic equivalent of the biblical 6th commandment: "You shall not kill any man whom Allah has forbidden you to kill, except for a just cause." Nizar Hindawi was going to blow up his intended and his own as of yet unborn son — his own flesh and blood for a just cause: bringing down an El Al airliner.

As I was finishing to relate this little piece of news which was only briefly mentioned in the U.S. press, I noticed a young Christian woman in the church sitting with my Egyptian born wife (who was accompanying me on that lecture circuit) in the first row. They were having an animated discussion.

As I concluded the questions and answers, the young lady's parents approached me in tears and said to me: "Save our daughter!"

"What do you mean?" I answered.

"We are about to lose our daughter! Save our daughter!" They were hysterical.

Finally, they calmed down enough to tell me her story. She was a student at the University of Texas in Austin, and had met a Saudi prince at a flying school there. On their second date, the Saudi prince proposed to her. He seemed the man of any American girl's dreams. Tall, dark, and handsome, and fabulously rich with a palace and chauffeurs back home in Saudi Arabia. A real Rudolf Valentino sheikh of Araby.

The young lady herself asked him how she could live in Saudi Arabia without being allowed to drive a car, because it is against the law for a woman to drive a car in Saudi Arabia. His answer was swift: "You don't need to drive. We have chauffeurs."

Finally, as people were leaving the church, the young lady, her parents, the pastor and my wife and myself, sat together to discuss this.

We told the young lady that the moment she left the sovereign territory of the United States with this Saudi prince, that she no longer enjoyed the rights America has to offer her because Saudi Arabia lives by different values.

"Would you share your husband with three other wives?" we asked, continuing, "You know that he is entitled to four wives according to the Koran. And the Koran is the law of the land in Saudi Arabia. You know your children will be Moslems, because that, too, is the law of the land. You know that you will have to completely cover yourself with the veil from head to toe, because that, too, is the law of the land. You know that eventually, pressure will be brought to bear on you to convert to Islam because you are a Christian infidel defiling the holy Islamic land of Saudi Arabia, and that if you are unhappy with this, you really have no choice, and if you are disobedient, it says in the Koran that your husband is commanded to beat you. And if you do not like this, your body might be found at the bottom of the royal swimming pool with chains wrapped around it. And nobody will be very interested in investigating the matter in the Saudi judicial system, because justice there, really means something entirely else. Once you leave America for any Islamic country, you lose almost all the rights you may have had in America."

After visiting Brownsville, Texas again in July 1997, I was gratified to meet this young lady again and to know that we saved the young woman from making the wrong decision in life. But there are many such American women who marry Moslem men and realize too late they got more than they bargained for, even while living in America, and then find themselves in an often intolerable condition in Islamic lands which are very antagonistically prejudicial against the status of these women, especially egalitarian western women.

But, returning to America, many of these Moslem men do stay here with their American wives. Many of the women do convert to Islam thus resulting in a spurious growth of this most rapidly expanding religious group in America and in the world for that matter.

From a small quiet minority, these new Moslem citizens press their right to vote, then to be heard and to influence their neighbors to accept more and more "Islamic" rights, and finally the aggressive, mutant form of Islamic activity which includes stifling any criticism of the Koran, buying out that criticizing voice when possible, and if that doesn't work, by threats, violence and even assassination.

The final threat to America is that Islam will stifle freedom of speech in America because, unlike Judaism or Christianity, fanatic Islam will make sure to it that anyone criticizing Islam will be silenced. Later on, as Moslems reach 20% and 30% and more of the population, it will utilize American democracy just as Hitler utilized Weimar German democracy to ascend to power or act as power brokers within the system and then eject the democratic system which is unacceptable to Islam and which cannot be reconciled with Islam. This can happen within a decade or two.

According to Seif Ashmawi, a moderate Moslem who publishes "The Voice of Peace" newspaper in the United States and whose life has been threatened numerous times by radical Moslems: "These people have their own doctrine. They could accuse you that you are not a Moslem. They could accuse you that you are an infidel. By saying that, which is the word 'Kafer', or infidel, you are being put out of the community, in other words, your blood has become lawful. Anyone could kill you and if he does did so in the way of God. Hitler came to power in a democracy means. Mussolini came to power in a democratic means. Those people are using the democracy just to reach the power. Once they have the power, there will be no democracy. I heard this over and over and over again, from many of them. I read their publications. They are saying: 'There is no democracy in Islam.'" (Steven Emerson's "Jihad in America")

American and western democracy, as we know them, are the fruits of classical Greek democracy which was a democracy of the elite, broadened through Judeo-Christian civilization of the last two millennia into a universalist system including all races, religions, and, of course, both sexes. This is anathema to Islam.

The purpose of this book is to serve as an introductory guide on the threats of fanatic Islam to the perplexed American, to the religious, pious citizen, be that person Christian, Jewish, Hindu, Buddhist, or even a Moslem who believes in democracy and the Judeo-Christian ethic and wants to defend the traditional way of American life as he or she knows it.

I say also Moslem because the first person to suffer from the fanatical brand of mutant Islam is the Moslem himself or herself who is forced to forego a modern, progressive, and open lifestyle in the American way and of the 21st century for a "new world order" that Islam wishes to impose first on the Moslem, then on the infidel.

According to Adel Yousef, a moderate Sudanese Moslem, who knows some of those convicted for the Trade Center bombing: "They (the fanatic Moslems) believe all the Westerners are the enemies of Islam, all the Christian and Jewish groups are the enemies of Islam.

And they believe even there are some Islamic groups working with those western people, they are enemies of Islam, and they said those are even (more) dangerous than the Westerners themselves." (Emerson's "Jihad in America")

In the Moslem world itself, one only has to think of the kind of life that the simple people must suffer with under the yoke of the ayatollahs — especially to half the population — the women who are degraded to a level worse than slavery, who must veil themselves from head to toe because it is a sin to be seen, who cannot drive a car, and who must accept forced arranged marriages or live according to the whims of fathers or brothers or face a death penalty for bringing dishonor to the family name. These are just a few examples unacceptable to western and civilized norms, where moral standards and punishments long ago abolished in civilized countries are still the norm; where even the slightest criticism or attempt at objective thinking critical of the "divine and infallible" Koran is punishable by death, such as in the case of Salman Rushdie and his book, "Satanic Verses," and several other cases in which prominent good Moslems were assassinated by fanatic co-religionists.

In the western world, those of us who consider ourselves religious Jews or Christians cringe when criticism or worse is leveled at the Bible, but as Voltaire said, "I may not agree with what you say, but I defend with my life your right to say it." This is our Judeo-Christian tradition. God will deal with the doers of good and evil in due time. But we, as democratic people believing in freedom, allow one and all a fair say in a spirit of debate and academic integrity.

This is not the case in Islam. The Koran cannot be changed by one letter, comma or iota. Everything that appears in the Koran must be taken literally because Moslems see their book as divine and infallible directly revealed by God to his prophet Mohammed. Any deviation or irreverence is punishable by death.

Can America tolerate such a situation? If so, then it is a death sentence for American democracy and freedom of speech as well. This is indeed the reason I write this as a clarion call to Americans to wake up to this Islamic threat before it is too late.

In Israel, Moslems are full and accepted citizens active in Israel's army, government, public life, and politics. Israel's lifestyle is open and western in style. It also has Jews and Christians of all denominations in its army and public life. This would not be the case if the roles were reversed and Jews and Christians in the Holy Land were minorities under Islam.

In fact, though Jews and Christians are considered the "People of the Book" to be protected by Islam, while all other religions are considered pagan and their adherents immediately put to the sword, Jews and Christians are understood by Islam to be subjugated and, eventually — at the end of days — converted to Islam or also put to the sword as the other pagans. Therefore, it is clear that Islam is not universal or tolerant of any other religion — and therefore is anti-democratic, un-American and even inhuman.

Chapter Five

Is Islam Un-American?

If one opens up the Koran, the book holy to Moslems, to verse 51 in Chapter V known as "The Table" (p. 116 in the Penguin Classics Koran), one is astounded to read the following:

"Believers, take neither Jews nor Christians for your friends. They are friends with one another. Whoever of you seeks their friendship shall become one of their number. God does not guide the wrongdoers."

Again, as I said in the introduction, one cannot question or change even one letter in the Koran. This cannot be interpreted in any way other than it appears in the Koran.

The Judeo-Christian tradition teaches us to "love thy neighbor as thyself," to do unto others as you have them do unto you and not to do to others as you would not have them do unto you. Again, the question of belief or unbelief in God is an entirely personal question between a person and his or her conscience. It is, of course, understandable and acceptable to try to convert an "outsider" to a cause or religion -but this has nothing to do with friendships.

But in the Koran, a Moslem is commanded not to take a Jew or a Christian as a friend. This is outrageous and patently un-American. After all, what is America? Why was it created? Judaism and its sister religion, Christianity, teach to love one's brother, friend, or neighbor. Not being able to be friends is hateful. And if a Moslem says he is my friend, either he is ignorant of his Koran, or betraying either me or his holy book.

Another aspect of how the Moslem views his "infidel" neighbor can be seen on page 206 of the Penguin Classics Koran in verse 123 of chapter IX called "Repentance": *"Believers make war on the infidels who dwell around you. Deal firmly with them."* This must have been the motto of Sheikh Abdul Rahman of New Jersey and his followers who were convicted of attempting to blow up the twin towers of the World Trade Center in New York City. What other explanation can there be for such a senseless crime?

Actually, a Washington-based researcher Dr. Laurie Mylroie has written a book based on the minutes of Sheikh Abdul Rahman's trial and all the evidence paves a trail straight back to Saddam Hussein and Iraq. Ramzi Yousef, the "engineer" behind the New York City bombing is a Baluchi Moslem under the employ of Saddam. Saddam wanted and is still seeking to avenge the deaths of hundreds of thousands of Iraqis because of his defeat in Desert Storm and the aftermath which the terrible deprivation in Iraq caused by world economic sanctions imposed by the UN at the initiative of the US.

By the way, Dr. Mylroie, also said in an August 1997 interview with Don Wiedeman and Avi Lipkin on American Freedom Network Radio that Saddam Hussein promised the world a surprise for Iraq's National Day in August 1996. The following day of Iraq's holiday was capped off with the shooting down of TWA-800 by a missile off the southern shore of Long Island.

In Chapter VIII "The Spoils" verses 12-16, we are further shocked to read:

12. *God revealed His will to the angels, saying: "I shall be with you. Give courage to the believers.*

13. *I shall cast terror into the hearts of the infidels. Strike off their heads, strike off the very tips of their fingers!"*

14. *That was because they defied God and His apostle.*

15. *He that defies God and His apostle shall be sternly punished by God. We said to them: 'Taste this. The scourge of the Fire awaits the unbelievers.'*

16. *Believers, when you encounter the infidels on the march, do not turn your backs to them in flight. If anyone on that day turns his back*

to them, except for tactical reasons, or to join another band, he shall incur the wrath of God and Hell shall be his home: an evil fate.

In Chapter II entitled "The Cow", Moslems are told:

216: Fighting is obligatory for you, much as you dislike it. But you may hate a thing although it is good for you, and love a thing although it is bad for you. God knows, but you know not...

Idolatry is worse than carnage.

217: They will not cease to fight against you until they force you to renounce your faith — if they are able. But whoever of you recants and dies an unbeliever, his works shall come to nothing in this world and in the world to come. Such men shall be the tenants of Hell, wherein they shall abide for ever.

Steven Emerson shows Sheikh Omar Abdul Rahman, convicted together with his followers of attempting to blow up and destroy the twin towers of the World Trade Center, in his documentary as saying clearly at an Islamic rally held in Detroit in 1991:

"The obligation of Allah is upon us to wage Jihad for the sake of Allah. It is one of the obligations that we must undoubtedly fulfill. And we conquer the lands of the infidels, and we spread Islam by calling the infidels to Allah. And if they stand in our way, we wage Jihad for the sake of Allah."

In Emerson's "Jihad in America" we also hear Sheikh Abdallah Azam addressing the First Conference of Jihad in Brooklyn in 1989 saying: "The Jihad, the fighting is obligatory on you wherever you can perform it. And just as when you are in America you must fast, unless you are ill or on a voyage, so, too, must you wage Jihad... The word Jihad means fighting only, fighting with the sword."

We hear and see Sheikh Abdul Walid Zindani, director of the Al-Kifah Refugee Center in Brooklyn speaking about fighting the "idol-worshippers" (a reference to Christians and Jews).

"Allah, the most high and exalted, ordered us to kill the idol-worshippers, the enemies of Allah. Fight the idol worshippers all together just as they fight all of you. When you go into battle, fight the idol worshippers wherever you find them. Pursue them, and finish them off." (Ibid)

We see and hear Sami Dhafar, head of the Islamic Charity Project speaking at an ICP radical Islamic convention saying: "We want this small Muslim community to serve as a dagger in the center of the this (US) civilization." (Ibid)

Finally, in verse 56 of Chapter IV "Women" it says:

"Those that deny our revelations we will burn in fire. No sooner will their skins be consumed than we will give them other skins, so that they may truly taste the scourge."

Is this democratic or the American way!

In verse 34 of Chapter V, "The Table", it says:

Those that make war against God and His apostle (Mohammed) and spread disorder in the land shall be put to death or crucified or have their hands and feet cut off on alternate sides, or be banished from the country."

I think President Bush had a taste of this during his narrow escape from an Iraqi hit team while visiting Kuwait after the 1991 Gulf War, because "he made war against God and His apostle and spread disorder in the land (Iraq) and was almost put to death."

Over 1,000 Palestinians were brutally executed by fellow Palestinians for alleged "cooperation" with Israeli authorities during the Intifada (uprising) between 1987 and 1994. Many hundreds of them were found with "their hands and feet cut off on alternate sides," as well as other parts of their bodies. Why? Because the Koran commands it.

The final quote from the Koran is on page 284 from the 33rd verse of chapter XVII, "Night Journey," where the Islamic equivalent of one of the Ten Commandments appears:

"You shall not kill any man whom God has forbidden you to kill, except for a just cause." So much for the absolute "Thou shall not kill" in the Judeo-Christian Bible. Also, if you can kill for a just cause, so, too, can you lie, steal, rape, destroy, and enslave for a just cause. Something is very wrong with the Koran.

The above quotes were taken very literally from the Koran — the written law of Islam, as well as from speeches radical Muslim leaders make here, on American soil.

When Hitler wrote *Mein Kampf* while in jail in 1923, people scoffed with disbelief. They thought this book was comic, and when Hitler came to power in 1933, nobody believed he would really do as he said he would in his book. But Hitler did exactly as he promised. He wrote what he meant, and he meant what he wrote.

My premise is that when one reads the Koran, Moslems consider "infallible" and unchangeable, followed by the Islamic Oral tradition, it is enough to set my hair on end, and from what other Jews and Christians say when they hear or read the above, theirs, too. Very unfortunately, most American Jews and Christians, and I would dare to say even Moslems, are not well versed in the Koran and Oral Tradition.

My suggestion, therefore, to all humanity is to read and study what the Koran preaches and be warned. Ignorance is the first enemy in this battle to defend democracy and the American way.

According to a *New York Times* article by Ari Goldman on U.S. prisons from September 6, 1993, an established 17% of the U.S. jail population is Moslem. Whether they be Moslems originating from the Middle East or American born, they must be made to read the above quotes and to say to their fellow Americans if that is what they really believe. I think that many who call themselves Moslems are unaware of what the texts really say, but have been "spoon-fed" with what the Islamic preachers want them to know only. Should they become aware, many would immediately disassociate themselves from Islam if they are humanists, but if they are aware, and really believe the above quotes, then look out! Because the quotes indeed are un-American and are inimical to everything America stands for.

Finally, Iran, which is behind this international Islamic takeover bid, says in its daily newspapers: "America is the Great Satan, America is doomed. Death to America! It is only a question of time." This may sound comic to Americans, but for someone like myself who lives in the Middle East and deals daily with Islamic radio, TV and press, that is all we hear. The Moslem extremists say and mean it. **It is the Islamic *Mein Kampf*.** And for them, the way to strike at Israel, America's surrogate, is by striking at the Great Satan, America, the puppeteer pulling Israel's strings and supporting it.

Chapter Six

Israel's Striving for Peace in the Middle East vs. Fanatic Islam

Very often, people in Israel, Jews, Christians and Moslems ask whether peace is attainable in the Middle East, considering that two peoples — Arabs and Jews — are fighting over a very small piece of land in a very large territorial sea of Islam.

The Jews, whose last revolt against Rome in A.D. 135 led to the final loss of Jewish sovereignty in the Holy Land for almost two millennia, have known terrible persecutions, expulsions, tortures, and unnatural deaths. The purpose of this book is not to document all of these sorrowful pages in Jewish history — which include the Crusades, the expulsion and inquisition in Spain, the massacres of the Ukrainian leader Cmielnicki of 1648, nor of the Russian pogroms, nor of the Nazi Holocaust of 1933 to 1945 — but to draw a conclusion that there is no people that seeks peace and safety more than the Jews. Ironically, it is this people that knows peace the least and desires it the most.

The Jews almost uninterruptedly maintained a presence in the Holy Land even after the failed Bar Kochba revolt of A.D. 132 to 135, but the massive return of the Jewish people to its land began only about a century ago.

With the awakening of Arab-Islamic fanaticism after WWI came the first pogroms (anti-Jewish) riots in Palestine of 1920, 1921, the infamous riots of 1929 in Hebron, and finally, the Arab revolt of 1936 to 1939 against the British mandatory authorities in Palestine. Hundreds of Jews were slaughtered and mutilated during these riots and revolts. All of this was even before the creation of the Jewish State of Israel in 1948. Ironically, though, for every Jew the Arab terrorists killed, they killed ten of each other in internecine terror.

With the United Nations' decision in 1947 to partition Palestine into a Jewish and an Arab state came agreement by David Ben Gurion of Israel and rejection by all the Arab parties to the dispute. Seven Arab armies invaded the fledgling State of Israel on May 15th after irregulars had already been fighting the Jews for over six months.

The War for Independence lasted over a year. By some miracle, Israel survived — and on land greater in size than the U.N. partition plan. A cease fire was achieved after the Rhodes talks in 1949, but not a peace agreement. For years, fedayeen (Arab infiltrators) wreaked havoc on Israeli settlements and even travelers in buses and private vehicles. By 1956, Israel found itself in need of stopping these fedayeen infiltrations and terrorist attacks.

At the same time, Egyptian President Gamal Abdul Nasser was massively arming Egypt with Soviet and Eastern bloc weaponries in preparation for a war with Israel. Nasser blocked the Straits of Tiran to Israeli shipping which in itself was a casus belli, and then poured tens of thousands of his troops into Sinai to attack Israel. Since Nasser also nationalized the Suez Canal, Israel together with Britain and France participated in the Sinai Campaign against Egypt. This was Israel's second war.

President Eisenhower forced Israel to withdraw from the Sinai in 1957, but promised Israel U.S. military intervention and support should the Straits of Tiran be again blocked by Egypt, which is precisely what happened in May, 1967. But the U.S. claimed it could not find the agreement in the safe of the State Department and so it balked at fulfilling this solemn agreement. At the same time, the Egyptians were again massively rearming with Soviet weaponries, pouring over 100,000 troops into Sinai and finally, with the expulsion of the U.N. peace keeping troops from Gaza and Sinai, it became evident to Israel that it was facing a third war with Egypt.

Due to a series of Arab miscalculations and blunders, Israel was again cornered into a war for its survival. It preemptively attacked Egypt. It warned Jordan to stay out of the fray, but when

King Hussein refused to heed these warnings and ordered the shelling of Jerusalem as well as the Jordanian Legionaires' incursion-invasion into Jerusalem across U.N. held Government House in Armon Hanatziv near Talpiot, the Israeli response was to defend itself leading to the liberation of Jerusalem and the West Bank (Judea and Samaria). When the Syrians continued their artillery bombardment of the Israeli settlements in the north of Israel, Israel decided on the fifth and sixth days of the Six Days War to silence the Syrian artillery by taking the Golan Heights. The result of this war was that the 1949 map of Israel (which was greater than the map of the U.N. partition) was now again increased to include Sinai, the West Bank (Judea and Samaria), as well as the formerly Syrian Golan. This was war number three for Israel in twenty years of existence.

Israel, however, immediately declared that it was willing to return the land it had to take through war in its own self-defense in order to arrive at a peace agreement with the Arab world. The Arabs' answer came at the Khartoum conference in 1968: "No recognition, no negotiations, no peace."

As a result of this refusal by the Arabs to even consider talking to the Israelis, it was decided to begin modest settlement of the newly acquired territories by Jewish settlers. This was a decision of the Labor government of Levi Eshkol in 1968.

At the same time, an unofficial and unpublicized war of attrition was taking place between Israel and Egypt across the Suez Canal. This went on from 1968 to 1970. Hundreds of Israeli soldiers were killed or wounded.

In October, 1973, war number four took place (not including the above war of attrition). Egypt and Syria surprise-attacked Israel on Yom Kippur, the holiest day of fasting in the Jewish calendar. Over 2,500 Israeli soldiers were killed and the same amount made invalid for the rest of their lives.

In 1982, war number five took place in Lebanon. The aim of Operation Peace in the Galilee was to free Lebanon of the PLO terrorist presence and mini-state in Lebanon. Over eight hundred Israelis died in this operation, as well as the Israeli occupation of the areas south of Beirut over a period of three years.

The reason I mention these five wars between Israel and the Arabs is not to try to attempt to give a history of Israel's military history, but to put into perspective certain quotes by Syrian President Hafez Assad, who has gone on record as saying:

"The Arabs have lost five wars against Israel. We can afford to lose ninety-nine wars — we only need the hundredth war."
or:

"We Arabs waited two hundred years to kick out the crusaders from the Holy Land. The Israelis have only been here fifty years — so we can wait another one hundred fifty years."

or, in light of the present Israeli attempts at reaching peace with the Palestinians on the one hand and Jordan on the other:

"Anyone who gives up one inch of Arab land (Jerusalem) will be considered a traitor, and we all know the destiny of traitors in the Arab world." (*Time Magazine*, November 22nd, 1992).

Finally, Israel is often equated with the Christian West. During the Gulf War from January to March, 1991, as the scud missiles were falling on Tel Aviv, Moslem residents of Ramallah would stand on their roof tops cheering the missiles on as they flew overhead from east to west, chanting:

"Ya Saddam, Ya Habib
Idrab Tel-Abib
Ya Saddam, Ya Habib
Idrab El-Selib."

Which translated means:

"Oh Saddam, Dear Saddam,
Strike at Tel Aviv
Oh Saddam, Dear Saddam
Strike at the cross."

Chapter Seven

Israel's Dilemma in Returning Territories

There is a rabbinical tale of a judge who had to hear a case. When the plaintiff completed his arguments, the judge immediately said: "You are right." After the defendant completed telling his side of the story, the judge also replied: "You are right." A third and independent party corrected the judge, saying: "It cannot possibly be that both sides are right." The Judge replied: "You, too, are right!"

In 1995 in Israel, the argument is raging between an almost equally divided nation as to whether any territories can be returned for peace. The right wing, led by the Likud, believes in providing autonomy to the Palestinians, but that surrendering sovereignty over any territories west of the Jordan River or the Golan Heights would threaten Israel's existence; the left wing, led by the Labor party, believes that the best security for Israel is not territories but peace agreements with the Arabs.

Both are right. And when I speak in uniform as an Israel Defense Forces spokesman in my reserves service, I represent both sides and try to present a consensus because the army must be neutral and apolitical. The vicissitudes of Israeli politics are such that either the Likud or Labor could exchange power at virtually any time, but the military realities on the battleground remain the same.

The Likud subscribes primarily to the military strategy that the armor, artillery, infantry and air forces require strategic depth in order to maintain security. From Amman, the capital of Jordan, it takes attack aircraft three minutes to reach and bomb Jerusalem, another three minutes to attack and bomb Tel Aviv, and another five minutes to fly back to Amman — a total of eleven minutes, which is equivalent to scramble time in the U.S. Air Force.

Another example of the close proximity of borders between Israel and the Jordan River, for example, is that it takes about twenty minutes to drive from the Allenby Bridge on the Jordan River up to Jerusalem. It does not matter if it is a private car or a military vehicle such as a tank or armored personnel carrier. Finally, as in the days of the Bible, one can even walk up to Jerusalem from the Jordan River in a matter of hours, something especially easy for well trained invading commandos. These same points involving aircraft, road vehicles or infantry apply all along the Jordan River border between Israel and the Kingdom of Jordan, and all along the Judea-Samaria mountain ridge which dominates Israel's coastal plain, a total of about sixty miles from the Jordan River to the Mediterranean Sea. Therefore, for the Likud, maintaining Israel's military presence along the Jordan River is critical for protecting Israel from any invading army coming from the east.

The previous borders of pre-1967 left a "narrow waistline" of only nine miles between the then Jordanian held West Bank towns of Kalkilya and Tulkarm on the Arab side, and Hadera and Netanya on the Israeli side. An invading army of a million or so "Islamic" volunteers would be unstoppable were it to cross such a border. Therefore, Israel, according to the Likud, must never return to the pre-1967 borders. In fact, Saddam Hussein occupied Kuwait in six hours. (Kuwait is the size of the West Bank). It took six months for the U.S.-led coalition to dislodge him. Israel, according to the Likud party, says, and rightfully so, that Israel would not be able to wait six months for salvation from the U.S. in the event of an Arab army occupation.

As for the Golan, the sixteen miles separating the Syrian territory starting in Kuneitra and the Jordan River and Sea of Galilee prevent Syrian artillery from taking pot shots at Israel as it did before the Six Day War in 1967, as well as other hostile combatant activity which forced Israel to take the Golan Heights in an act of self-defense. Military assessments today concur that a Syrian army crossing over the Jordan River as a border would probably be unstoppable before it reaches Nazareth or maybe even Haifa, only an hour's drive away. So goes the Likud argument.

Labor's strategy is that missiles fired from Syria recognize no borders on the Golan, and that Syria's thousand or more stockpiled improved Scud and Frog missiles can hit virtually any target inside Israel with absolute accuracy, that unlike Saddam Hussein's missiles which carry warheads of 250 kgs, Syria's missiles carry the full payload of 1,250 kgs, and that instead of six minutes to reach Israel from Iraqi bases H2 and H3 in western Iraq, Syrian missiles can reach Israel in a mere two minutes.

At the same time, these missiles would wreak havoc on Israel, killing and wounding perhaps hundreds of thousands of civilians as well as military people in addition to the material damage in the first two minutes of the next war, God forbid. The question is asked: Could or would Israel retaliate? And if so, to what extent? What would be the world or America's response to this? And finally, would it make a difference in the world's concept of fulfilling UN Resolutions 242 and 338 calling on Israel to return territories in exchange for recognition and a negotiated peace? So Labor's approach is to try to avoid the Syrian missiles from being fired in the first place because in the final analysis, the world will require Israel to return the Golan to Syria anyway.

In fact, in 1971, Sadat hinted that he would be willing to make peace with Israel if Israel returned Sinai to Egypt. But Israel, under the Labor party at that time, and with the tacit agreement of the Likud party said: "Better Sinai without peace than peace without Sinai." In 1973, Egypt and Syria secretly attacked Israel. Israel lost 2,500 soldiers killed as well as number even greater in wounded, 2,000 tanks and hundreds of aircraft in the first three weeks of war. President Nixon and Secretary of State Kissinger immediately ordered an American airlift of war materiel to Israel - without which Israel could not have continued fighting until its military victory a few months later. There was a price tag attached, however. Israel had to return Sinai to Egypt and part of the Golan to Syria - which it did.

In fact, Israel did fulfill 91% of U. N. Resolutions 242 and 338 by returning Sinai, and another 2% by returning half the Golan to Syria. Today's negotiations regarding the Golan Heights involved another 2% of territory and the West Bank and Gaza represent another 5%. So Israel has already compromised 93% on the territories and the present Labor administration in Israel may be willing to compromise more now, before another war breaks out -again, because if a war breaks out, it will not change the bottom line, that the world will require Israel to compromise even more on these territories, and no one will be able to bring the casualties back to life, so it is best to cure a war by preventing one.

So went the Labor administration's policy between 1992-1996. And indeed, war was prevented. The only fly in the ointment was that the majority of Jews in Israel (close to 60%) opposed what was considered giving away too much too quickly to the Palestinians under the Oslo I & II agreements. So in the May 1996 elections, the Likud party was returned to power at the head of a more conservative right-wing coalition with the intention of "applying the brakes" and slowing down the return of territories to the Palestinians. Fortunately or unfortunately, in a democracy, the majority rules.

At the time of the updating of this edition in the fall of 1997, it is still too early to know which direction Benjamin Netanyahu's government will take, or which direction the peace process will take, but we all know that a war could break out at any moment with either the Likud or Labor at the helm of government because the Arab neighbors of Israel including the Palestinian Authority have all been arming and preparing for war regardless of Labor or Likud being in power. Egypt is the key player in this new war.

Also, it must be remembered that though Egyptian President Anwar Sadat was the first Arab leader to conclude a peace agreement with Israel in 1979, it was Anwar Sadat, suspected of pro-Nazi leanings during World War II, who said in 1971, two years prior to the 1973 Yom Kippur War, that he was prepared to sacrifice up to a million Egyptian soldiers to regain the Sinai for Egypt. Israel did not take that threat or promise seriously, and Sadat indeed did keep his word to attack Israel. Had the Labor government of Golda Meir taken Sadat seriously in 1971 and returned Sinai to Egypt then, the 1973 war might have been averted. But, both Likud and Labor parties in 1971 followed Moshe Dayan's famous adage: Better to have Sinai without peace than to have peace without Sinai.

At this point, I feel it incumbent on me to add a personal note to the above. When Anwar Sadat was assassinated by Islamic radicals in October 1981, my wife, who as I mentioned at the beginning of this book, lived the first twenty years of her life in Egypt, remarked, "This is a black day for Israel."

When I asked her why, she explained: "Vice President Hosni Mubarak, who will now replace Sadat, will one day wage war against Israel. He hates Israel, is even more megalomaniac than former Egyptian President Abdul Nasser was, but smarter than Nasser and will attack Israel within twenty years, but only when Egypt is ready to do so. He will methodically prepare Egypt for that day."

I disagreed with my wife. After all, in 1981, Israel was still in the final stages of returning the Sinai a third time to Egypt. And Mubarak pledged to remain loyal to the peace process. But my wife insisted: "You see, in America, it is usually baseball or football players who are the role models. In Egypt, it has always been the military. We have always known who Hosni Mubarak was. He was groomed for leadership. He was always on radio, TV and in the press. He has gone on record again and again, that he would complete what Nasser failed to complete... the destruction of Israel. He was trained in Moscow, was a war hero, and commander of the air force. He will make war with Israel when he is ready."

Since familiarity breeds contempt, as the saying goes, I found it hard to believe my wife. But now I believe she is a prophetess, and God sent her to me to be my wife to give me the insights into the Egyptian, Arab and Islamic psyche that otherwise I would be lacking.

Indeed, ten years later, in the summer of 1990, I was surprised to discover from first hand information that Hosni Mubarak indeed signed an agreement with Saddam Hussein to attack Israel two weeks after Iraq did. This agreement was also reported on a number of times by the Israeli press. So my wife was not far off target.

But a strange thing happened. As I mentioned before, a few days before the Iraqi invasion of Kuwait, Saddam Hussein met with former American ambassador to Iraq April Gillespie, and either understood or misunderstood America's intentions. But "God made Pharaoh's heart stubborn", and caused Saddam to attack

Kuwait, something which was not cleared first with Egypt's Mubarak, and which caused Egypt financial losses in excess of $7 billion (paid for by the US taxpayer when this amount in Egyptian debt was forgiven) and the displacement and flight of over a million expatriate workers from Iraq and Kuwait.

It is kind of like two bank robbers agreeing to rob a bank at 2 PM, and meanwhile the first robber decides on his own to rob another bank by himself at 10 AM, sounds the alarm, is chased down the highway by the police. The hypothetical question as to whether another bank will be robbed at 2 PM as per the original plan with the robber's partner seems a moot point. My belief is that God acted supernaturally to deflect the wrath of those who hate Israel away from Israel. The Saddam Hussein-Hosni Mubarak strategy was deflected away from Israel. And even though forty-three scuds were fired at Israel, by God's miracle only one person died from a direct hit, and that, too, because the victim refused to go into the air raid shelter. Otherwise, he, too, could have been saved from death.

It was a fact, though, that throughout Operations Desert Shield and Desert Storm, Israel, under the Shamir Likud Administration was warned very clearly by the US not to retaliate against Iraq in spite of forty-three Scud missiles falling on Israel so that the UN-US-Arab alliance would not become unglued, or better stated, that Egypt and Syria would not be provided an excuse to attack Israel, as had been the original plan in the first place, and for which they had been systematically preparing.

In November 1993, I received reliable reports in Israel as to the latest developments in the Egyptian and Syrian armaments and war preparations programs. These were among some of the points I learned:

1. Syria received $4 billion from Saudi Arabia for its participation in Desert Shield/Desert Storm at the behest of U.S. Secretary of State James Baker III. Instead of using these funds to improve the lot of the Syrian people and improving Syria's basket case economy, hundreds of Scud missiles, 300 T-72 tanks, former Soviet submarines, as well as other non-specified biological, chemical and conventional weapons capabilities were acquired.

2. Israel had no anti-missile missile capable of defending its skies from these Syrian scuds, the Patriot missile having been an

almost total failure. Israel was literally in a pre-Hiroshima Nagasaki scenario.

3. Egypt's army, according to reliable sources was now armed with state-of-the-art US weaponries and doctrines, much of which had been upgraded due to Israeli input, instead of Soviet weaponries; and that Egyptian training maps used during maneuvers show that Israel - not Libya or Sudan - was the target of the Egyptian army maneuvers.

4. Israel was cutting training and weapons acquisitions budgets under the "red line" for its air, armor, artillery and infantry. Basically, while the Arabs were arming and training for war with Israel, Israel was disarming — much like France and England disarming while Hitler's Nazi Germany was arming for war, in order to send a message to the Arab states neighboring it that its intentions were peaceful.

While the Arab countries were mortgaging their economies for the next one hundred years in order to make war with Israel, Israel was redirecting its meager financial resources into economic development and infrastructure, because it basically realized it could never win the arms race against the Arabs, nor could it win out in continued wars of attrition or, God forbid, apocalyptic ABC wars. It's like a matador in a ring turning his back on a seething bull and walking away. He might come out of it alive, but then, again, he might not.

I will never forget a studio tape recording made of US President Ronald Reagan prior to a routine radio interview which went like this:

"Testing 1-2-3 testing. Fellow Americans, I am proud to announce that Congress has just passed a law banning Russia forever. Bombing starts in five minutes."

As hilarious as it would seem to an American, the Russians took it very seriously. A couple of weeks later, Soviet President Michael Gorbachev announced perestroika and the end of the Cold War with the West. Russia realized that there was no way it could keep up with the West, either with its military, technology or economy. Better to bury the hatchet, because, Gorbachev realized, Russia would lose.

Deep down, I have a feeling, that this is precisely what motivated former prime ministers Yitzhak Rabin (z"l) and Shimon Peres to sue for peace even under the unfavorable conditions which caused the Israeli public to vote Labor out of office in 1996. There just was this fear of an arms race Israel could not win, a fear of how Israel could survive the future high-tech type wars with the Arabs and Moslems (including Iran) and their unlimited petro-dollars.

This is why it causes me great consternation when in Israel as outside Israel, among Jews and Christians, there are those who condemn the late prime minister Yitzhak Rabin and then prime minister Shimon Peres for their handling or mishandling of the peace process — depending on the viewpoint. Rabin's experiences as Israel's ambassador to the U.S. during the late 60's and early 70's surely exposed him to the ideology of bodies such as the Dallas Council on World Affairs or New York's Council on Foreign Relations, that Israel was indeed all alone, and that Israel had not the wherewithal to keep up with the massive investments into high tech weaponries that our Arab neighbors were making. Therefore, like Russia's Gorbachev, we must seek perestroika or rather peace.

To those "gung-ho" Christians in their churches I would quote from the Gospel of Luke Chapter 14 verses 28-32:

28. For which of you, intending to build a tower, sitteth not down first, and counteth the cost, whether he have sufficient to finish it?
29. Lest haply, after he hath laid the foundation, and is not able to finish it, all that behold it begin to mock him.
30. Saying, This man began to build, and was not able to finish.
31. Or what king, going to make war against another king, sitteth not down first, and consulteth whether he be able with ten thousand to meet him that cometh against him with twenty thousand?
32. Or else, while the other is yet a great way off, he sendeth an ambassage, and desireth conditions of peace.

I do not envy any leader of Israel, be he Labor or Likud party member. The next war in the Middle East, God forbid will be unlike any war ever experienced before.

But what perturbs me so much is in spite of Israel having such a "user-friendly" to Arabs government, I still encounter such quotes in the Egyptian press as:

"The war with Israel is a certainty and we are ready." (Former Egyptian Minister of War Amin El Huwaidi, January 29, 1995 in Egyptian weekly "Rous el Yusef")

or

"In spite of the fact Israel has atomic weapons, Egypt will know how to cut off the arm of the enemy when the time comes." (Present Egyptian Minister of War Field Marshall Mohammed Hussein Tantawi, January 29, 1995 in same article as previous quote).

These two statements above appeared in the Egyptian weekly "Rous el Yusef", this specific edition of which was devoted entirely to the question of war with Israel.

It was illustrated with photographs of the Egyptian army crossing of the Suez Canal during the 1973 Yom Kippur War; a day remembered in Egypt as the most glorious in Egypt's military history, but in Israel, it will always be remembered traumatically as a Pearl Harbor "sneak attack" on the holiest day of the Jewish calendar.

The contents of "Rous el Yusef" are dictated directly from the office of President Hosni Mubarak.

In the months February-March-April 1995, there was great consternation in Jerusalem, when both Egyptian President Mubarak and Foreign Minister Amr Musa condemned Israel's refusal to sign the NPT (non-proliferation agreement) opening up its nuclear facilities to the world thus compromising Israel's capability to maintain a deterrent force and thus maintain peace, saying that the deterioration in relations with Israel (under Labor) was such that no one could predict where this would lead, i.e. another war.

In September 1995, even with the signing of the second stage of the Israel-Palestinian accords, there was a scandal brewing both in Egypt and in Israel regarding alleged executions of Egyptian prisoners in Sinai in 1967 during the Six Day War. There are those in Egypt calling for a suspension of diplomatic relations with Israel and a complete freeze or even an end to the peace process.

So it seems, Egypt is looking for an excuse to end the peace process and initiate a war with Israel.

Basically, Israel's strategy is to create peace and strengthen peace with the Palestinians, the Jordanians, and finally with the Syrians (this includes Lebanon which is under Syrian rule).

In spite of the signed agreements with the Palestinians, the Jordanians and even the Egyptians, the final question, and possibly the straw that breaks the camel's back, will be the question of Jerusalem. Then the Egyptians will indeed have an excuse. The building at the Har Homa neighborhood in southern Jerusalem as well as the Ras El Amud neighborhood may be the last straws.

Again, it must be emphasized that Jerusalem is mentioned 616 times in the Old Testament, 195 times in the New Testament but never once in the Koran. Yet the Moslems lay claim to Jerusalem as the capital of Palestine, a city now, all of a sudden, holy to the Islamic faith.

PLO chief Yasser Arafat has said numerous times that his goal is a Palestinian State with its capital Jerusalem. He has been persistent and honest about this, from the beginning. Israel officially refuses to consider these two possibilities though there are those Jewish leaders who privately and not so privately express their acquiescence to such a Palestinian plan.

I think it behooves such leaders to read a report which appeared in "The Jerusalem Post" (English language daily) of February 23rd, 1996:

"Arafat Sees Israel's Demise"

Yasser Arafat told a closed meeting of Arab ambassadors in Stockholm recently that he expects Israel to collapse in the foreseeable future, according to the Norwegian daily "Dagen" of February 16th, 1996.

The PLO leader was in the Swedish capital on January 30th to celebrate a peace prize shared by Peace Now, Labor Young Leadership and Fatah Youth.

According to "Dagen", the report has been confirmed by Swedish sources, which traced the information to one of the diplomats attending the meeting with Arafat following a festive dinner. Assuring his audience that the establishment of a Palestinian state is imminent, Arafat was quoted as declaring that both Prime Minister Shimon Peres and Minister Yossi Beilin would support such a (Palestinian) state, as long as religious freedom is guaranteed its Jewish inhabitants.

But he predicted Jews would not want to live under Palestinian sovereignty. "They will give up their dwellings and leave for the U.S.," he said, adding, "We Palestinians will take over everything, including all of Jerusalem. Peres and Beilin have already promised us half of Jerusalem. The Golan Heights, too, have already been given away (to Syria), subject to just a few details. And when they are returned, at least a million rich Jews will leave Israel."

Arafat said he expects civil war to erupt in Israel, in which Russian immigrants, "half of whom are Christians or Moslems," will fight for a "united Palestinian State." He also asserted that the "so-called Ethiopian Jews" are Moslems.

Outlining his strategy, he said, "The PLO will now concentrate on splitting Israel psychologically into two camps. Within five years we will have six to seven million Arabs living on the West Bank and Jerusalem. All Palestinian Arabs will be welcomed by us. If the Jews can import all kinds of Ethiopians, Russians, Uzbekistanis and Ukrainians as Jews, we can import all kinds of Arabs. We plan to eliminate the State of Israel and establish a Palestinian state. We will make life unbearable for Jews by psychological warfare and population explosion. Jews will not want to live among Arabs.

"I have no use for Jews. They are and remain Jews. We now need all the help we can get from you (Arab ambassadors) in our battle for a united Palestine under Arab rule," he concluded.

Since 60% of the Jews of Israel voted in May 1996 against such a scenario that the Labor government was promoting, there is now a rethinking or restructuring of the entire peace process, which could be the excuse Israel's war seeking enemies might seize to carry out the war for which they have been so diligently preparing.

All Arabs, not only the Palestinians, seek Jerusalem as the capital of the Palestinian state, and when this does not happen, there could be riots, suicide bombers, and a renewed "intifada" in the streets of East Jerusalem, thus causing the peace agreement between Israel and the Palestinians to implode, followed by a domino effect with Jordan, Egypt and the other Arab states with which Israel has so laboriously worked to establish relations. The whole peace process could come down like a house of cards.

Obviously, Israel has no choice but to remain committed to the peace process, but my belief is that between the question of Jerusalem, Palestinian aspirations for an independent state, and a backlash from the Jewish population of Israel, the peace process could end virtually at any time.

When Yasser Arafat said in a mosque in Johannesburg, South Africa, immediately after the signing of the PLO-Israel agreement, that this agreement was good only for two years similar to an agreement signed between the prophet Mohammed and the tribe of Quraish in Mecca 1,300 years ago and annulled after two years, many people were outraged that Yasser Arafat was a double-crosser and that he was proud of it. He also called for a holy war to liberate Jerusalem and that Jews would be banned from Jerusalem in a way similar to an agreement between Caliph Omar the conqueror of Jerusalem in the 7th century and the Patriarch Sophronius, Christian leader of Jerusalem at the time of Conquest 638.

Is Israel to take Yasser Arafat seriously when he speaks in Johannesburg, in Gaza or in Washington?

Changing to the more mundane, and putting aside the antics of Yasser Arafat, his problem is not only taking Jerusalem away from the Jews, but of paying salaries to his people in Gaza and Jericho and possibly later in the rest of Judea and Samaria. The success of this whole peace process and experiment of Palestinian autonomy will hinge largely on economics — on whether Arafat will succeed in anything beyond rhetoric. Palestinian autonomy can only succeed if billions of dollars in infrastructure and industrially productive ventures are introduced. Jerusalem is a moot point if Arafat fails in putting the Palestinians on their feet economically. He seems to have failed at that miserably until now.

But as for returning territories, Israel's strategy has been to be prepared for some territorial concessions on the Golan to Syria, but not all of it.   There can be no withdrawal from the Jordan River as a boundary.   In other words, there can be no territorial contiguity between the Palestinian entity and the Hashemite Kingdom of Jordan. Should Israel be forced to move from this natural border, its defense against any invading enemy from the east will be made untenable. And the closer such a new border may be to Jerusalem, the greater the opposition from within the Jewish population will be.

The bottom line of the Israeli government will always be: What is the threshold of war? What is its price? Will territories thereafter have to be returned anyway? And what is the destiny of Iran's nuclear capability in the event the momentum of peace with Syria and other intransigent Arab states slows or is stopped?

And finally, my question is:

Given the fact that the powers that be today in Washington see Israel as an obstacle to steady oil prices and supply as I learned in Dallas, Texas;

Given that Rabin's experience as Israel ambassador in Washington in the late 1960's and 70's taught him the same hard facts about Israel being alone in its battle for survival;

Given the Arabs' continuing on-going weapons and hi-tech warfare acquisition capabilities programs, in spite of the peace process;

Given that Islamic religion and culture see Israel as an extension of the Christian West, and therefore to be purged sooner or later from the Islamic Middle East like the Crusaders centuries ago;

Given that the peace process is on the verge of melting down;

Given that such developments could lead to the intervention of these armed neighbors, especially Egypt and Syria;

Given a wide spectrum of Bible believing Christians in the U.S. and throughout the world supporting autonomy for the Palestinian Arabs, but also dedicated to Israel's survival.

Given all of these, is it not incumbent for Jews and Christians to come together at this time to strive for peace, support Israel, support Palestinian autonomy, and most important of all, to do everything to ensure that war will never again break out in the Middle East?

Are the Bible Christians of America not a force to be reached out to? My belief is that with a wise Christian leadership in Washington, a war can be avoided in the Middle East. A Christian voice in Washington would see to it that those Islamic forces seeking death and destruction would be intimidated enough by a leadership in the U.S. that would say, "Don't even think of attacking Israel."

My dream is of peace. I do not wish to see one drop of blood spilt in the Middle East. Not of Jew, Christian nor Arab. It is only a strong, forceful Christian leadership in Washington that can do this, not a petrodollar leadership which would look the other way, thus giving a green light to such an attack and/or exact such a bloody price from Israel, that its future defense and survival are called into question, all for the sake of oil or mammon.

Chapter Eight

Iran's Nuclear Capability, Subversive Activities in Europe and Persecution of Christians

Iran's Nuclear Capability:

Summary of a report from "Focus," a German magazine dated January 24, 1993:

North Korea is helping Iran to develop nuclear missiles and may be training Iranian pilots to fly nuclear bombers. Iran has two nuclear warheads, both of 40 kilotons, or twice as powerful as the bomb that destroyed Hiroshima, one nuclear bomb and one nuclear shell. Iran wants to manufacture medium range missiles with the aid of North Korea and China.

Iranian pilots trained in Wonsan, North Korea, are at an air base not far from Teheran, where the nuclear bomb is stored. The bomb can be dropped from a Mig-27 aircraft.

Iran assembled its nuclear devices using parts imported from former Soviet republics, such as Kazakhstan and Tajikistan. A German company helped the missile development project by supplying guidance equipment.

(Above article taken from the periodical of the Jerusalem Institute for Western Defense, Jerusalem, Israel, Vol. 5, Digest 3, March, 1993).

Iranian Training of Israel-Attacking Suicide Pilots

Excerpt of an interview with Iranian political leader in exile Manoushar Ganjee by Orli Azulai Katz writing from Paris for Israeli daily "Yediot Aharonot" weekend supplement (February 17th, 1995):

"A secret training base has been established in Iran for Kamikazi type suicide pilots whose target would be objectives in Israel. It was not written in the reports I received what their nationalities were. According to this report, four such pilots have just completed their training and have left Iran in order to prepare for the mission."

Iranian Backed Islamic Terror in Europe:

Summary of a report from Al-Watan Al-Arabi, Lebanon, published in Paris (December 24, 1993):

Some days ago, French and German and other West European security services received a secret warning that terrorist cells had infiltrated their countries to prepare the ground for military operations together with fundamentalists and other extremists already there. The terrorist underground is controlled and financed by Iran.

The report noted that the following organizations took part in recent meetings with Iranian intelligence in Teheran:

- Fatah Revolutionary Council; leader Abu Nidal
- Popular Front for the Liberation of Palestine — General Command; leader Ahmed Jibril
- The Japanese Red Army
- The Secret Irish Army (the reference may be to the I.R.A.)
- The Secret Army for the Liberation of Armenia
- The Lebanese Revolutionary Organization; leader Mirshad Shabu
- The Lebanese Hizbollah

All of the afore mentioned were represented by senior commanders. The commander of Iran's Revolutionary Guards participated in the meetings, together with Mohammed Mussawi, who is responsible for Iranian propaganda at Iran's Beirut Embassy. Upon receiving orders from Iran, the above-mentioned groups are now ready to carry out operations against U.S. and western interests or to assassinate politicians and diplomats. This will be done whenever Iran is attacked or subjected to international threats intended to isolate it politically and economically, causing internal instability.

Since the signature of the Gaza-Jericho agreement on September 13, 1993, plans were made to upset it by terrorism. A prize of several million dollars has been offered for the murder of Yasser Arafat. In recent weeks, western intelligence has reached the conclusion that in reaction to the Israel-PLO agreement, there will be an intensification of terrorism - first in the occupied territories, then among Palestinians generally, still later in Lebanon and finally in various parts of the world, especially Europe.

Iran has opened training camps, including one at Qaranji near Qum, for commando units of the Hizbollah, the Hamas and the Palestinian Islamic Jihad. Simultaneously, Iran requested Sudan to open training camps for Arab veterans of the Afghan war and North African fundamentalists presently in Europe. Activity in Hizbollah camps in western Beka'a valley (Lebanon) has also been intensified. There, instructors from Iran train new arrivals in guerilla warfare, the use of explosives and the preparation of car bombs. The presence of elements of the Japanese Red Army has been confirmed in the Beka'a valley and in Beirut, where they are stationed with the PFLP (General Command) of Ahmed Jibril. The commander of the Iranian Revolutionary Guards in Lebanon has been meeting Hizbollah's operational command regularly.

Many of the terrorists are already stationed all over the world and have received their orders. Abu Nidal's plan to assassinate an Arab official in India this month was discovered, leading to the proclamation of an alert by the security services of many western states. There are reports of suspicious activities of terrorist networks in Germany and France. In Germany, there are Hizbollah activists who are German nationals or are married to German women. Fundamentalist and radical Kurds are also participating in the realization of these Iranian plans.

During recent investigations in France, it was established that many Algerian fundamentalists have connections with the Lebanese Hizbollah and that the ties between Algeria's Islamic Salvation Front and Iran are now closer. Sudan's Hassan Al-Turabi helped to bring this about. The French are worried about the possibility of Iranian terrorist operations on their soil.

Germany is the main base of fundamentalists and extremists, including the Kurdish PKK which is allied with Iran, members of the Muslim Brotherhood and other fundamentalists - Turks, Pakistanis and Arabs -resident in Hamburg, Munich and Cologne. There has been much internal and external criticism of Germany for the concessions it has made to Teheran within the framework of a security pact signed recently in Bonn with Iran's Minister of Intelligence, Ali Plahiyan. Iran's relations with western Europe have deteriorated.

This article was taken from the March, 1994, digest of the Jerusalem Institute for Western Defense, Vol. 6, Digest 3.

Iran's Worldwide Terrorism Diplomatic Network

Excerpts of Article by Knut Royce and Saul Friedman of "Newsday" (The Long Island Newspaper) of September 7th 1994.

Washington — At least two dozen of the Iranians who seized the U.S. Embassy in Tehran in 1979 and held 52 Americans hostage for more than a year are now government officials and ambassadors, and many are suspected of spreading terrorism throughout the world, knowledgeable U.S. sources have told "Newsday".

According to those sources, who have access to government intelligence, the Iranian officials and their embassies in Latin America, Europe and the Middle East have been responsible for bombings aimed at Jewish interests, the assassination of Tehran opponents living abroad and the recruiting of Arab terrorists.

Their global designs include the spread of Islamic fundamentalism among South Asia's Muslims and terror bombings in New York City.

One of those officials, Hosein Sheikh-ol-Islam, is described as a "key leader" in the U.S. Embassy takeover. Now, according to administration officials, Sheikh-ol-Islam is Iran's deputy foreign minister for Afro-Arab affairs and vice director-general of its foreign service. From those posts, according to Kenneth Katzman, a former intelligence analyst who is now an Iran specialist for the Congressional Research Service, "He is the kingpin, the patron of the radicals and former hostage holders, the man who assigns them to their jobs overseas, in embassies and elsewhere.

Katzman, author of "Warriors of Islam," a book on Iran's Revolutionary Guard Corps, said that under Sheikh-ol-Islam's guidance the former hostage-holders — was well as other Iranian officials — have used embassies to finance, arm and provide logistics and cover for acts of terrorism and the spread of their brand of Islamic fundamentalism, controlling government and society.

He rejects the notion that they are merely former revolutionaries who went on to serve in the government they helped create. "The difference," Katzman said, "is that these men have taken their ideologies and their terrorist tactics abroad."

For example, one of Sheikh-ol-Eslam's colleagues among the hostage-takers, Ali Reza Deyhim, has been Iran's ambassador to Mexico since 1993 and is serving concurrently as Tehran's envoy to Belize. The Iranian government has said it is interested in expanding its relations with all of Latin America.

Terrorism expert Vince Cannistraro, a former director of the CIA's counter-terrorism center who served as a staff member of the National Security Council during the Reagan administration, said U.S. intelligence sources "are worried because the Iranians are building up an infrastructure in Latin America." Mexico is especially important, he added, because "it is strategically placed and is as close to the U.S. as Iran can get."

Cannistraro said intelligence sources here believe that the July 19 bombing of a Panama commuter plane that killed twenty-three persons, most of them Jews, "was directed out of Mexico."

Secretary of State Warren Christopher, relying on U.S. intelligence agencies, has blamed the bombing on Hezbollah, the radical Islamic group Party of God, which, he said, is financed and largely controlled by Iran.

Christopher also has blamed the Hezbollah and Iran for the July 18, 1994 bombing of a Buenos Aires building housing Jewish agencies, in which nearly one hundred people were killed. He charged it was part of an effort to undermine the Middle East peace process. After Argentinian investigators charged that the bombing was the work of Iranian agents, Tehran lodged a denial and pulled out its ambassador, Hadi Soleimanpur. Cannistraro and Katzman say Soleimanpur was one of the 1979 hostage-holders, although intelligence sources have been unable to confirm that.

"The operation (bombing) in Buenos Aires may not have been directed by the ambassador," said Cannistraro, "but the embassies supply support, logistics, passports, visas, even weapons, and the ambassador is usually aware of what's going on."

The CIA and State Department have followed the careers of some of the hostage-holders as they've gone on to key posts, mostly in Iran's foreign ministry, and have tracked their continued involvement in terrorist activities. Indeed, since 1979 the CIA has written three classified reports on the issue.

The State Department, in its latest annual report on "Patterns of Global Terrorism," calls Iran, "the most active state sponsor of terrorism" which has been "implicated in terrorist attacks in Italy, Turkey and Pakistan." In addition, the report said, "Iranian intelligence continues to stalk members of the Iranian opposition in the U.S., Europe, Asia and the Middle East."

The report also added another nation to its list of states that sponsor terrorism — Sudan. And it notes that Majid Kamal, Iran's ambassador in Khartoum until July, 1994, was largely responsible for helping to organize, finance and equip terrorist groups operating in and from Sudan. Several Sudanese were arrested last summer as part of a plot to bomb prominent sites in New York City.

Before his assignment to Sudan in 1990, Kamal served as Tehran's top diplomat in Lebanon, where, according to the State Department, he "guided Iranian efforts in developing the Lebanese Hezbollah group," which was responsible for holding Americans and other Westerners hostage for several years.

On another front, the State Department in 1986 lodged a protest to the Swiss government's acceptance of the credentials of the new Iranian ambassador, Muhammad-Hussein Mala'ek, because of his involvement in hostage taking. Another hostage holder identified by Katzman and Iranian dissident organizations was also stationed in Switzerland — Sirus Naseri, Iran's United Nations representative in Geneva.

On August 24th, 1990, during the tenure of the two Iranians, the head of the local Iranian dissident organization, Kazem Rajavi, was slain in Geneva. Swiss authorities implicated 13 Iranians who had entered the country with diplomatic passports.

Similarly, Katzman and Cannistraro say that 1979 hostage holders have served as ambassadors to Germany, Italy and Turkey, where Tehran's agents have stalked and killed dozens of opponents of the regime in Iran.

According to U.S. intelligence sources, Afghanistan — where radical Islamic fundamentalists are fighting to control the war-shattered government — and Pakistan have become priority targets for Iran's efforts to gain influence in Muslim south and central Asia. And Katzman said that Iranians operating in Pakistan are seeking to recruit terrorist agents from among the radicals who have been fighting in Afghanistan.

Thus the Iranian diplomats in those countries have been trusted radicals assigned there by Tehran's foreign ministry. The current Iranian ambassador to Pakistan, Mohammad Mehdi Akhondzadeh-Basti, is a former hostage holder, as is the consul-general in Lahore, Ali Nikan-Qomi. And two previous ambassadors to Islamabad are former hostage holders who were leaders of the revolutionary guards who stormed the U.S. Embassy.

Former hostage Barry Rosen, the U.S. embassy's press officer, now a teacher of a course on Iran at Brooklyn College said he has given up hope for now that Tehran will take a more moderate course. He added, "It's easy to see Iranians under every bed. But it's not surprising that these people who held the hostages should still be active now. They still have the same ideological vision and mission."

Berlin Mosque Used To Plan Terror Attacks

(Reuters news service article appearing in *The Jerusalem Post* of November 13th, 1994)

Bonn — Islamic militants have been found to be using a Berlin mosque to plan attacks on Israeli targets, the German news weekly "Focus" reported yesterday.

A telex from Berlin's regional counter-intelligence service said members of Hamas, Hizbullah and Syria's Moslem Brotherhood had met in the mosque to plan attacks on Israeli premises, Focus reported.

In an advance release from this week's edition, the magazine said the intelligence service had cautioned that the militants planned attacks as soon as vigilance at Israeli premises slackened.

Berlin security officials declined comment on the report.

In September "Focus" and the news weekly "Der Spiegel" said security forces were on the alert for possible Palestinian terrorist attacks against Jewish targets in Germany.

At the time German media also reported federal police and the federal intelligence agency BND had uncovered plans by militants led by Abu Nidal to hit Jewish targets including an EL AL flight at Tempelhof Airport.

Iranian Terrorist Infiltration into South America

Article by James Brooke taken from *The New York Times*, July 26, 1994.

As the death toll reached eighty today, Argentines asserted that Iran wielded a secret hand in the truck bomb that demolished the main community center here for Argentine Jews one week ago.

"Suspicions fall very heavily on Iran," Ruben Ezra Beraja, a Jewish group leader, said today after meeting with the Argentine President, Carlos Saul Menem. Mr. Beraja is president of the Delegation of Argentine Jewish Associations, a federation of Jewish groups that was housed in the building destroyed by the bomb.

In addition to the confirmed dead, twenty-four people are listed as missing and fifty-two remain in hospitals.

Today, the Argentine judge investigating the bombing, Juan Jose Galeano, questioned a dissident Iranian diplomat in Caracas, Venezuela, about Iranian links to bombings in South America. On July 14, 1994, the Venezuelan Government expelled four Iranian diplomats on the grounds that in early July, they kidnapped at pistol point the dissident diplomat and five family members and held them against their will in a Caracas hotel.

After the expulsion order, the Iranian Ambassador to Venezuela described Venezuela's accusations against his subordinates as "totally fallacious." In reprisal, Venezuela on Wednesday expelled the Ambassador, Seyyed Reza Zargarbashi.

Venezuela officials are investigating to see if there are any ties between Iranian diplomats and the truck bomb attack here.

Today, a newspaper here, Clarin, published excerpts of what it said was a Venezuelan intelligence agency report on links between Iranian diplomats in Caracas and underground cells in South America of the Party of God, the fundamentalist guerilla group supported by Iran.

Iranian diplomats provided terrorists with "logistical support, arms and explosives, using the diplomatic pouch for such ends," the document read. "In some cases, the explosives were delivered to the terrorists through Shiite communities living in the south of Brazil or in Uruguay."

Iranian diplomats here have denied any involvement in the Buenos Aires bombing. In Teheran today, Iran's supreme leader, Ayatollah Ali Khamenei, accused the world's powers of fighting a propaganda war against his country with forged news. Today, Iran's Ambassador to Argentina, Hadi Suyleiman Pour, delivered to the Foreign Ministry officials here a letter of condolence from Teheran.

...It was unclear if the van was driven by a suicide driver or exploded by remote control.

Investigators discovered the big toe of a right foot that did not belong to any of the known victims. Studying the calluses on the toe, experts concluded that it belonged to a brown-skinned man of medium height who often walked barefoot or who wore leather sandals.

Argentina Probes New Bombing Leads

(From Article by Thomas O'Dwyer in *The Jerusalem Post*, July 26th, 1995)

Argentina's foreign minister said yesterday that his country is absolutely determined to find those responsible for the bombing of the Israeli and Jewish targets in Buenos Aires.

Guido Di Tella told "The Jerusalem Post" that two Lebanese in a group of six men and one woman extradited from Paraguay to Argentina on Monday are "definitely more suspect" than the others. He declined to elaborate.

No one has been convicted for the March 17th, 1992 bombing of the Israeli Embassy, in which twenty-nine people died and 225 people were injured, or for the attack a year ago on the Argentine Israel Mutual Aid Association (AMIA), which killed eighty-six people and injured 120. One man, Carlos Telleldin, has been charged with selling the car used to bomb the AMIA building.

The suspects Paraguay extradited were named as Mohammed Hassan Alayan, Johnny Moraes Baalbay, Luis Alberto Nader, Sergio Salem and Fadil Abdul Karim — all of Lebanese extraction — and Brazilians Roberto Ribeiro Ruiz and Valdirene Vieira.

They were questioned yesterday about an arms cache found in 1994 on an island near Buenos Aires belonging to Argentine neo-Nazi Alejandro Sucksdorf, a former military intelligence officer. Sucksdorf was arrested on Parana Island, 50 km north of Buenos Aires, and is under arrest.

The suspects are being held at Campo de Mayo army base on the outskirts of Buenos Aires. Judge Roberto Marquevich said they will be questioned with Sucksdorf about allegations they received paramilitary training on his island to carry out the embassy attack.

Paraguayan intelligence officers say the group has links to Hizbullah, and at least three of those extradited may be connected with the embassy bomb. The seven were arrested in January, 1995, and held on charges of drug-trafficking and arms possession in a remote Paraguayan border town long believed by diplomats to be a hideout for Middle Eastern outlaws.

German Court Blames Iran In Berlin Killing

(Taken from news agencies report in "The Jerusalem Post", p.6 of April 11, 1997)

A German court ruled yesterday that Iran's top leaders were behind the assassination of an Iranian-Kurdish opposition figure in Berlin, shaking the foundations of Germany's policy of close ties and continued trade with the Teheran regime.

Within hours, Bonn recalled its ambassador to Iran and ordered the expulsion of four Iranian diplomats. In a statement, the Foreign Ministry said the verdict indicated "a flagrant breach of international law" by Iran.

Iran also recalled its ambassador to Bonn for consultations, Iranian television reported.

The German court convicted two men of murder and two of being accessories to murder in the Sept. 17, 1992 killing of Kurdish leader Sadiq Sarafkindi and three of his colleagues in the Mykonos restaurant.

Presiding Judge Frithjof Kubsch said, however, that the men acted not on their own, but on orders from Teheran. "The Iranian political leadership is responsible," he said, adding that its goal was to eliminate political dissidents.

Judge Kubsch said in his ruling that the assassination of the four Kurdish leaders ordered by a secret special operations committee whose members included Iran's president, its religious leader, intelligence minister and the head of foreign policy.

He stopped short of explicitly naming Iranian President Akbar Hashemi Rafsanjani and religious leader Ayatollah Ali Khamenei, who had been accused by prosecutors of ultimate responsibility for the attack in Berlin's Mykonos restaurant.

The verdict marked the first time that a European court had clearly attributed political responsibility for any of the dozens of assassinations of Iranian opposition figures abroad since the Islamic revolution in 1979.

Iran quickly dismissed the verdict as political, and withdrew its own ambassador for consultations.

This accusation is not true,' Iranian parliamentary speaker Ali Akbar Nateq-Nouri told reporters during a visit to Moscow.

"We have asked the German leadership many times if there is any evidence and if so to present it to us. But until now they haven't. The trial had a political tinge."

Operators at the Iranian Foreign Ministry in Teheran said no one was available to take phone calls, and an embassy spokesman in Bonn said they had no comment.

While Washington has sought to isolate Iran as a state sponsor of terrorism, Germany and other European Union countries have for years pursued a "critical dialogue" policy, continuing to do profitable business with Iran while discussing issues of terrorism and human rights.

Washington, which has sought to isolate Iran for sponsoring such terrorist acts, called on European governments to move to "choke off trade with Iran." "The 'critical dialogue' has not succeeded in moderating Iran's behavior," State Department spokesman Nicholas Burns said.

"There is no evidence that the 'critical dialogue' has made a difference."

The Foreign Ministry said Germany will "not participate for the foreseeable future" in that policy, and said it was in close contact with its E.U. partners. It was unclear what the impact of the decision would be.

Germany is Iran's biggest Western trade partner, with trade exceeding 3 billion marks ($1.8 billion) last year, and had been one of the strongest proponents in the E.U. for keeping the controversial "critical dialogue" policy alive.

Iran Long-Range Missle Slated For 2000

(Article by Steve Rodan in *The Jerusalem Post*, p.2 of April 15th, 1997)

Israel plans to raise Russian aid to Iran's medium-range ballistic missile project during this week's visit by Russian Deputy Foreign Minister Victor Posuvaliuk. Officials here said they increasingly regard Moscow as a strategic threat to Middle East stability.

The officials said that despite numerous Israeli appeals, Russia is continuing to provide massive aid to Iran's missile project.

They said Teheran is developing a missile, with a range of up to 1,500 kilometers, that can hit any part of Israel.

"Just two weeks ago, the Iranians held tests, albeit ground tests so far, with the Russians to develop a missile with a range of 1,500 km that can have Iran reach Israel through the use of ballistic missiles," Air Force Commander Maj.-Gen. Eitan Ben-Eliahu said on Sunday.

The officials added that the missile will be able to carry a non-conventional, including nuclear, warhead and that Teheran plans to test launch it within three years.

"We view this project gravely," a senior official said. "It's a serious Iranian effort and, with Russia behind it, this project can be completed on schedule."

The officials said Russia was invited to help Iran with its ballistic missile, after North Korea was apparently unable to supply its Nodung I missile. The Nodung, with a range of 1,300 km., is believed to have been fired once and never reached the stage of deployment.

"Iran tried to get Nodung I, but it never arrived," Efraim Kam, deputy director of Tel Aviv University's Jaffee Center for Strategic Studies said. "Maybe it was because of financial difficulties in North Korea. Maybe there were political difficulties with the Americans. This leaves Russia now as the number one supplier to Iran."

Prime Minister Binyamin Netanyahu visited Moscow in early March and met with Russian President Boris Yeltsin. They agreed to clarify the extent and type of help Russia is providing Iran.

But Israeli and Russian diplomatic sources agree that Netanyahu was not successful in changing minds in Moscow. They said both the Foreign Ministry and the Russian military lobby are united on selling weapons and nuclear technology to Iran.

"Russia is a serious strategic problem for Israel," an official said. "Despite all the warm meetings reported, I doubt there is love between us and Russia."

Diplomatic sources said Israel is closely following reports that Iran and Russia have concluded a deal in which Teheran would buy Russian weapons for Syria — the first stop on Posuvaliuks's tour. The deal is meant to solve Syria's inability to pay its $11 billion debt to Moscow.

"Our assessment is that the only thing that is stopping continued Russian arms shipments to Syria is the debt," an official said. "But if Iran provides the cash for new weapons, then Russia will sell to Syria."

U.S. and Israeli officials are said to agree on the extent of Russian aid for Iran's ballistic missile project. The two countries discussed Israeli intelligence on the Iranian ballistic missile project during a visit by senior Israeli defense and intelligence officials in January.

Reuter adds:

Iran said yesterday it would soon start mass-producing a fighter aircraft which it said had been locally designed and built. State-run Teheran Radio quoted a deputy head of Iran's Armed Forces Joint Chiefs of Staff as saying the aircraft was the result of efforts by Iranian air force experts and had been successfully tested.

An Eye For An Eye: Khomeini's Revenge

(Article on p.5 from *The New York Post*, July 6, 1997, reported by Brian Blomquist in Washington, Uri Dan in Jerusalem and Devlin Barrett and Tracy Connor in New York. Written by Connor .)

A revenge-crazed Ayatollah Khomeini gave the order for the bombing of Pan Am Flight 103 over Lockerbie, Scotland, in 1988, a former top Iranian spy reportedly has told investigators.

The ex-operative claims the late despot demanded the terrorist slaughter as retaliation for the deadly U.S. downing of an Iranian passenger jet six months earlier, the German magazine Der Spiegel reported.

All 290 people on board were killed when the USS Vincennes shot down the Iran Air jet over the Persian Gulf in a tragic case of mistaken identity.

Bent on payback, Khomeini supposedly asked Libya and master Palestinian terrorist Abu Nidal for help with the Pan Am bombing — which killed 270 people on December 21, 1988.

A German representative of Iran Air smuggled bomb parts through airport security so they could be shipped to London and placed aboard New York-bound Flight 103 there, Spiegel reported.

That account does not jibe with British and U.S. investigations, which found that the bomb originated on an Air Malta flight.

The tip — which comes from Abolghassem Mesbahi, the cofounder of Iran's intelligence service — is being checked out by German officials, the magazine said.

The White House had a cautious response to the report, saying the world won't know exactly what happened until two Libyans indicted for the bombing are tried.

"This is a case which has been investigated very thoroughly by our law-enforcement agencies, and all the evidence we've been able to uncover points to individuals located in Libya as being culpable," White House spokesman David Johnson said.

"The way to get to the bottom of this is for those individuals to be extradited to either the U.S. or Scotland and to stand trial.

"We've seen a lot of effort in this case to push people away from where the evidence leads. One can't ever know. But the way to find out is to bring the people who are accused — the people against whom the evidence points — to trial."

The report seemed plausible to Israeli anti-terrorism expert Yigal Presler.

"The vicious circle of terror connecting Iran, the terrorist Abu Nidal, pro-Syrian terrorist organizations and the Libyans to the Pan Am bombing has been repeatedly traced during the probe," Presler said.

"The Iranians and Abu Nidal used to have close connections, including training of terrorists in Iran. The Iranians kept in close contact with terrorist organizations in Syria and the Libyans."

The families of Flight 103 victims also were not surprised by the report.

"That was one of the earliest theories," said Paul Hudson, an Albany lawyer whose daughter Melina, 16, was killed.

He said the indictment of the two suspected Libyans does not rule out Iranian involvement.

"There is still a current theory that the bombing could have been subcontracted by Iran to Libya," he said.

Victoria Cummock of Families of Pan Am 103 Lockerbie, said her group always believed Khomeini played a major role in the blast that killed her husband.

"My three children don't feel safe knowing that the bad guys are still out there," Cummock said. "All we need is one person to come forward to start the thing unraveling."

She also said the U.S. should be doing more to find all the alleged partners in the plot, not just the Libyan "bagmen" accused of placing the bomb on the plane.

Hudson agreed.

"The criminal case has been stalled for more than five years, and I would hope lead our government to redouble its efforts to solve the crime, he said.

Lawyer Lee Kreindler, lead counsel on the legal team that represented Flight 103 families in lawsuits against the airline, was skeptical of the report.

"It has always been possible that Iran was involved, but there's never been any strong evidence," he said.

Until Mesbahi's story can be corroborated, "it will be just another rumor," Kreindler added.

Testimony from Mesbahi last year helped German prosecutors link Iran's rulers to the 1992 assassination of four exiled Iranian dissidents in Berlin.

The Palestine Liberation Organization in 1992 claimed that Iran was the culprit, but U.S. and Scottish authorities have said they have found no links to Teheran.

Chapter Nine

Iranian Persecution Of
Its Own Christian Citizens

Article taken from page A5 of *The New York Times International Edition* of Thursday, January 27, 1994:

"Christian Bishop in Iran is Reported Missing."

Cairo, January 26 - A leader of Iranian Christians has disappeared in Teheran after speaking out against persecution of Christians, a New York based human rights group said today.

The leader, Bishop Haik Hovsepian Mehr, was last seen in the Iranian capital on January 19 on his way to the airport, the group, Middle East Watch, said in a statement.

Bishop Hovsepian has been General Superintendent of the Assemblies of God churches in Iran for 12 years.

The rights group said it suspected that the 48-year-old Bishop was being held by one of Iran's security agencies. No one has taken responsibility for his abduction, and Iranian authorities have denied knowledge of his whereabouts, the group added.

"It's the first development of its kind affecting a religious minority in Iran," said Andrew Whitley, the executive director of Middle East Watch.

The Bishop disappeared three days after the Rev. Mehdi Dibaj, another Assemblies of God cleric, was freed by the authorities, according to the rights group. Mr. Dibaj spent nine years in prison for apostasy.

Middle East Watch said the Bishop told the group the day before he disappeared that Iran had closed down several Protestant churches.

"Missing Iranian Bishop Found Dead" From Teheran AP Report of February, 1994

An Iranian Bishop who reportedly was missing in Teheran after criticizing the government's treatment of the Christian minority in his country has been found dead.

Members of Bishop Haik Mehr Hovsepian's Protestant church, the Assemblies of God, said yesterday that police emissaries informed them that their spiritual leader's body had been recovered.

They said they were notified of the death of Hovsepian, an Armenian, on Sunday, 11 days after he was missing on his way to the airport. But they said they did not know when or how he died.

"We don't know what caused the death," Henry Manoukian, an aide to the Bishop said. "We were told an autopsy will be carried out today."

However, Middle East Watch, which was first to report Hovsepian's disappearance on January 19, then the recovery of his body, said Sunday the Bishop had died January 20.

Iranian officials, who have not commented on Hovsepian's disappearance, have yet to announce his death. The state media has ignored the issue.

Middle East Watch, a New York-based human rights group, quoted a statement issued by the Assemblies of God regional director in Cyprus as saying photographs of Hovsepian's body showed stitches in the abdomen, suggesting a post-mortem examination had been done.

It urged Iranian authorities to make their findings public and to also allow an independent autopsy.

Asked what the impact of the news has had on the parish, Manoukian said: "We are worried that this may be directed against us." He refused to explain.

When told of Hovsepian's death, Archbishop Ardak Manoukian, of the Armenian Orthodox Church, said he was surprised that he hadn't heard it from other sources.

Archbishop Manoukian, of no relation to Hovsepian's assistant, said reports of religious persecution in Iran were incorrect, at least not in the case of the sizeable Armenian Orthodox minority. "There is religious tolerance here," he said. "The Armenian community has no problem whatever with the Iranian government and people."

Middle East Watch said that there has been no explanation for the delay in informing Hovsepian's relatives and followers of his death.

Hovsepian, 48, vanished shortly after leading a successful campaign to free a fellow Assemblies of God clergyman, the Rev. Mehdi Dibaj, who had been sentenced to death for abandoning his Moslem faith.

Dibaj spent ten years in jail before being convicted of apostasy last year. Iran announced his release January 16, days after the U.S. State Department called for him to be freed.

As part of his campaign to draw world attention to Dibaj's case, Hovsepian recently had stepped up his criticism of Iranian authorities for what he said was their long history of harassing and persecuting evangelical churches in Iran, Middle East Watch said.

Protestant Leader Killed In Iran

The Jerusalem Post - Israeli English language publication of July 4, 1994:

A group defending persecuted Christians worldwide said this week that a Protestant leader had been murdered in Iran - the second this year.

Portes Ouvertes (Open Doors), founded in the Netherlands in 1955, appealed to United Nations High Commissioner for Human Rights Jose Ayala Lasso to intervene with Iran on behalf of Christians in the country.

It identified the dead man as Tateos Michaelian, a 62-year-old Presbyterian preacher who was acting chairman of the Council of Protestant Ministers in Iran.

In that post, he had succeeded Bishop Haik Hovsepian Mehr of the Iranian Assemblies of God church who was found murdered near Teheran in January.

Exile and church groups accused Iranian authorities of involvement in Hovsepian's death, alleging it was part of a campaign against Christians, especially those who had been born Moslems.

Iranian authorities have denied the charges.

Portes Ouvertes was active in the past in the defense of Christians in the Soviet Union and other communist countries. Michaelian, a former general secretary of the Iranian Bible Society, disappeared on June 29th.

On July 2, according to the group, his son was summoned by the Iranian police to identify his body, which had several bullet wounds in the head.

(News Agencies).

Crisis For Iran's Intellectuals

Article by Middle East Correspondent Nicholas Goldberg on p. A 15 from the June 2nd, 1997 edition of *Newsday*)

Teheran — On March 29, a little more than a month after he disappeared, Ibrahim Zalzadeh's body turned up at the morgue in the city coroner's office.

In another country, his family might have assumed the 49-year-old magazine publisher had been the victim of a car accident or some other relatively innocent tragedy. But in Iran, thoughts tend toward the sinister.

Indeed, a few days later, when friends of the family finally saw the body and reported that Zalzadeh had been stabbed three or four times in the chest, the family's suspicions deepened. "He was stabbed in the heart," said a close friend who asked not to be identified. "It certainly wasn't an accident."

No one knows for sure whether Zalzadeh was killed by Iran's hard-line Islamic regime. But he had been on the bad side of the government lately, having publicly criticized it for censoring authors. His own magazine, *Mayar*, had closed after the government cut its supply of newsprint, and in the weeks before he disappeared, he told friends he felt threatened by the government.

What's more his death came in the wake of similar misfortunes that have befallen writers and intellectuals such as Ghaffar Hosseini, Ahmad Mir-Allai and Ahmad Taffazouli, among others. In all, more than a half-dozen of Iran's intellectual elite have been mysteriously killed in the past two years here.

"It's all very, very suspicious," said Daryush Farouchar, a long-time opponent of the Iranian regime. "Zalzadeh is not the only one who has died recently."

All these years after the mullahs took power in Iran, it's hardly news that the government has no soft spot for writers and intellectuals. Since the Islamic revolution that brought Ayatollah Ruhollah Khomeini to power eighteen years ago, the government has refused to tolerate movies, books, magazines or other artistic endeavors that make use of sexual imagery or are perceived as excessively "western," unfavorable to Islam or even slightly antigovernment. For those who didn't get the message, there was the Salman Rushdie affair in 1989, in which Khomeini issued a religious decree calling for the death of the British author for writing a novel deemed blasphemous to Islam.

The most recent crackdown — the so-called black period, which began about two years ago and has meant imprisonment and, in the opinion of many Iranian intellectuals, death for a group of those who would not be silenced — is a new low, part of what human rights groups call a concerted official effort to clamp down on thought and expression perceived as dangerous to the Islamic republic. Human Rights Watch, in a letter to the head of the Iranian judiciary last month, expressed concern about "a pattern of repression directed against independent writers and publishers."

The regime is determined not to see the reality that is before them," said Abas Maroufi, an Iranian writer and publisher whose magazine, Gardoun, was closed down and who was himself sentenced to twenty lashes and a six-month prison term for an article that supposedly criticized the regime and insulted its leaders. "They know that writers are like a mirror, and that if you let them write, you cannot any longer ignore the reality."

Yet despite the heavy-handed tactics of the regime, the battle goes on. One publisher said in an interview last week that he had thirty-five books — some with thousands of copies already printed, others in manuscript form — currently gathering dust in the office of the censors at what is euphemistically known as the "Ministry of Culture and Islamic Guidance," and that he had been refused permission to distribute them to bookstores. Films are routinely cut and changed by bureaucrats in the office of film censorship. Books of poetry, some of which have been published for decades, are being banned or changed in their ninth or tenth edition. Famous Iranian writers have been deleted from the latest issues of the Iranian Encyclopedia of Literature. In the last year and a half, Farouhar said, some twenty publications have lost their licenses to publish, and editors have been punished.

The latest wave of repression began after Ali Akbar Saidi-Sirjani died in detention under mysterious circumstances in the end of 1994. A coroner's report was never released. Then, when 134 writers and intellectuals signed a letter to President Hashemi Rafsanjani protesting the handling of the case, every single one of the signers received anonymous death threats. One of the signers, Ar. Ahmad Mir-allai, an editor at the magazine Zendehroud, died in suspicious circumstances in Isfahan in October, 1995, according to Human Rights Watch. In the months that followed, security agents raided the houses of writers and broke up meetings. A number have been sentenced to lashings and prison terms. Zalzadeh, Hosseini and Tafazoulli have all died since the beginning of the year.

Perhaps nothing is as eerily symbolic of what's going on as the melting of books. It's happened on numerous occasions: The Ministry of Culture and Islamic Guidance takes books that have already been printed, but not yet distributed, and they hold them in a warehouse while reviewing the content. If they decide the book should not be allowed into the stores, they take all existing copies — in one case, there were 11,000 of them — and bring them by truck to a cardboard plant, where they are washed in a big pot to get the ink off. The pages are then shredded, and finally are cooked into a paste. The paste is then recycled into cardboard.

"They've burned my store down and they've arrested me and they've taken my books and put them back into the pot and made them into dough," one publisher said. "But the funny thing is, I still love my job, because I feel I haven't made any compromises to them.. The problems here have happened gradually and we've become resistant or used to them, or we just learned to survive them"

There are numerous responses to the repression. Some publishers have gone ahead with their work, like Zalzadeh and Maroufi, and have been punished for it. Many writers and intellectuals, particularly in recent days, have left the country altogether. Many others have learned to censor themselves.

"Self-censorship is extremely common," said one person in the book industry. "First, the writers kill their own creativity and suppress their talent so their books will be acceptable to the regime, and then the editor makes further changes. You can imagine what the result is."

But the crackdown has not completely chilled free expression. Writers and publishers still gather at people's houses and read their work to one another. Poems that have been banned are photocopied and distributed. Western books are smuggled into the country and duplicated. Like the samizdat publishing endeavors of the former Soviet Union, entire books are copied unofficially and passed hand-to-hand through Teheran. Underground newsletters are distributed by fax.

"The government is frightened, of course," Farouhar said. "In any atmosphere this oppressive, the writers, artists and intellectuals are the ones who best convey the suffering of the people, the emotions they're feeling — and dictators are afraid of that. But they won't be able to stop it."

Salman Rushdie: Europe's Shameful Trade In Silence

(Salman Rushdie's article in *New York Times* OP-ED Edition of Saturday, February 1997)

Europe begins, as the Italian writer Roberto Calasso reminds us in "The Marriage of Cadmus and Harmony," with a bull , and a rape. Europa as an Asian maiden abducted by a God (who changed himself, for the occasion, into a white bull), and was held captive in a new land that came, in time, to bear her name. The prisoner of Zeus's unending desire for mortal flesh, Europa has been avenged by history. Zeus is just a story now. He is powerless; but Europe is alive.

At the very dawn of the idea of Europe, then, is an unequal struggle between human beings and gods, and an encouraging lesson: While the bull-god may win the first skirmish, it is the maiden-Continent that triumphs, in time.

I have been engaged in a skirmish with a latter-day Zeus, though his thunderbolts have thus far missed their mark.

Many others — in Algeria and Egypt, as well as Iran— have been less fortunate. Those of us engaged in this battle have long understood what it's about. It's about the right of human beings — their thoughts, their works of art, their lives — to survive those thunderbolts and to prevail over the whimsical autocracy of whatever Olympus may presently be in vogue. It's about the right to make moral, intellectual and artistic judgements without worrying about Judgement Day.

The Greek myths are Europe's southern roots. At the Continent's other end, the old Norse creation-legends also bring news of the supplanting of the gods by the human race. The final battle between the Norse gods and their terrible enemies has already taken place. The gods have slain their foes and been slain by them. Now, we are told, it is time for us to take over. There are no more gods to help us. We're on our own. Or, to put it another way (for gods are tyrants, too): We're free. The loss of the divine places us at the center of the stage to build our own morality, or own communities: to make our own choices; to make our own way.

Once again, in the earliest ideas of Europe, we find an emphasis on what is human over and above what is, at one moment or another, held to be divine. Gods may come and gods may go, but we, with any luck, go on forever.

This humanist emphasis is, to my mind, one of the most attractive aspects of European thought. It's easy, of course, to argue that Europe has also stood, during its long history, for conquest, pillage, exterminations and inquisitions. But now that we are being asked to join in the creation of a new Europe, it's helpful to remind ourselves of the best meanings of that resonant word. Because there is a Europe that many, if not most, of its citizens care about. This is not a Europe of money or bureaucracy. Since the word "culture" has been debased by overuse, I'd prefer not to use it. The Europe that is worth talking about, worth recreating, is anyhow something broader than a culture." It is a civilization.

Today, I am listening to the melancholy echoes of one small, intellectually impoverished, pathetically violent assault on the values of that civilization. I refer, I'm sorry to say, to the fatwa imposed upon me by Iran's Ayatollah Ruhollah Khomeini eight years ago yesterday, and to the latest barbaric notices about "bounty money" emerging from the Iranian Government's front organization, the 15 Khordad Foundation. I'm also sorry to say that the European Union's response to such threats has been little more than tokenist. It has achieved, in one word, nothing.

The Europe for which Europeans care would have done more than simply state that it found such an assault unacceptable. It would have sought to place maximum pressure on Iran while removing as much pressure as possible from the lives of those threatened. What has happened is the exact opposite. Iran is under very little, if any, pressure on this matter. But for eight years, some of us have been under a fair amount of stress.

During these eight years, I have come to understand the equivocations at the heart of the new Europe. I have heard German's Foreign Minister say with a shrug that there is a limit to what the European Union is prepared to do for human rights. (A few months after this statement, Germany, then Iran's biggest trading partner, gave a red-carpet welcome to Iran's terrorist in chief, Intelligence Minister Ali Fallahian. My Norwegian publisher, William Nygaard, was shot the week after Mr. Fallahian's triumphal tour.)

I have heard Belgium's Foreign Minister tell me that the European Union knows all about Iran's terrorist activities against its own dissidents on European soil. But as to action? Just a world-weary smile; just another shrug.

When Italy held the rotating presidency of the European Union last year, the Italian Foreign Ministry refused to answer — even to acknowledge — our letters on this issue. In the Netherlands, I actually found myself obliged to explain to Foreign Ministry officials why it would not be a good idea for the European Union to accept the fatwa's validity on religious grounds!

I have been refused entry to Denmark, on the spurious grounds of a trumped-up "specific threat" against my life, a threat that mysteriously vanished in the face of a public outcry. But I know that Denmark, already a major exporter of feta cheese to Iran, is trying hard to increase trade with that country.

Ireland, too, is looking to expand trade with Iran. During the just-concluded Irish presidency of the European Union, I was offered a meeting with Dick Spring, the Irish Foreign Minister, which oddly took six months and a lot of pushing actually to arrange. In this meeting, Mr. Spring assured me that a strong statement about the fatwa would be made at the European Union's summit in Dublin. No such statement was made.

This new Europe does not look to me like a civilization. It is an altogether more cynical enterprise.

Leaders of the European Union pay lip service to the great European ideals — free expression, human rights, the Enlightenment, the right to dissent, the importance of the separation of church and state. But when these ideals come up against the powerful banalities of what is called "reality" — trade, money, guns, power — then it's freedom that takes a dive. When it's Danish feta cheese or Irish halal beef against the European Convention on Human Rights, don't expect free expression to win. Speaking as a committed European, it's enough to make a Euro-skeptic out of you.

Soon Britain will take over the presidency of the European Union and will then have a real opportunity to resolve this problem. I hope — I think after so long a wait I have a right to expect — that the British Government will, during this period, be a good deal more active than it has been. So much of diplomacy, I've learned, is a matter of nods and winks. The extreme passivity of the British Foreign Office has permitted the rest of the European Union to go to sleep on this issue, and has given the Iranian people the sign that there is really no need for them to do very much at all. I am, of course, pleased that the Foreign Office has condemned the new bounty offer, but a few stiff words once a year are no substitute for a policy.

Like so many of my fellow Britons, I hope there will soon be a new Labor Government. I have long been urging that government-in-waiting to understand the importance of the arts in convening a sense of national renewal, which Labor must seek swiftly to create.

On the occasion of this tawdry anniversary, I ask Tony Blair, the Labor leader who may become Britain's next Prime Minister, to come to the aid of this one particular artist. As he knows, and has been good enough to tell me, the principles involved go far beyond the survival of a single individual. I ask him to bring a new spirit of urgency to the fight against the Zeus of Iran and his attempt to kidnap our freedoms, and to show Labor's commitment to the true spirit of Europe — not just to an economic community or to a monetary union, but European civilization itself.

Chapter Ten

Islamic Persecution of Christians in the Holy Land

In the first week of January, 1992, I happened to be reading *The Jerusalem Post* and came across on the first page of this English language daily, an article written about a Catholic priest George Abou Khazen, who had just written a controversial article in the Franciscan Order magazine "La Terra Santa." What was unusual about this article was that, for the first time, an officially sanctioned Catholic Church article was blasting the Moslems and not the Jews for the exodus of Christians from the Holy Land.

A day or two later, another article appeared in *The Jerusalem Post* that through a plea-bargain with the fanatic Islamic Jihad, the life of Father George Abou-Khazen was spared on the condition that the November-December 1991 Terra Santa magazine featuring his article attacking Islamic buyouts of Christian properties be recalled from the newsstands in Jerusalem and withdrawn from circulation — in other words, Islamic censorship, intimidation, and muzzling of the free press.

Naturally, my curiosity was aroused, and I immediately went to the renowned Ludwig-Mayer bookshop in Jerusalem to order myself a copy of that controversial magazine. Ludwig-Mayer promised that if anybody could get me a copy of that magazine it was they. However, after four months of waiting, I realized I would have to do some private investigation type work to land myself a copy.

So I gathered up my courage, went down into the Christian Quarter of the Old City of Jerusalem to the offices of the Franciscan Order and told them that I was student at the Seminary of Judaic Studies in Jerusalem for an MA program and studying beginner classical Greek as well as introductory courses on classical Greece and Rome at the Hebrew University of Jerusalem. I told them I had a research project for which I needed all six bi-monthly editions of their magazine for 1991. The best lie is the truth! So I purchased all six magazines though I only needed the last bi-monthly for November-December 1991. No sooner did I get my hands on a copy, that I immediately took a bus to Tel-Aviv to the Israel Defense Forces Army Spokesman's Office where I serve in the reserves and submitted photocopies of the article in the original in Italian for the military to translate into Hebrew. An Italian speaking reserves officer was mobilized to translate the article into Hebrew. Copies of this article were distributed to all members of my unit. I then retranslated this article from Hebrew into English for all of you now reading my book. This book is the only book in the world with the contents of Father George Abou Khazen's article:

A. From article by Father George Abou-Khazen o.f.m. appearing in Vatican sanctioned Franciscan Order magazine, "La Terra Santa," of November-December, 1991, published in Jerusalem, and later recalled from the shelves because of Islamic death threats issued against Father Abou-Khazen.

"The Bitter Exodus of Christians from the Holy Land"

The dream that one day there will be a dialogue of life and peace and cooperation between Christians and Moslems has never abandoned the Franciscans in the Holy Land, who inherited this spirit from the world conference (of the Church) of St. Francis, the hero of a famous friendly meeting with the Sultan.

The difficulties facing the Christians are caused by the Moslem takeover spreading more than ever over the land in order to block the living space of the Christians. George Abou Khazen, a regional Bethlehem priest, cries out for the Christians of the Holy Land.

The Christians are abandoning the Middle East. Regrettably, this is an undeniable fact. Many have analyzed this phenomenon, others prophesy that in another thirty years there will be no more Christians in the Middle East. It is clear that the Jewish presence has alarmed the Arabs, and more than anything else, the commercial, cultural and technological contacts of recent years have caused a confrontation between western civilization and middle eastern culture, or as is commonly known Islamic culture against Judeo-Christian. This has sharpened today's Islamic approach: All lands must be Islamic.

For this reason, the first to adopt this approach were the Arabs of the Galilee, who celebrate "Land Day." This commemoration started on March 30, 1977, to remind one and all that on this date, as a result of demonstrations protesting land appropriations, five Arabs were killed and dozens injured. Commemorations of this incident spread throughout Israeli Arab communities and even into the formerly Jordanian territories administered by Israel.

We Christians also say that every being is called to defend the faith, but we say this to all people under any kind of regime, culture or state who can believe freely and to convert to Christianity should they so wish.

The Moslem religion (Islam) is both a religion as well as a society, religion and state as one. Whoever is not a member of this religion is considered a foreigner and outsider. According to Islam, at least for the foreseeable future, no pluralistic or democratic society can exist.

Islam cannot and must not agree to any non-Islamic rule. Just as Islam is considered citizenship, it is also the House of Islam; all lands on which Moslems live or were ever conquered by Muslims are considered part of the House of Islam.

Today, the geographic entity known as Palestine is considered WAKF or Moslem trusteeship (land ownership). This, we say, is a principle that the Jews also hold regarding Palestine. In Saudi Arabia, for example, it is forbidden to build a Christian church, or to bury a Christian, simply because it is forbidden to profane Moslem soil. The call to prayer is also territorial: it must be heard throughout all the neighborhoods of the city.

Since the Moslems are not capable at this time of implementing a homogenous Islamic society on the entire nation regarding a way of life, legislation of laws, they are attempting to "Islamicize the land," i.e., that the land be the property of Moslems.

In order to carry out this program, considerable amounts of money have been allocated over the decades by Muslim countries, during a summit meeting of Moslem states which took place in Baghdad in 1978, and in which it was decided, inter alia, to acquire lands in Beit Jala, and to build a mosque there, as indeed has happened.

Many such instances occurred in the '70s and '80s; a campaign was carried out to purchase stores in the Christian quarter of the old city of Jerusalem, and they were successful in their endeavors.

The sensational and much publicized event involving St. John's Hospice in the old city of Jerusalem, which was the property of the Greek Orthodox Church, and in which Israelis settled during Passover of 1990, exemplifies what I have been claiming. When the Israelis moved into the building, the Moslems initiated a popular chain reaction and blamed the Greek Orthodox for this. But every time that the Greek Orthodox sold lands to the Moslems, the "People" did not protest.

In any case, the Moslems continue with their tricks in order not only to take over lands but to acquire the lands; they paid astronomical amounts in Bethlehem. In the areas under the jurisdiction of my church, a Christian family wanted to sell a parcel of land. Moslems arrived, but the family advised them that they prefer to try to sell to other Christians. They finally succeeded in doing so, but after a short period, the Moslems tried to burn their house down. Who committed the arson? "Children," they said. Luckily, this time the owners of the house noticed the fire as it began and quickly put it out. But two stores were torched by two street cleaners in Jerusalem and were completely gutted.

As can be seen, the idea of Islamicizing the land causes great tensions and at the same time narrows more and more the living room available to Christians. The present day political problems, the limitations imposed on the Christians as a result of continuing strikes, the dramas of the intifada (Palestinian uprising against Israel), have brought the Moslem Arabs considerable aid from "sister" Moslem countries while the Christians were told: "You have your churches!" (which collect charity on Good Friday and which is not based on oil wells).

If this situation continues, young Christian families will find themselves more and more unable to be owners of lands and of homes, and, therefore, will be unable to sink roots into their homeland and they will be forced to join the wave of emigration of Christians from the Holy Land.

Christians Attacked By Moslems
On The Streets Of Jerusalem

From an article by Jim Hutman appearing in *The Jerusalem Post* on July 18, 1994 (page 1).

Recent attacks by Moslems on Christian targets in Jerusalem's Old City have sparked the concern of government officials.

"Moslems are increasing their attacks on Christians in Jerusalem in an effort to show their dominance in the city," Uri Mor, the Religious Affairs Ministry Advisor on Christian Affairs, told the *Jerusalem Post* yesterday.

He said Hamas leaders had verbally threatened Christian leaders at least twice in the past six months.

"We look upon the situation that has developed with much concern," Mor said.

According to Mor, the matter is to be raised today at the weekly cabinet meeting.

Over the weekend, a gang of Moslem youths ransacked a pool hall near the Church of the Holy Sepulchre, which is frequented by Christian youths. Four of the Christians were stabbed and lightly wounded; one of them required hospitalization.

Witnesses said about fifty Moslem youths marched through the Christian Quarter to the pool hall Saturday afternoon, chanting anti-Christian slogans. They attacked the Christians inside, broke chairs, tables, and other objects.

Mor said the matter was brought to the attention of Police Inspector-General Assaf Hefetz, who ordered the investigation into the attack be made a top priority.

Old City Police Chief Dep. Cmdr. David Givati confirmed that there have been a number of attacks by Moslems on Christian targets recently. He could not, however, say whether this represented a substantial increase from the past.

Arab residents of the Old City often do not report crime to police, Givati noted. Mor said that according to reports he has received, Saturday's attack was the most severe of a string of such attacks in recent months.

Mor maintained that the attacks were politically motivated. Police, however, said that often social and religious issues were at issue, such as Christians serving liquor, which is forbidden by Islam.

Police sources, meanwhile, said that police protection has been beefed up at Christian holy sites, particularly during holidays, to prevent attacks by Moslem extremists.

Article from *Jerusalem Post* supplement *In Jerusalem* on July 22, 1994 (page 3).

Moslems Attack Christians

Several Christian residents in the Old City contacted *In Jerusalem,* informing us they have become the subject of increasing and regular attacks at the hands of gangs of Moslems. This past weekend, three Christians suffered knife wounds and had to be treated at Hadassah Hospital, where they were reported in moderate to good condition. The residents complained the police arrived at the scene, but never in time to catch the perpetrators. Residents intend to step up efforts to protect themselves and are preparing a petition to give to city leaders which calls for more police protection.

Kidnapping and Torture of Palestinian Christians by Palestinian Authority in Jericho

First article

Excerpt from an article by Steve Rodan and Bill Hutman in Israel's English daily *The Jerusalem Post* on May 19th, 1995.

"Meanwhile, another Palestinian has been reported kidnapped by the Palestinian Authority. He was identified as Shaker Mustafa Daoud Saleh, 37, of Sarta near Nablus.

Family members say Saleh, a Moslem who recently converted to Christianity, was ordered to appear in Jericho for questioning by the Palestinian police. He arrived in Jericho ten days ago and never returned.

Family members were allowed to visit Saleh on Wednesday at the Jericho police station, where they discovered that his jaw and leg were broken.

In an interview, Jibril Rajoub refused to discuss the kidnapping.

Second Article

Excerpt from an article by Nadav Haetzni in the May 1995 *Yesha Report Supplement*, Jerusalem, Israel

"About three weeks ago, on Sunday, Victor Elias, a 22-year-old from Bethlehem went out to root for the local basketball team in a game in Jericho against the Ramallah team. He did not imagine that he would make the return trip lying down, with every broken bone in his body reminding him of the special treatment he received at the hands of the Palestinian police force.

"Unfortunately for Victor, he got caught in a riot that broke out on the edge of the basketball court. Red-bereted soldiers serving in Jericho's military police were called out to restore order. Eyewitnesses at the court said that the soldiers began hitting anyone they happened to come across. They fired shots in the air and that only further inflamed the situation. Young Victor Elias stood the whole time beside a soldier spraying fire. In his innocence he asked the soldier: 'Why are you shooting? You are wreaking havoc in the crowd; even the Israeli soldiers would not have shot in a place like this.'

"That was a serious mistake. What happened immediately afterward, Elias told his friend and even detailed in a letter sent two weeks ago to the chairman of the Palestinian Authority, Yasser Arafat. The soldier firing shots called his colleagues and together they dragged the insolent youth to a military vehicle standing nearby, while beating him with clubs and cursing. The Palestinian Minister of Sport, Umi Shueihi was present and tried to intervene, but the soldiers did not give him so much as a glance.

"Elias was brought to the Jericho prison and thrown into a cell where the real treatment began: 'They broke three clubs on me,' he later related. 'Every time I fell on the ground from the many blows, they would step on me, lift me up and continue beating. During the beatings, my shirt was torn and the cross hanging on a chain around my neck was noticed. Then they became even more violent. 'We came here specially from Lebanon to teach the Christian dogs,' they said. And then while beating me, they forced me to repeat the sahaduta three times: 'There is no god other than Allah and Mohammed is his prophet.' After I said that, they informed me that 'now you are a Moslem, and now we will teach you what it means to be a Moslem.' And then the blows began coming.

"After hours of this nightmare, Victor was rescued from the prison by his friends, not before Palestinian minister and Bethlehem Mayor Elias Freij frantically appealed to Arafat's office and asked for his intervention. Victor was rushed to a Bethlehem hospital where he was hospitalized with numerous fractured bones and swellings all over his body. For some time, he had difficulty standing up.

"Following that incident, Elias sent a letter of complaint to the PLO chairman demanding an investigation and trial for those responsible. No investigation was opened, but the complainant was summoned to the office of Jibril Rajoub, the strong man in Jericho. Rajoub assured him that the abusive soldiers apologized and made it clear to Elias that he could not talk about the incident with anyone."

Arab Christians Under The Palestinian Authority

Article by David Blewitt, executive director of the National Christian Leadership Conference for Israel, New York City, NY. Reprinted from *Midstream*, May 1996, by permission.(Taken from *The Jewish Political Chronicle* - August/September, 1996.)

In January 1996 I was in Bethlehem with a group of Christian tourists. We left the buses to enter the Church of the Nativity and were confronted by a two-story banner of a smiling Yasir Arafat looking down on Manger Square. The banner had been left since Christmas when Arafat had stood on the roof of the church next to a Palestinian flag and greeted Christian pilgrims by saying, This is the holy city, the city of the Palestinian Lord, the Messiah of Peace and Freedom." The Muslim leaders of the Palestinian Authority had then crowded the church, making it virtually impossible for Christians to attend Christmas services.

After the tour, I returned to Bethlehem to meet with Palestinian (Arab) Christians and was shocked to discover how the peace process is affecting them. (It is still difficult for me to call Arabs "Palestinians" because the word referred to Jews in the land of Israel until 1948 — the year the U.N. made them Israelis.

Israel has withdrawn from all areas where Arabs are in the majority, and for the first time in history, 450 villages and all major cities in Gaza, Judea, and Samaria are under Palestinian (Arab) Authority. During a press conference with President Bill Clinton on 11 December 1995, Prime Minister Shimon Peres said, "Israel has implemented one of our greatest moral promises — not to rule other people." (*Near East Report*, 18 December 1995)

Most of the world press heralded Israel's withdrawal as a victory "for all the oppressed Arabs," but one group of oppressed Arabs is not celebrating. Palestinian Christians in Judea and Samaria admit privately that they view the change from Israeli to Palestinian rule with fear.

The new Palestinian Authority is said to represent all Palestinians, but in reality it is controlled by Muslims who have shown little or no concern for the Christian minority. (Arab Christians are a distinct minority in Judea and Samaria, numbering about 50,000 people or 2.4 percent of the total population, down from 20 percent in 1948. ((The *New York Times*, 31 December 1995)) The Eastern Orthodox are the largest group, followed by Catholics who have the most powerful voice due to Vatican-Israel relations. Protestants are a tiny, fractured, hardly measurable group with no significant native voice who rely on their various church leaderships to make their voices heard abroad.) They follow the dhimmi system of Islamic law that permits only a restricted life to Christians and Jews ("People of the Book"); consequently, the Arab Christian minority in Israel is shrinking. (According to Catholic figures, Bethlehem was around 79 percent Christian from 1931 until 1967. The latest unofficial figures, compiled by Father Ignacio Pena in 1984 for the Catholic publication, "Holy Land Review," revealed that Bethlehem's Christian population had shrunk to 40 percent: 5,150 Eastern Orthodox, 4,400 Catholics, 180 Protestants, and one

Copt. (*The Jerusalem Post Magazine*, 15 December 1995)) It is estimated that the Christian population has now shrunk to 32 percent.) Since they tend to have better educations, higher incomes,
fewer children, and family ties abroad, they can travel almost anywhere in the Western world and assimilate into Christian communities.

Israel has often been accused of causing Christian Arabs to
emigrate, but the Christian population in Israeli towns and cities
has more than quadrupled since 1948 — from 30,000 to 146,000 as
of 1993. ("Jerusalem", seventh edition; Israel Information Center,
1995)

Many Palestinian Christians had openly criticized Israeli rule
in the past because they feared the PLO more than they feared
Israeli rule. But now they are concerned about their future because
they are afraid they will no longer have Israel to protect them. They
have been moved into an overwhelming Muslim society, where
they are seen not only as inferior but as potentially disloyal to Islamic authority, especially in light of a growing radical fundamentalism.

Christian Arabs wonder: What place will they have as
dhimmis in Muslim society under Palestinian Authority? Present
indications are not encouraging. Several Christian lay people in
Bethlehem told me they have to be "one with the tongue, one with
the heart," by which they mean that although their hearts are often united with Israel, they must speak in unity with their local
leaders. This is not new. For many years, they have had to prove
their loyalty to local leaders by joining in defying Israel. I was told
by several Arab Christians that this is the price they must pay for
security. One man told me, "When we go East (into the Arab states)
we have to shut our mouths, when we go West (into Israel) we can
open them."

Arab Christians are an intimidated minority who find it difficult to oppose their Palestinian leaders. They know what has been
done to others who disagreed with PLO policies, and they remember Arafat's January 1989 threat of "ten bullets in the chest for any
one who collaborates with Israel." They know that he has arrested
and threatened journalists, intellectuals, and human rights activists who have angered him by documenting abuses by the Palestinian security service. ("Boston Globe," January 1996)

They know what happened to the editor of "Al-Quds," the leading Palestinian newspaper in Jerusalem. Maher Alami was imprisoned for a week because his paper ran a flattering article about Yasir Arafat on page three rather than on page one, where Arafat thought it belonged. ("Dispatch from Jerusalem, January-February 1996; "Jerusalem Insider," 4 February 1996) They recall that at the height of the intifada, three times as many Arabs were killed by Arabs than by Israelis. The "New York Times" reported that when Palestinians hear a knock at the door, they are relieved to see an Israeli soldier rather than a masked Palestinian. ("Myths and Facts," p.170; "The New York Times", 12 June 1991) And they understand what is meant by the graffiti on a wall in Beit Zahur: "First the Saturday people, then the Sunday people." ("New York Times Magazine," 24 December 1995, p.40)

I was told that during the intifada pilgrims walking to the Church of the Nativity in Bethlehem were sometimes stoned, but the Greek Orthodox patriarch dared not report it. I was also told that a statue of Mary had been taken from the Beit Jala convent near Jericho and burned. When questioned about it, the nuns were shocked and asked, "How did you know? We did not report it!" And when asked why, a nun put her finger to her lips and whispered, "We were told not to."

Such incidents do not reach the Western press, but can you imagine the uproar if Israel were responsible for such outrages? More than once, I heard people say in various ways, "Our condition is not so bad as it could be without Israel's presence. Everyone who spoke to me indicated that their only hope within the present situation still lies with Israel.

The problems, as I see them, are: 1) because of their fear of what will happen to them and their families, local Christians must say whatever the Palestinian Authority tells them to say; 2) most mainline Protestant churches in the U.S. hear what Palestinian Christians are forced to say and, unaware of threats of intimidation, believe them; 3) church leaders have invested much of their own credibility in support of the Palestinian Arabs' cause. They have portrayed Israel for so long as the troublemaker, the obstacle to peace in the Middle East, could they now admit that the only real friend Arab Christians have in the area is Israel? Could they admit that they have been used and are still being used to spread anti-Israel propaganda? Their continuing to bash Israel, the Arab Christians' only hope for assistance, does nothing to help the Arab communities the church leaders claim to support; 4) and finally, the turning over of Bethlehem to the Palestinian Authority has created a potential bombshell. An Israeli leader told me he was afraid that their giving up Bethlehem — without any protest from the Christian world — could set a precedent that would lead to the redividing of Jerusalem. And a Christian with the same concern said that Israel's abandonment of Bethlehem has given misinformed Christians an argument for the abandonment of Jerusalem. If there is no Christian reaction to the Palestinian Authority controlling Bethlehem, why should there be any problem with their controlling part of Jerusalem?

We must remember that only under Israel have all peoples of all religious faiths had access to Jerusalem. We must also remember the PLO has still not changed its stated goal of ridding the land of Jews — or that Christians are also regarded as dhimmis to be mistreated.

What is the challenge to Christians in the U.S.? Our need to support Israel remains unchanged, but it is given new impetus as we consider our responsibility to our Christian sisters and brothers who feel alone and abandoned under the Palestinian Authority.

True peace cannot come to the region through jihad, which Arafat continues to promote when he speaks in Arabic (and which he says means "nation building" when he speaks in English). It can only come through learning to live and work together, the policies that Israel has promoted since its inception.

PA Police Denying Entry To Greek Orthodox Clergy

(Article from *The Jerusalem Post,* November 12th, 1996)

Greek Orthodox clergymen wishing to visit their communities in areas under the control of the Palestinian Authority have, on occasion, been stopped and turned back by the Palestinian Police, a ranking official of the Greek Orthodox Church has charged.

Metropolitan Timothy, secretary of the Greek Orthodox Patriarchate in Jerusalem, said that on Sunday night he and a Greek

Orthodox archbishop had been on their way to Ramallah when Palestinian policemen stopped them and told them to return to Jerusalem.

"I have heard reports of similar incidents in the past, but I did not really believe them until it actually happened to me," he said.

Timothy said that when they were stopped, the only identification he had was his driver's license, although the archbishop had his Greek passport.

When he objected to being stopped and said that he was expected for an appointment in Ramallah, the policemen told him to turn around and go back to Jerusalem

Timothy insisted on taking the name and number of the policemen who stopped him and refused to leave for thirty minutes until the commander arrived. He told him that he could not have the details and turned him back.

Church Heads Discuss Wakf Fray With Prime Minister Netanyahu

Article by Haim Shapiro from p 20 of *The Jerusalem Post*, Friday, April 25, 1997.

As thousands of Orthodox Christian pilgrims filled the Old City of Jerusalem in preparation for their Easter this Sunday, the heads of the two major Orthodox churches, together with a leading Roman Catholic, met yesterday with Prime Minister Binyamin Netanyahu to discuss a Moslem incursion into the holiest site in Christendom.

The Christian leaders, Greek Orthodox Patriarch Diodoros I, Armenian Patriarch Torkom Manoogian, and Franciscan Custos of the Holy Land Joseph Nazzaro, had earlier written to Netanyahu to enlist his support. The Christian leaders complained that, during its renovations to the Hanqa Mosque adjacent to the Church of the Holy Sepulcher, the Wakf (the Moslem religious trust) had built a toilet above the roof of the church. In addition, the Wakf had broken into and appropriated two rooms in the Greek Orthodox Patriarchate.

Netanyahu told the leaders that the government could not accept any change in the status quo in Jerusalem, and in particular the part of the Old City where the church and mosque are located.

"It is our duty to look after the future of Jerusalem and we will work to restore the status quo that has existed in the area for more than a hundred years, ' the prime minister said. He promised them the government would handle the matter with the utmost responsibility.

Also attending the meeting were Deputy Minister of Religious Affairs Yigal Bibi, Jerusalem Mayor Ehud Olmert, and Jerusalem police chief Cmdr. Yair Yitzhaki.

Meanwhile, the Jerusalem District Court yesterday issued an injunction ordering the work at the mosque to stop. The order was issued at the request of the Jerusalem Municipality, which maintains that the renovations have been undertaken without a permit.

Christian-Moslem Dispute Escalates

Article by Haim Shapiro in *The Jerusalem Post* of Thursday, May 1st, 1997.

The confrontation between Christian and Moslem institutions in Jerusalem's Old City escalated sharply yesterday with charges by a church leader that Moslems had attempted to break into the Church of the Holy Sepulchre.

The Moslem leader responsible for the disputed construction work, which Christians said encroaches on their property and violates the sanctity of the ancient church, denied Moslems had taken over any Christian area and refused to recognize the right of the municipality to stop the work.

In the dispute, which relates to construction work at the Khanka Salahieh Mosque, which abuts the church, representatives of the three historic churches — Greek, Orthodox, Armenian, and Roman Catholic — allege that the Moslem WAKF had constructed toilets over the church. This would violate the status quo which has tempered interreligious relations in the city for over two centuries.

In addition, the Greek Orthodox said that the Moslems had broken into and occupied two rooms in the Greek Orthodox Patriarchate.

However yesterday, in a press tour of the disputed area organized by the Government Press Office, Metropolitan Timothy, secretary of the Greek Orthodox Patriarchate, said that the Moslem workmen had attempted to break into the church. Relating that church officials had found stones and debris from the church wall, Timothy said that he did not know why the workmen had tried to break in.

The tour revealed a maze of interconnecting structures, with rooms carved out of buildings representing different layers of history and often not serving their original function. On the Greek Orthodox side, one walked through a winding series of passages and rooms to find two doors which open onto doorways roughly blocked with stones and cement blocks.

On the Moslem side, an equally convoluted passage leads up a flight of stairs, past a living area, to what apparently once had been a Crusader hall, and now is functioning as a mosque. According to one version, it was only the small hall at street level which had constituted the original mosque, while according to another version, the upstairs mosque had served dignitaries, including Saladin.

At the entrance to the upstairs room, Sheikh Yakoub Rajaby, who is responsible for the mosque, pointed to a newly plastered wall in what now constitutes the entrance hall, defying media representatives to find the two rooms described by the Greek Orthodox.

"The Priests said here were rooms and we stole them. You see this is the main entrance of the mosque," he said.

Clearly the newly plastered area had originally been one room and it had apparently been connected to the hall now serving as a mosque, but whether this had been the case since Saladin captured Jerusalem in 1187 or even for the past century or two, is unclear.

On the other side of the entrance, along a wall abutting the northern edge of the Church of the Holy Sepulcher, the work on the new toilet complex is continuing, despite an order to stop issued at the request of the Jerusalem Municipality. Rajaby said the WAKF will not honor the request.

"The municipality has no authority here, only the Moslem WAKF. Only God can stop the work here," he said.

It was virtually impossible to determine whether the new toilets actually extended over the Christian sanctuary, as the Christians insist, or whether the outer wall of the church is as much as 18 or 20 meters from the construction area, as Rajaby averred. Photographers scrambled over walls and onto rooftops in a vain attempt to actually see how far the church extended.

According to the Government Press Office, which described the building work as "illegal construction in the heart of the Christian Quarter," the incident began two years ago when the WAKF "took control" of what it described as an underground hall (apparently the Crusader hall) under the Church of the Holy Sepulcher, an act which later led to the appropriation of the two rooms in the Patriarchate.

The GPO also said that the toilet complex, built of reinforced concrete, damages the ancient character of the site and could lead to future deterioration of the original structure

Greek Orthodox-Wakf Dispute Remains Unresolved

Article by Haim Shapiro in *The Jerusalem Post* of Tuesday, July 8th, 1997

Despite a recent Jordanian report that a solution had been found to the dispute between the Greek Orthodox Patriarchate and the Moslem WAKF in Jerusalem, there is still no solution in sight.

The dispute arises from an incursion by builders, carrying out renovations at the Khanka Salahieh Mosque in the Old City, who annexed two rooms belonging to the Patriarchate. The rooms had been used by the Greek Orthodox Patriarch Diodoros's representative in Istanbul, who was away. When officials of the Patriarch tried to visit the rooms, they found the doorways blocked with cement and the representative's belongings flung into a nearby corridor.

Mosque representatives say the area is part of an ancient mosque.

Metropolitan Timothy, the secretary of the Greek Orthodox Patriarchate, said yesterday that the Jordanians had indeed sent a delegation to meet with Diodoros.

"The Jordanian delegation visited his beatitude and stressed the desire of the Jordanians to solve this problem amicably. We all feel that it should be solved amicably," he said.

The Jordanians had proposed exchanging the two rooms for St. George's Church in Kerak, east of the Dead Sea, he said. The church, he said, had been a place of worship for both Christians and Moslems, but a Jordanian court had ruled that it belonged to the Moslems.

According to Timothy, Diodoros asked the Jordanians to put their offer into writing. So far, he said, the Jordanians had failed to do so.

"The matter is not yet solved. The case is not over yet," Timothy said.

Palestinian Authority Police Intervene In Russian Church Property Dispute In Hebron

Article by Haim Shapiro in *The Jerusalem Post* of Wednesday, July 9th, 1997.

In an unprecedented action, the Palestinian Police this weekend broke into the Russian Orthodox Abraham's Oak Monastery in Hebron, evicted the clerics of the New York based Russian Orthodox Church Outside of Russia, and turned it over to representatives of the Moscow-based church.

The action, a representative of the Russian-based church said yesterday, was the result of a promise made by Palestinian Authority Chairman Yasser Arafat to Patriarch of Moscow Alexei II during the latter's visit here last month.

Although Russian Orthodox Church property in pre-1967 Israel has been in the hands of the Moscow-based Church, the New York-based mission had controlled such property in the West Bank and eastern Jerusalem since the early 1950's, when the Jordanian government ruled that it was the rightful heir of the Russian Orthodox Church. After the Six Day War, Israel respected the status quo.

According to Archimandrite Bartholomew, head of the New York-based mission, for over a month, Palestinian security forces had visited the monastery almost daily, demanding that the residents leave.

On Saturday, he said, the Palestinian Police broke into the living quarters and demanded that the three priests and four monks there gather their belongings and leave. The latter refused to do so. Meanwhile, Bartholomew himself arrived with two nuns.

Bartholomew said representatives of the Russian-based church and the Russian consulate watched as Palestinian policemen dragged the clerics from the building. Women police officers, assisted by their male counterparts, dragged and beat the nuns, he said adding that one nun had been hospitalized.

According to a press release issued on Monday by Archbishop Laurus, secretary of the New York-based Church Synod of Bishops, the Church is an American legal church body, incorporated under the laws of the state of New York.

However, a U.S. consular official in Jerusalem said yesterday that there was no reason for the consulate to interfere in the matter. Ann Casper, deputy head of the consulate's press section, said the consulate had a duty to see that American citizens were treated justly under local laws, but no such protection extended to a church.

Palestinian Authority spokesman Nabil Abu Rudeineh said yesterday that he was not aware of the incident, but that in principle the PA did not interfere in church affairs.

A Bloody Week In A Galilee Village

Excerpts from an article by David Rudge on p.10 of *The Jerusalem Post* of Friday, May 2nd, 1997.

Violent clashes this week between two families in Turan village in Lower Galilee have raised the specter of MoslemChristian strife in the Arab community.

Village leaders in Turan maintain that the bloody, week-long feuds, in which a Christian resident was killed and three Moslems seriously injured, are not based on religious differences, but were sparked by a dispute between family clans.

Nevertheless, Dr. Elie Rekhess believes that there are signs of a growing rift between Moslems and Christians.

Israeli Arab leaders have taken pains to play down even hints of division among religious lines in their ranks, according to Rekhess, an expert on Israeli Arabs at Tel Aviv University's Oayan Center.

"Generally speaking, Moslem-Christian relationships in the Israeli Arab community have in the past been characterized by peace and quiet," says Rekhess. "In recent years, however, tensions have occasionally risen, especially during Moslem and Christian holidays, such as Id al-Fitr (at the end of the month-long Ramadan fast), Id al-Adha (the Feast of the Sacrifice) and at Christmas and Easter."

This growing tension, which can sometimes be exacerbated by clan disputes or squabbles, is partly related to the expansion of the Islamic Movement within the Arab community in Israel, Rekhess notes.

Rekhess maintains that the Islamic Movement's slogans, such as "Islam is the Truth" and "Islam is the Solution," have irritated certain sectors of the Christian community.

"Islamic leaders try to minimize religious differences and continue to present the Islamic Movement as an all-Arab entity.

"Some Christian leaders are concerned about the changing winds, although nobody is prepared to talk about this publicly," says Rekhess.

Arab leaders too, in their public announcements, have vehemently rejected any indications of a Moslem-Christian rift, although some cracks have been appearing, even in places like Nazareth and Kafr Yasif, according to Rekhess.

According to Turan local council chairman Nagi Nessar, the riots that have broken the peace and normally harmonious relations between residents of the village, located on the Nazareth-Tiberias road, are the outcome of what he describes as juvenile hooliganism.

Nevertheless, a continuation of the fighting, which has been primarily between members of the Moslem Dahleh and Christian Khouri families, could have far-reaching ramifications for Turan's 9,000 inhabitants — ninety percent of whom are Moslems and the remainder, Greek Orthodox Christians.

Chapter Eleven

Palestinian Authority: Realities

'LIKE BEING IN HELL' (Article by Uri Dan and Dennis Eisenberg from *The Jerusalem Post* of Thursday, September 5th, 1996)

We agreed that we would call him Mustafa. He is a decorator and works at the Jerusalem home of a writer of this column. Last week he suddenly announced: "I've applied for Israeli citizenship.

This was a surprise, as he had been jubilant when Yasser Arafat signed the Oslo accords in Washington three years ago. He said then: "We will have a Palestinian state and you a Jewish state. We will be like brothers living in peace.

Now he spoke in a voice full of bitterness. "Living under Arafat's secret police is like being in hell. I would rather live under the Jews. My people are fearful every day and night of their lives, for the most terrible things are happening to us.

"Jibril Rajoub's thugs are kidnapping young girls in areas under Arafat's control, in Ramallah and other cities, even in Jerusalem, raping them and then killing them to prevent them from talking. Human life is cheaper than dirt from the gutter."

"That sounds like a rumor," we told him. "We deal only in facts."

"I'll tell you facts if you hide my identity," he answered.

"On August 19, Rajoub's heroes in their leather jackets walked into a neighbor's house in the Arab Quarter of the Old City of Jerusalem, near the Damascus Gate.

"In my neighbor's house was a girl, 18 or 19 years old, a relative from Gaza who had come to stay with them around the beginning of the month. My neighbor, who is a cousin of my wife, told her that the girl had quarreled with her parents. They had wanted her to marry a rich old man, a builder in Gaza. She hated him and ran away. She threatened to kill herself if she was sent home.

"Rajoub's thugs marched right into the house. They grabbed the girl and hit her on the head and around the face when she screamed. They threatened her with their guns if she didn't shut up. They dragged her off and drove away with her in their car."

"Mustafa" went on: "There are several hundred of Rajoub's men operating quite openly in Jerusalem. They take what they want from shops — radios, food, cigarettes — and sometimes grab money from the till.

"The shopkeepers dare not protest. If they go to the Israeli police they know they will be dead within 24 hours. If they try to protect themselves Rajoub's officers take them to Ramallah or Jericho.

"Everybody knows about the torture chambers there. Those who have survived say it is better to die than end up in the hands of Rajoub's `interrogators.' So shopkeepers now say thank you to his men and keep their mouths closed."

Mustafa said he only heard about the incident a week later.

"I asked a lawyer friend who handles such matters. He knows of about a dozen girls who have been taken away by Rajoub's men and never been seen again. With a lot of money you can bribe them to bring the girls back sometimes. But not in this case.

"The lawyer told me that the girl's family had paid Rajoub's officers NIS6,000 to return her to Gaza. They drove through the Israeli barriers with her in the car. All four had raped her on the way.

"The girl's brother paid Rajoub's men. You ask what happened to her? Her brothers called her a prostitute for running away and killed her. They threw her body into a ditch. It was a case of family honor."

We were told by an Israeli security official: "There is nothing we can do. We have reported many cases like this to the government, particularly when they happen in Jerusalem. But when Israeli Arabs are involved we can't go and look for them in Palestinian areas. We've been blind there, ever since we were forced to stop using Palestinian informers.

"So we try to get information from Arafat's security people. They tell us nothing; they are laughing behind our backs. It's humiliating.

"Recently a TV team went to Ramallah to do a program about life in 'independent Palestine.' The cameramen wanted to take pictures of the police station because they were impressed by the fine cars parked outside. There were Volvo's, Mitsubishi's, BMW's and so on — all expensive vehicles, all fairly new. They refused to give us permission.

"The vehicles were all stolen. Some even had their original Israeli license plates." A second security source we talked to backed up this account. A major problem is that many of Arafat's police and security men have only the vaguest connection to the Palestinians. They were brought in with Arafat from Tunis, where they had it easy. There they were called "naval police" because they sat on the beach all day.

They hate their present work. They are badly paid and the locals ignore them.

Security sources told us about three incidents during the past month that ended in murder.

Recently two of Arafat's policemen saw a youth leave a discotheque in Ramallah at midnight and get into his BMW. He turned on his radio full blast. It was playing the latest rave music. They told him to turn it down. He refused. They dragged him out of the car. His body was found next morning in a nearby lane.

In Nablus a local intifada hero annoyed the "naval police." He was found slashed to pieces. He was taken to an Israeli hospital to give the impression that it was the Jews who did him in.

In the village of Bidou people complained about rival families screaming, shouting and fighting each other in the middle of the night. Finally the Palestinian police arrived and settled the matter immediately. They turned their guns onto one member of each family, shot them dead, and that was that.

One of the most notorious centers is where Rajoub has stationed members of Arafat's Force 17 unit. Every Palestinian is well aware of a cellar in Abu Dis on the outskirts of Jerusalem where kidnapped men and women are taken before being "transferred" quite openly to either Ramallah or Jericho.

Israeli security men who raided the village recently found bloodstained wooden clubs. Residents told them that the local people take a roundabout way instead of passing by the building containing Arafat's men.

We were told by a senior intelligence officer: "Resentment and even hatred is building up against Arafat because of the way he treats his own people. There are hundreds of others like your decorator who have applied or wish to apply for Israeli citizenship. They are doing it secretly, fearing revenge.

"The government is fully briefed about what is going on, particularly in the Jerusalem area. It is frustrating for us. Nothing whatsoever is being done. It's not only shameful, it's dangerous so close to major Israeli centers."

Wasn't it the prophet Hosea who warned: "He who sows the wind will reap the whirlwind." The Oslo accords were the wind brought into play so thoughtlessly three years ago. Now the whirlwind of barbaric cruelty, rape, torture and death by club and bullet presses on all sides of the Jewish state.

A Legacy Of Violence

Article by Jon Immanuel on p.2 of *The Jerusalem Post* of Tuesday, February 4th, 1997.

The following list of Palestinian deaths in PA custody is compiled from the December joint report of B'Tselem and the Palestinian Human Rights Monitoring Group:

1. Farid Jarboa of Gaza died in Gaza Prison on July 6, 1994. Palestinian Justice Minister Freih Abu Medein announced that Jarboa died as a result of violence. Four police officers were arrested and later released.

2. Salman Jalaytah, 40, of Jericho, died in Jericho Prison on January 18, 1995. According to his family, he was severely tortured by members of the Preventive Security Service, and there were indications of violence on his body.

3. Youssef Sa'arawi, 21, from Gaza, was shot in the head on May 26, 1995 during interrogation. According to Attorney General Khalid al-Qidra, a weapon misfired and the officer responsible would be tried. To date, no one has been tried.

4. Mohammed Amour, 50, of Khan Yunis, died at A-Shifa Hospital on June 21, 1995 after being held for two months by the Preventive Security Service. According to his family, there were signs of burns on his body. An autopsy was conducted and a commission of inquiry established, but no findings have been released.

5. Tawfik Sawarka, 36, of Gaza, died in the central Gaza Prison on August 27, 1995. It was announced that he died of a heart attack. A commission of inquiry was established and it was announced that two interrogators were suspended.

6. Azzam Mosleh, of Ayn Yabrud near Ramallah, was detained by the Preventive Security Service on September 27, 1995. On September 29, his family received his body. An autopsy was performed. According to his family, there were signs of beatings on his body. The Palestinian authorities announced that three officers were charged; two were sentenced to one year in prison and the third to seven years in prison.

7. Mahmoud Jumayel, 26, of Nablus, died in Hadassah Hospital in Jerusalem on July 31, 1996. Jumayel was arrested on December 18, 1995 and eight days later transferred to Juneid Prison in Nablus. He was beaten with electric cables and clubs, and given electric shocks. PA Chairman Yasser Arafat ordered an investigation, the results of which have not yet been published. Three interrogators were tried and each sentenced to 15 years imprisonment.

8. Nahed Dahlan, 24, of Gaza, died in hospital on August 7, 1996, after being interrogated by Palestinian intelligence for a week. An official announcement stated that an autopsy found he had committed suicide by swallowing pesticide; his family has not received the autopsy report.

9. Khaled Habal, 60, from Hirbata near Ramallah, died in the Ramallah Police station on August 11, 1996, after being arrested the day before following a dispute with neighbors. On August 13, his body was transferred to his family, who said they saw marks of violence on the body. The Ramallah public prosecutor ordered an autopsy — the results of which have yet to be provided to his family- while the police announced that Habal committed suicide.

10. Rashid Fatiani was shot to death in Jericho Prison by a Palestinian Police officer on December 3, 1996, after being arrested on January 15, 1995 by the Preventive Security Service. According to his family, he was severely tortured. According to prison au-

thorities, a dispute broke out between Fatiani and a police officer, in which the officer shot Fatiani 13 times. The officer was suspended and it was announced that he would be tried.

11. Fayez Qumsiyeh, 53, a cab driver from Beit Sahur, died on January 17, 1997, 11 months after being arrested in connection with the murder of 15-year-old Bassem Rishmawi 15 years earlier. Police said he died of a heart attack. The family members said he had a heart condition but seemed healthy when they visited him the morning of his death. They claimed he had a broken left hand and bore other signs of beating.

12. Yosef Baba, 32, property dealer arrested by military intelligence January 3, died on February 1 in Rafidiye Hospital, Nablus. As Baba was clearly tortured, the PA prosecutor-general promised an inquiry.

Palestinian Authority: Some Final Quotes And Thoughts

Yasser Arafat:

1. "The goal of our struggle is the end of Israel, and there can be no compromise." March 1970 *The Washington Post*

2. "Peace for us means the destruction of Israel." February 1980 *El Mundo*, Caracas, Venezuela.

3. "The victory march will continue until the Palestinian flag flies in Jerusalem and in all of Palestine." December 1980 - Speech at the University of Beirut.

4. "We still have before us the task of completing the comprehensive withdrawal from all the occupied territories, at the forefront of which is Holy Jerusalem, the capital city of our independent state." December 1993 — "Voice of Palestine" — Algiers

5. "The Jihad (Muslim holy war) will continue.. - You have to understand our main battle is Jerusalem... It is not their capital. It is our capital." May 1994 — Speech in Johannesburg, South Africa.

6. "I will never give my hand to the annulment of one paragraph of the Palestinian National Charter." August 1994 — Radio Monte Carlo.

7. "Jerusalem is the capital of the Palestinian state, whether they like it or not. If they don't like it, let them drink out of the Sea of Gaza. October 1994— Speech in Gaza.

8. "In order to obtain the goal of returning to Palestine, all of us sometimes have to grit our teeth (a reference to the "peace process). But it is forbidden that this harm the continued struggle against the Zionist enemy... The speedy retreat of Israel from the occupied territories is only the first stage in establishment of a Palestinian state with its capital in Jerusalem. Only a state like that can then continue the struggle to remove the enemy from all Palestinian lands." November 1994 — *The Jerusalem Post*

9. "We are going to continue the Palestinian revolution until the last martyr to create a Palestinian state." January 1995 —Speech in Gaza

10. "I say once more that Israel shall remain the principal enemy of the Palestinian people not only now but also in the future." May 1995 — Speech in Gaza

11. "All of us are willing to be martyrs along the way, until our flag flies over Jerusalem, the capital of Palestine. Let no one think they can scare us with weapons, for we have mightier weapons — the weapon of faith, the weapon of martyrdom, the weapon of Jihad." June 1995 — *Parade Magazine*

12. "We will continue this long jihad, this difficult jihad. .. via deaths, via sacrifices. August 1995 — *The Jerusalem Post*

13. "By Allah I swear... that the Palestinian people are prepared to sacrifice the last boy and the last girl so that the Palestinian flag will be flown over the walls, the churches, and the mosques of Jerusalem." September 1995 — *The Jerusalem Post*

14. "To whomever of the believers gives his life and money for Allah, to kill and be killed, as it is written in the Torah, New Testament and Koran, Allah has promised them Heaven. September 24th, 1996 — Speech in Gaza.

Nabil Sha'ath:

"If the negotiations reach a dead end, we shall go back to the struggle and strife, as we did for forty years. It is not beyond our capabilities. . . As long as Israel goes forward (with the process), there are no problems, which is why we observe the agreements of peace and non-violence. But if and when Israel will say: `That's it, we won't talk about Jerusalem, we won't return refugees, we won't dismantle settlements and we won't retreat from borders,' then all the acts of violence will return. Except that this time we'll have 30,000 armed Palestinian soldiers."

Speech at a March 1996 symposium in Nablus.

Mufti Ikrama Sabri:

Article by Jay Bushinsky from "The Jerusalem Post" of Monday, July 14th, 1997.

A vitriolic sermon by Palestinian Authority-appointed Mufti Ikrama Sabri, in which he branded Israeli settlers "sons of monkeys and pigs" and called for America's destruction, was assailed yesterday by senior government officials as a grave violation of the Oslo accords.

Addressing Moslem worshippers in Jerusalem's Al-Aksa Mosque, Sabri charged that the U.S. "is ruled by Zionist Jews" and that President Bill Clinton "is fulfilling his father's will to identify with Israel."

"Allah will paint the White House black!" said Sabri, who the PA appointed as the supreme Moslem religious authority in Jerusalem to supersede his veteran Jordanian-backed counterpart, Abdel Kader Abdin, who is still in office rivaling Sabri.

"The Moslems say to Britain, France, and all the infidel nations that Jerusalem is Arab. We shall not respect anyone else's wishes regarding her.

"The only relevant party is the Islamic nation, which will not allow infidel nations to interfere."

Government officials cited Article 22 of the Interim Agreement of September 28, 1995 (known as Oslo II) which states that Israel and the PA "shall seek to foster mutual understanding and tolerance and shall accordingly abstain from incitement, including hostile propaganda against each other. -.

Article 22 also obligates them to "take legal measures to prevent such incitement by any organizations, groups, or individuals within their jurisdiction."

This raises a delicate issue inasmuch as Al-Aksa is within the boundaries of Jerusalem, which is under Israeli jurisdiction, but

by Victor Mordecai

also is subject to the direct and exclusive administratı
Moslem religious trust or Wakf.

Sabri's rhetoric escalated as his sermon proceeded, rۦ
his pejorative plateau- "Allah shall take revenge on behalۦ ʋr his
prophet against the colonialist settlers who are sons of monkeys
and pigs."

He went on to ask Allah to forgive the Moslems "for the acts
of these sons of monkeys and pigs who sought to harm your sanctuary."

Victor Mordecai: The above hatred is taught in Chapter V of
the Koran "The Table":

*57: Believers, do not seek the friendship of the infidels and those
who were given the Book before you, who have made of your religion a jest
and a diversion. Have fear of Allah, if you are true believers.*

*58: When you call them to pray, they treat their prayers as a jest
and a diversion. This is because they are devoid of understanding.*

*59: Say: 'People of the Book' (Jews and Christians), is it not that
you hate us only because we believe in Allah and in which has been revealed to us and to others before, and because most of you are evil-doers?'*

*60: Say: 'Shall I tell you who will receive a worse reward from God?
Those whom God has cursed and with whom He has been angry, trans-
forming them into apes and swine, and those who serve the devil. Worse
is the plight of these, and they have strayed farther from the right path.'*

Ibrahim Makadama:

"Nothing can stop Israel except holy warriors carrying explosives on their bodies to destroy the enemies of God. We will not
liberate Jerusalem through negotiations; we will not liberate Jerusalem through demonstrations and rallies. We will liberate Jerusalem through continuous jihad (holy war), and with the help of Allah, blessed be his name, we will continue on the path of jihad.

"Our people must chase them, whether they live in Tel-Aviv
or Latin America. The new intifada (uprising) is a different kind of
intifada, and just as Rabin, in the past, wanted Gaza to drown in
the sea, we must make Netanyahu curse the day his mother gave
birth to him, and we must make Netanyahu hope that Jerusalem
will drown in the sea.

"Do not fear the strength of your enemy. Do not fear his planes or his atom bombs. Do not fear America or the other heretical nations that support it.

"Allah is with us, Allah is the greatest, Allah is with us, Allah is the greatest."

March 21, 1997 — Ibrahim Makadama, chief of the secret military wing of the Hamas terrorist organization speaking the same day as a Hamas suicide bomber murdered three Israeli women and wounded more than forty people in a Tel-Aviv cafe.

Chapter Twelve

Israel's Moral Duty Towards Christian South Lebanon

Article by Colonel Sharbel Barakat, a historian, is a former officer of the Lebanese Army and Middle East Director for the World Lebanese Organization (WLO). Reprinted from *Middle East Intelligence Digest*, July 1995//*The Jewish Political Chronicle* — October 1996).

Fear is growing among Israel's Christian allies in southern Lebanon that they are about to be sacrificed on the altar of an Israeli-Syrian peace deal. If Lebanon's Christians are betrayed, no moderate Arab leader who has placed his life on the line to make an agreement with Israel will ever be able fully to trust Israel again.

On October 13, 1990, the Syrian army and its allies, the Hizballah and Islamic factions, invaded Lebanon. Under the weight of 30,000 troops, heavy artillery and hundreds of tanks, and crushed by the Soviet-made bombers, the Christian resistance was annihilated. Six hundred prisoners and dozens of civilians were executed by the invaders. Since that date, Lebanon has been under Syrian domination, and Lebanon's Christians submitted to a political oppression.

Only in South Lebanon, in the so-called security zone, have 180,000 Lebanese in general, and Christians in particular, felt safe under the protection of the South Lebanon Army (SLA) and their

Israeli allies. In 1976, the Christian population of the border area with Israel was attacked by the PLO and Muslim militia. With no contact with Christian East Beirut, and nowhere to go except south, the Christian resistance opened the gates of its villages to their Hebrew cousins. It was through the famous Good Fence' — the open border between Israel and Lebanon — that free south Lebanon was able to survive.

In 1985, in the wake of Israel's withdrawal from central Lebanon, the SLA drew a line north of the city of Jezzine (pop. 80,000). The massacres endured by the Christians in the Shuf and Iqlim mountains after the IDF pullout was a lesson for their southern brethren. The enclave of free south Lebanon was born out of two commitments:

* A Christian commitment to resist the Syrian-Islamist aggression in Lebanon.

* An Israeli commitment to protect the security of its northern borders, and of its allies in south Lebanon.

The "security zone" became a symbol of cooperation, and a blood alliance between the Jewish and Christian peoples in the Middle East.

Atop a thousand-meter high mountain, the city of Jezzine was perceived as a formidable stronghold for the free Lebanese. It cuts the Shi'ite Beka'a Valley off from the Hizballah bases in the south, preventing what would otherwise be an unbroken Islamist stronghold.

After the fall of Damour in 1976, Zgorta in 1978, the Shuf in 1983, the Zahle in 1985, and East Beirut and Ba'abda since 1990, Jezzine is the last free Christian center in the country; the last not under Arab Muslim control.

If Jezzine falls into the hands of the Syrian-controlled government:

* The Christian resistance will cease, not only in the town, but all over the security zone. No Christian will fight after the fall of Jezzine.

* Syria will be in control of the entire Israel-Lebanon international border, increasing the threat of blitzkrieg against the Jewish state.

* Islamist guerrillas will be able to penetrate the Galilee, and infiltrate the Golan Heights — an area potentially under U.S. sur-

veillance. It is thus possible to foresee massacres of Christians in southern Lebanon, killings of Jews in northern Israel, and assassinations of U.S. personnel on the Golan.

Furthermore, abandoning Jezzine to Syrian-occupied Lebanon will have incalculable consequences on an international level. Apart from the definite and final loss of Lebanon as a pro-Western, free and democratic country, another effect is perceivable.

For eighteen years, Israel's support of free south Lebanon has embodied the alliance between Jewish people and Christians in the Middle East. The image of Lebanese Christian soldiers shedding their blood together with Jewish soldiers to defend both countries was the basis for much international Christian support for Israel. If Israel, for any reason, including its perceived political interest, should hand over the "security zone" — and particularly Jezzine — to a Syrian-Islamist-controlled government in Beirut, millions worldwide could think twice about continuing their support for the Jewish state. America's powerful Christian community should be alerted. America's Congress is the only power on earth able to bring awareness to this issue. If sensitized, the U.S. government can make a difference by drawing the lines north of Jezzine.

Israel has a moral and historical duty, not only to stand by its allies, but to reject any Syrian blackmail to undermine the Christian resistance in Lebanon. To the Lebanese Christians, Jezzine is the final red line. It is fair that no Israeli soldier should remain in that area. But at the same time, no deal should dismantle the city's resistance. In other words, until Lebanon recovers its freedom and sovereignty, the South Lebanon Army should remain the only guarantor of this Christian city. And that commitment should be Israel's contribution to its duty towards its faithful ally.

Chapter Thirteen

Massacre Victims Mourned

Article on p. A17 in *Newsday* of February 14, 1997. Combined News Services

Abu Qurqas, Egypt — Some 5,000 people attended funerals here yesterday for nine Christian religious students shot in their church in an Islamic militant attack that was condemned across Egypt's political spectrum. A tenth victim died later in hospital.

Shocked residents, Christian and Muslim, gathered in this southern village for a memorial service for the students killed Wednesday night when gunmen stormed Saint George's church and attacked a group of Coptic Christians. Four wounded Copts remained hospitalized.

The priest conducting the ceremony in this farming village, where 9,000 Christians and 4,500 Muslims live, called for "national unity" between the two communities.

As the cortege made its way along the 2.5-mile route between the church and cemetery under police security, crowds shouted slogans against armed Islamists who have been waging a five-year campaign of violence against Egypt's secular government.

In the wake of the killings, police stationed armored vehicles around churches in southern Egypt, put Abu Qurqas under curfew and searched Minya province for suspects, arresting about 80.

It was the latest Islamic attack against Orthodox Christians in the Minya region, about 190 miles south of Cairo, and it sparked condemnation by groups ranging from the Marxist Tagammu party to the Muslim Brotherhood, which has carried out attacks in its campaign to set up an Islamic regime but has renounced violence.

Some 110 Copts have been slain since the outbreak of Islamic fundamentalist violence in March, 1992, that has claimed the lives of a total of 1,141 people. Most of the victims have been police or militants.

Minya has over the past two years become the key stronghold of the main armed Islamic group in Egypt, the Jamaa Islamiyya.

A Coptic priest in Minya said security services stopped posting police guards at the Coptic religious places in Minya almost a year ago and had replaced them with mobile patrols.

The police themselves are the main target of the Jamaa Islamiyya and Jihad militants, followed by Copts.

The decade's worst anti-Copt attack was in May, 1992, when 12 Orthodox Christians were killed in the southern town of Sanabu by Jihad militants. Last February, six Copts and two Muslims were killed when Islamic fundamentalists fired automatic weapons at residents in Etmanya.

Copts make up 5.8 percent of Egypt's 63.5 million people. The Minya area, where Wednesday's killing occurred, has 485,000 Copts, the largest concentration outside Cairo.

Three Christians Are Slain In Attack In Egypt

Article from *The New York Times International Edition* of Saturday, February 15, 1997.

Attackers shot and killed three Christians in southern Egypt, the Interior Ministry said today. The attack came despite stepped-up police security after a deadly raid on a Christian church.

The bodies of the three men were found Thursday night in El Zuheir, a village in Minya Province, the ministry said.

The police stationed armored vehicles around churches after gunmen burst into the Mar Girgis church on Wednesday and opened fire on a charity meeting, killing ten people.

Coptic Christians, who make up 10 percent of Egypt's 60 million people but are a large minority in southern Egypt, have been the target of Muslims on the ground that they are heretics.

Murder On The Nile

Article by Richard Engel of Reuter Business News in *The Jerusalem Post* Money Supplement of April 16, 1997, p.3.

Amgad, a Christian from a village in middle Egypt, has been in hiding in Cairo for more than a year, another victim of a protection racket that is tearing apart the social fabric of his birthplace.

What did the trick for Amgad was the third threatening letter from the Gama'a al-Islamiya (Islamic Group), Egypt's largest Islamist militant organization.

"We demand 10,000 pounds ($3,000) from you tomorrow. We will not accept one piaster less and if you bring the money a day late it will be 15,000. If you can't bring it within these days... you know the punishment for that," the letter said.

The Islamists, starved of funds for their campaign of violence against the government, had picked on him as a source of finance on the pretext that Egypt's Christians should all be paying gizya, the ancient Islamic tax on non Moslem subjects.

Gizya, abolished by the government at least 100 years ago, has come back in a virulent form indistinguishable from the extortion money collected by mafias all over the world.

"They (the Islamists) take whatever they need. When they need weapons they take money from the Christians," said Samir, who declined to be named in full for fear for his safety.

Samir, who continues to live in a village close to Amgad's, is the victim of a secondary and possibly more pervasive form of the same phenomenon — extortion by a local Moslem mafia- style boss who may have picked up the practice from the Gama 'a.

"Everyone pays, everyone. But what can we do?.. I am scared I will be killed. Even if I was killed, no one would say anything, even a witness, he said.

Some of them have been killed and Copts, members of the Christian minority that has survived centuries of Moslem domination, say the police are doing nothing about it.

"We only know the people killed. We never know the people who are paying because if they tell they are dead. A doctor was killed recently because he refused to pay. We didn't know he had been paying," said Talaat Hamed, a doctor from Abu Qurqas.

"Many Copts are afraid of informing the police, and I doubt the police officers are interested in stopping them because their inner feeling is `let the Copts pay,'" said Rifaat Said, a Moslem member of parliament from the leftist Tagammu party.

The practice appears to be confined mainly to the central provinces of Minya and Assiut, where the proportion of Copts is especially high and where the Gama'a is most active in fighting the government.

In the bishopric of Qusiya, a Nile Valley town 300 km. (185 miles) south of Cairo, the gizya racket has become routine for many of the 100,000 Coptic residents, says Bishop Thomas.

The bishop, who has kept track of more than 100 villagers forced to pay, suggested that extortion by local bosses was now more pervasive than that by the Islamists.

"He (the boss) sends a message to send an amount of money. They don't need secret letters. He will pass by (a Christian's house or shop) and say `You send me 1,000 pounds ($300).'"

They are mafia bosses and it is well known that only Christians are paying," the bishop said.

Milad Hanna, a prominent Coptic intellectual and campaigner for good relations between Copts and Moslems, said he thought the practice was more dangerous in the long term than the occasional massacres of Christians by suspected militants.

There have been two such massacres this year — one of 10 young Copts in a church near Abu Qurqas and one of 13 people, eight of them Copts, in a rampage through the streets of a village near the southern town of Nag Hammadi.

"The phenomenon of gizya... is the true fundamentalism. The wicked and filthy incidents (of extortion) mean that there is no government in Egypt. It means we are living in a fundamentalist state like Iran or Saudi Arabia," said Hanna.

"I accuse the (ruling) National Democratic Party... because for the last 20 years they have excluded the Copts from political life," he added.

Hanna said the gravity lay in the damage the practice could do to relations between the two communities and the demographic change it would bring about as Copts left the area.

"It is a system that has destroyed development," added Bishop Thomas. The Copts, he said, had to pay gizya on every business transaction, even when they harvested or returned from abroad.

Samir tried to do business instead in the Nile Delta, away from the clutches of his mafia boss. But the boss followed him.

I am very sad because a lot of people are leaving because the situation is not sound," he said.

"This is hell but I don't pay," said a Coptic pharmacist in Qusiya. He said he would love to leave but could not afford it.

U.S.-Egyptian Ties Under Growing Strain

Excerpts from article by Steve Rodan on p.14 of *The Jerusalem Post* of April 18, 1997.

Rose El Youssef is the magazine of Egypt's liberal elite and every Sunday it appears with a diet of juicy conspiracy stories, cutting cartoons and an occasional interview.

Last Sunday, the subject of interview was the supreme guide of the Moslem Brotherhood, Egypt's largest Moslem fundamentalist group. In this interview, the fundamentalist leader, Mashoor, as he is commonly known, called on the government to purge Christians from the military and called for them to be forced to pay a religious tax (gizey) once levied on non-Moslem minorities.

In Washington, U.S. officials monitoring Egypt cringed. The interview, they said, is the latest ammunition for the growing number of critics in Congress who want to see U.S. aid to Cairo cut on the grounds that the government of President Hosni Mubarak is drifting further away from American interests and no longer shares a common regional agenda.

"Over the past few years, public discord and private frustration between Egypt arid the United States have increased," says a new study of the Washington Institute of Near East Policy called "Building for the Security & Peace in the Middle East: An American Agenda.

"At times, these tensions reflect clear policy differences based on the national interests of the two countries; at other times they mirror broader frustration within the two societies.

For more than a year, key members of Congress and their aides have been quietly warning Mubarak and his foreign minister, Amr Moussa, that their hostility toward Israel and Cairo's opposition to many areas of U.S. policy in the Middle East are endangering the $2.1 billion in aid Egypt receives from the U.S..

In January, the heads of the Appropriations subcommittee that deals with foreign aid in the Senate and House, Mitch McConnell and Sonny Callahan, conveyed this message to Mubarak during their visit to Cairo.

Congressional aides who monitor Egypt said that didn't help. They said Mubarak's visit to Washington last month failed to improve U.S.-Egyptian relations. So now, the congressional warning is becoming public as Republicans and Democrats on key congressional committees are warning of a break with Egypt.

The lightning rod of criticism came at a hearing on April 10 of the House International Relations Committee. House committee chairman Benjamin Gilman, a New York Republican, set the tone when he contrasted the Mubarak's government behavior over the last six months with its signing of the peace treaty with Israel in 1979.

The latest example of discord occurred most recently, when under Egyptian leadership, the Arab League recommended that its member states cease normalizing relations with Israel and restore the old economic boycott," Gilman said. "Egypt's leadership role in that vote puzzles and dismays many of its friends in the U.S.."

Gilman said Congress has numerous grievances with Egypt. They include Egypt's advocacy that U.N. sanctions be lifted from Libya, which has refused to extradite its agents suspected of bombing the Pan Am passenger jet over Lockerbie, Scotland, in 1988. Egypt has derailed the multilateral talks on regional security by insisting on discussing Israel's purported nuclear arsenal. Antisemitic attacks in the Egyptian press have become daily fare, with Israel accused of spreading AIDS to Egyptians.

In addition, Gilman referred to a report that Egypt's human-rights record has worsened over the last few years as Islamic attacks increase on Christians and government restrictions on churches are tightened.

Egyptian Court: Academic Must Divorce

Article from *The Jerusalem Post* of August 7, 1996. News agencies.

An Egyptian court this week threw its weight behind Islamists by upholding a ruling that a happily married university professor must divorce his wife because his writings make him unfit to be married to a Moslem woman.

He was found to have renounced Islam. The decision in the case of Nasr Abud Zeid drew immediate criticism from human rights activists and secular lawyers, who fear the decision will embolden Moslem fundamentalists to go after others who do not share their view of Islam.

"It is all the more dangerous because it gives regressive forces the opportunity to challenge others' personal, academic, scientific and religious beliefs in court," said a statement issued by the Egyptian Organization for Human Rights (EOHR). The group said it feared for the life of Abu Zeid and urged President Hosni Mubarak to overturn the "unjust" decision.

The court rejected Abu Zeid's appeal against a ruling ordering his separation from fellow academic Ibtihal Younis.

Moslem fundamentalists won their court case against Abu Zeid last year when a judge supported their claim that his writing had made him an unbeliever.

Mohammed Moneib, secretary general of the EOHR, said the court decision was a damaging blow to Egypt.

"This is a big shock to us. The ruling is a strike in the face of civil society in Egypt and to its development. It is another addition to the backward behavior in Egypt that is working to stop any real development and it strengthens the limitations on freedom of opinion and belief," Moneib said.

"We urge the president to intervene immediately and cancel this unjust ruling," he added.

Court sources said they had expected judge Mohammed Misbah Sharabiya to postpone his decision on the appeal until Abu

Zeid's lawyers had had a chance to include details of new legislation passed by parliament earlier this year that affects their case.

According to the legislation, any cases calling for the separation of a husband and wife must be investigated before they go to court if the plaintiff is not directly involved.

Abu Zeid and Younis moved to the Netherlands earlier this year to take up teaching posts. The court that made the decision is the last stop for appeals in Egypt and court sources say if the couple ever return to Cairo they will have to separate.

Human rights groups have expressed concern for Abu Zeid's life, saying they fear that Moslem militant groups fighting to turn Egypt into a strict Islamic state will take the ruling against Abu Zeid as a license to kill him.

The Egyptian militant Jihad group said last year that Abu Zeid should be killed in line with Islamic laws because he had abandoned his Moslem faith.

"Abu Zeid's life is in real danger now. There is no way he or his wife can return (to Egypt) because they (militants) are waiting to kill them immediately and they have a legal justification — this unjust ruling," EOHR's Moneib said.

Chapter Fourteen

Algeria:
Islamic Fratricide — Islamic
Self-Destruction

In the last few chapters dealing with persecution of Christians in Iran, the Holy Land and Egypt, I also added a small measure of radical, fanatic, fundamentalist Islamic persecution of fellow Moslem citizens.

In this chapter, I will give a small press survey of reports dealing with the civil war in Algeria, a country in which there are no Jews and virtually no Christians. The war there is a war between Moslems and Moslems.

Islamic ideology preaches that when all Jews and Christians, the People of the Book, embrace Islam, when the whole world is Islam, then utopia will be reached in this "Dar es-Salaam" or Islamic House of peace. Well, I think that the following articles will show the opposite — Hell on Earth.

Algerian Rebel Group Names Former Bosnian Fighter As New Leader

Article from AP News Service in *The Jerusalem Post* of Monday, December 9th, 1996.

Algiers, Algeria — A 28-year-old Moslem extremist who fought in Afghanistan and Bosnia has been chosen to lead the Armed Islamic Group (GIA), Algeria's most violent rebel faction, the group said yesterday.

Slimane Maherzi, also known as Abu Djamil, has replaced Antar Zouabri to lead the group's fight to install a fundamentalist Islamic government in Algeria.

It was not immediately clear why Zouabri was replaced, but he may have been killed by Algerian security forces, who have stepped up their operations against the militants in the past 15 days. More than 60,000 people have been killed in the four and a half year insurgency.

Zouabri was considered responsible for the killings of dozens of Algerians who were not strictly observing Islamic law. He in turn had replaced Djamel Zitouni.

More Killed In Algeria

Article from *The Jerusalem Post* of January 26, 1997.

Paris — Suspected Moslem rebels killed up to 59 people in more massacres in hamlets near Algiers, an Algerian Newspaper said yesterday, hours after President Liamine Zeroual spoke of "unequaled terror" in the country.

Algeria's main independent dailies all reported continued killings in the five-year-old conflict. "Le Matin" said more than 250 people had now been killed in the past two weeks.

Without giving details of the slaughter or new steps to stop it, Zeroual told the nation in a televised address on Friday night: "Innocent citizens, of all categories, are victims each day of a blind terrorism never equalled in other times or other places."

"Le Matin," quoting villagers, said: "Fifty-nine have been assassinated during this weekend in the center of the country, mostly in Berroughia and in douars (villages) of Benramdane, Saouala and Baraki (near Algiers.)

Zeroual blamed foreign circles for manipulating "criminals, traitors and mercenaries" — Algerian terms for Moslem fundamentalists.

Shock After Massacre

Article from Agence France-Presse on page A17 in *Newsday* of February 19, 1997.

Kerrach, Algeria — Among their burned-out homes, the survivors of one of Algeria's most brutal massacres gathered yesterday, shocked and weeping, after seeing 31 of their neighbors burned alive and hacked to pieces.

Attacks on remote spots like this have long been a part of the five-year-civil war between Islamic fundamentalists and the military-backed regime here.

But the brutality of the Sunday night massacre has shocked this north African nation.

The dead were 24 women, six men and one young girl — most of the male population had left the region in search of work elsewhere.

The victims were burned, shot and axed. They were turned, one survivor said, into "human torches."

The attack was instantly blamed on armed fundamentalists, who have been accused in earlier attacks in the five-year-war, which has cost the lives of more than 60,000 people.

A survivor, huddled yesterday with the others, described the assault on the hamlet, once a ski village. "They came across the mountains, probably from Medea, at around one in the morning," he said.

"They started at the bottom of the village, and then worked their way up. Some were dressed in camouflage gear, they had beards and Kalashnikovs (Soviet-made assault rifles), axes , swords."

The attackers, between 30 and 50 men, locked the terrified residents in their homes and then set fire to the building.

"A young girl came out of one of the houses, her clothes on fire. She tried to escape," a resident said. "One of the terrorists shot her before she could leave the courtyard."

Since November, several hundred villagers in places like this, just 30 miles south of the capital, Algiers, have been killed in the battle to overthrow the government of President Liamine Zeroual.

The daily "El Watan" said the death toll would have been higher had a villager not escaped and alerted security forces. It said the attackers waged a 10 minute gun battle with security forces and then fled, taking with them the bodies of at least eight rebels. Around 10 guerrillas were wounded, the paper said.

Islamic Group Massacres Thirty-two Civilians

Article from AP in *The Jerusalem Post* of Sunday, March 23, 1997.

Algiers — A group of Islamic militants armed with sabres and axes slit the throats of 32 civilians and then beheaded some of them independent newspapers reported yesterday.

The attackers took only half an hour on Wednesday to wreak havoc in a village near Ksar El Boukhari, 150 km south of Algiers, the French language dailies "El Watan" and "Liberte" reported.

The newspapers said the victims, including 16 women, came from four different families.

There was no immediate claim of responsibility for the attacks, which were not reported by the pro-government media.

The deaths come less than week after up to 18 civilians died in bomb attacks in and around the Algerian capital, according to hospital sources speaking on condition of anonymity. There was no claim of responsibility for the deaths, but the methods resemble those used by Islamic militants.

Islamists Kill Eighty In Algeria

Article of Reuters on p.4 of *The Jerusalem Post* of April 7th, 1997.

Moslem rebels massacred more than 80 villagers in Algeria, slaughtering some with chainsaws and dousing others in burning petrol during the weekend, newspapers said yesterday.

In the worst attack in the five years of Algeria's violence, rebels exterminated 52 inhabitants of Thalit village in Medea province, 70km southwest of Algiers, said "El Watan" newspaper.

About 40 rebels armed with axes, daggers and swords ringed the hamlet and moved in to kill everyone there, the paper added. "Liberte" newspaper said 52 people in the community had their throats slit, with only one person escaping.

In another raid, more than 40 gunmen armed with Kalashnikov assault rifles and shotguns and led by Algeria's ruthless Armed Islamic Group chief Antar Zouabri hacked to death 15 villagers in Amroussa village in Blida province, 50 km south of Algiers.

"The assailants broke into seven houses and cut up 15 people, including seven women and three children, with a chainsaw," survivors from Amroussa said.

It said some people who tried to flee were doused with petrol and set ablaze.

"My neighbor hid under a car, but was spotted. They set fire to the vehicle and he couldn't get out. He died there," the paper quoted a survivor as saying.

Another survivor said: "They killed my nephew in front of his mother, then one of them fired several times at my sister. Before they left, they set fire to the house.

"Liberte" said survivors loaded their belongings into vans and left the village.

In another killing, the newspaper said five civilians had their throats cut and seven were abducted in Sidi Naamane in Tizi-Ouzou province, 90km east of Algiers.

Moslem rebels cut the throats of four family members near the coastal town of Moretti, 40 km west of Algiers, said "El Watan."

Survivors Recount Slaughter Of 93 In Algeria

Article by Reuters in *The Jerusalem Post* of April 24, 1997

Stunned survivors of Algeria's worst massacre in five years of slaughter told in tearful testimony published yesterday on how Moslem rebels mercilessly hacked and shot 93 people to death in a nightlong bloodbath Monday night.

Nearly half of the dead were women and young girls.

Their throats were cut, heads hacked off and others shot in an orgy of savagery 25km from the capital Algiers that ended only as dawn approached.

"When they left, I got up. And there in the yard was only blood, bloodied bodies and heads everywhere. I fainted," said 14-year-old Radia, who had pretended to be dead as her whole family was slaughtered.

Witnesses quoted by Algerian newspapers said between 40 and 50 men took part in the raid on an isolated farming community, Haouch Bouglet-Khemisti, in Bougara district.

"A bomb explosion woke us. Some minutes later they started dragging us to the center of the village where they began cutting people's throats," said 33-year-old Houria.

"One held my head and another my clothes and they sliced my throat quickly. I fainted. One of them came and kicked me to see if I was really dead," she said in her account in the newspaper "Al-Khabar." "My husband was killed, his throat cut."

The government termed the massacre one of unprecedented savagery and said the killers were being hunted down. This is a savage act such as mankind has never before witnessed," Prime Minister Ahmed Ouyahia said on television.

Algerian Terror

Article in *The New York Times International Edition*, by Bob Herbert, September 30, 1997.

In an interview at *The New York Times*, Zazi Sadou spoke through a translator about the nightmare in her homeland - the murderous rampages in the name of God, the violent attacks on teachers and students and artists and intellectuals, and especially the horrendous ways in which women have been targeted, how they are raped and maimed and casually killed, or kidnapped and forced into sexual servitude.

Ms. Sadou is a feminist and veteran journalist in Algeria, a country that for the past several years has been soaked in the blood of innocents sacrificed by religious and political zealots, assorted crazed criminals and maniacal believers in masculine supremacy.

An estimated 60,000 people, many of them women and children, have been killed in armed clashes and outright massacres since the military Government voided elections in 1992 that probably would have been won by militant Islamic fundamentalists.

Prevented from attaining power by the ballot, the fundamentalists have attempted to seize it through terror.

"The violence has been so barbaric, so extensive, so extreme," said Ms. Sadou, "that it is taking the shape of genocide. These are crimes against humanity. And we need to hear, from everywhere, the firm condemnation of those who are responsible."

At least 98 people and perhaps as many as 300 were slaughtered in August when members of the Armed Islamic Group, equipped with shotguns, knives, swords and axes, invaded the village of Rais, which is just south of Algiers. Witnesses said the majority of the panicked victims were women and children. Many of the bodies were burned and some were decapitated. In some cases, the heads of victims were left on doorsteps.

The massacre was not an isolated occurrence. On Sept. 22 more than 400 people were slaughtered, again by members of the Armed Islamic Group, during an attack on the village of Bin Talna, which is also south of Algiers, in an area that has come to be known as the Triangle of Death.

Ms. Sadou noted that it is typical in such attacks for attractive young women and girls to be kidnapped for sexual purposes, and then killed late~. When the attackers left Rais they took nearly three dozen women and girls with them. An unknown number were taken from Bin Talna.

"In these attacks you might have 100 or 150 terrorists and they would divide up the tasks," Ms. Sadou said.

"One group would do the killing, the beheading. Another would choose the most beautiful women to take with them. And a third group would be outside waiting for anybody who tried to flee the village.

The extreme oppression of women and girls - including widespread public humiliation, maiming and killing has been a cornerstone of Islamist terror in Algeria for many years. Even before the aborted election, members of Islamic militias and other militant groups would torment and sometimes kill women who refused to wear the traditional veil. Women perceived to be living in "immoral" circumstances were also subject to savage punishment. And there were several cases of girls whose skirts were considered too short having their legs burned with acid.

"Women are seen as devils," Ms. Sadou said. "We are the permanent enemies."

"A recent A.P. story began: "Eight men who were apparently Muslim a militants descended on a village school in Algeria over the weekend, -shooting or slashing to death life-male teachers and a male instructor who tried to stop the killings as students watched, witnesses said today."

The main political party of the Islamic militants is the Islamic Salvation Front (or F.I.S., its French acronym). It has been weakened in its struggle with the Government over the past five years and many analysts now see it as a moderating force.

But Ms. Sadon warned that the F.I.S. has long been inextricably entwined with the most murderous elements in Algeria (including the Armed Islamic Group), that It has not backed away from Its profoundly destructive beliefs regarding women and girls and that it has never favored a democratic form of government.

The situation in Algeria needs to be seen for what it really is. The atrocities are, indeed, crimes against humanity - In other words, crimes against the whole world. It would behoove the rest of the world to pay closer attention.

Again, my heart goes out to the innocent Moslem people of Algeria. But this is what is to be expected from the Islamic system. There cannot be heaven in hell. So, too, there cannot be utopia or peace in the "Dar es-Salaam" of Islam. The next chapter will deal with Afghanistan, another Islamic utopia where there are no Jews or Christians. They have only their own Islamic system to blame for their suffering.

Chapter Fifteen

Afghanistan: Another Islamic Hell Bordering On The Ridiculous

Afghan Women Face A "War On Their Minds"

Article in the "Middle East " column of *The Jerusalem Post* of Wednesday, November 6, 1996.

Associated Press — Weeks ago when Kabul's new fundamentalist Moslem rulers closed down schools for girls and banned women from holding jobs, poet Khalileh Forooz wrote a poem entitled "Dagger in my Mind."

Like Forooz and her two sisters, life for thousands of women in this war-ruined capital has changed drastically since the ragtag Taleban militia drove government forces from the capital last month and imposed a strict version of Islam.

One day after the Taleban took over the city, Forooz and her family heard two important announcements on the radio that changed their lives: working women were advised not to report to work or university classes, and parents were told to keep schoolgirls home.

Forooz, 28, lost her job as producer of a literary program on state-run radio.

One sister lost her teaching position and the other had to give up her unfinished university degree.

"During the years of war, Afghans lost almost everything. But this is worse, it's a war on our minds," says Forooz. She and her sisters have not left their home since the Taleban stormed into the city.

The Taleban have ordered men to grow beards and wear turbans, like Islam's seventh-century prophet, Mohammed. And they want women to be neither seen nor heard.

Gun-toting Taleban guards, who roam the city, have whipped women for stepping out of their homes unaccompanied by their husbands or close male relatives.

Violators of the hejab, the Islamic dress code that requires women to be covered from head to toe in public, also have received public beatings.

Nevertheless, the Taleban — former seminary students turned fighters — insist they are not against women. They say they are enforcing Islamic teachings that women must be modest.

"You can see our respect for women by the fact that we have pledged to pay working women, even though they don't have to work anymore," says Taleban Information Minister Amir Khan Muttaqi.

As it is, most of the doctors, teachers and other professionals in Kabul are women, in part because nearly 20 years of war has left a good portion of the male population uneducated, except in the art of war.

As a result many boys' schools in Kabul also have remained closed because there are not enough male teachers to keep them open.

Hospitals have been particularly hard hit. When they lost their female nurses they lost the majority of their staff, yet the wounded only increased as fighting continued north of Kabul.

The few women who have been allowed to return to work in the hospitals have been forced to wear the full covering and treat only women. In the female wards, even the sickest woman wears the traditional Islamic head scarf.

Some, like the British charity Oxfam, have suspended their programs because of the restrictions on women.

Women Afghan employees of the International Committee of the Red Cross stayed away from the relief agency's Kabul compound this week after Taleban fighters threatened to hang them.

Several international aid groups have pulled out of Kabul saying it is impossible to work without their female staff. The United Nations and the Inter national Committee of the Red Cross have called on the Taleban to change their policies on women.

But Muttaqi said that's not possible. "Islam is not changeable," he said. The new rules are an outrage to educated women, and even their uneducated sisters are sneaking past Taleban guards to their jobs as domestic workers, too desperate to give up the $10 a month they earn cleaning homes.

At the city orphanage where most of the staff had been women, the older children now care for the younger ones.

War widows suddenly found themselves out of desperately needed work. The U.N. estimates 30,000 war widows have lost their jobs.

The Taleban say the widows should stay home and rely on the charity of others. But the charity isn't there and some of the widows are getting increasingly desperate and angry.

Afghans To Prosecute French Aid Workers

Article from AP in *The New York Times International Edition* of Thursday, February 27, 1997.

Kabul, Afghanistan — Two French aid workers arrested for fraternizing with Afghan women will be tried, the Afghan Attorney General said here today.

Frederic Michel and Daniel Lorente were arrested Friday after a luncheon given by the French aid group Action Against Hunger. Sixty Afghan women had also attended.

"They did not have the right to sit and eat with Muslim Afghan women," said Jalilullah Maulvi Zada, the Attorney General. "We will send them to court."

Troops were searching for the women, but several people in Kabul, the capital, said today that many of them had fled to Pakistan.

It is not clear what the punishment would be if the Frenchmen were found guilty, but leaders of Taliban, the militant Islamic movement that rules most of the country, have said that whippings would be a suitable punishment for lesser crimes.

Mr. Zada said the aid workers took photographs of the Afghan women and music was played at the luncheon, both crimes under the Taliban's interpretation of the Islamic law.

Afghan Religious Police On Beating Spree

Article of AP in *The Jerusalem Post* on April 30, 1997.

Kabul — The Taleban's religious police publicly beat 10 people in the Afghan capital yesterday for defying strict Islamic edicts.

The Taleban beat five men who had trimmed their beards, a crime in Taleban-run areas. Three women were beaten with electrical wires after they ventured outside wrapped in huge shawls rather than the all-enveloping burqa the Taleban require women to wear. Two taxi drivers also received public beatings after they picked up female passengers unaccompanied by men. According to the Taleban a woman must be accompanied by a male relative.

Chapter Sixteen

Global Conflicts With Ishmael — Islam

11. And the angel of the Lord said unto her (Hagar): "Behold, thou art with child, and shalt bear a son; and thou shalt call his name Ishmael, because the Lord hath heard thy affliction. 12. And he shall be a wild ass of a man: his hand shall be against every man, and every man's hand against him; and he shall dwell in the face of all his brethren.
Genesis 16:11-12.

In the last few chapters, I have pointed to the persecution of Christians by Moslems. But as I have emphasized throughout the book, the first and foremost to suffer from radical Islam are the Moslems themselves. This, too, has been shown in the book.

The purpose of this chapter is to widen the horizon to include the Buddhists, Hindus and other non-monotheists who represent half of humanity on this planet. The following is but a taste of things to come, for the hand of Ishmael will be against every man, and every man's hand against Ishmael, and he shall dwell in the face of his brethren as it has been foretold in the Bible. To dwell in the face of his brethren means perpetual war with everyone, hence Islam the global threat.

CHINA

500 Held During Lethal Chinese Moslem Riots

AP Report by John Leicester on p.4 of "The Jerusalem Post" of February 11, 1997.

Chinese police fired warning shots over crowds of young Moslems who beat people to death and torched cars during pro-independence riots in far west China, a police official said yesterday.

The riots last week were the worst to hit Yining, in the restive Chinese province of Xinjiang, since the 1949 Communist takeover, said the officer with the Yining city police.

He said four or five people, including Chinese and members of local ethnic groups, were killed and that others, including police officers, were injured.

Some of those killed were beaten to death, said the officer, reached by telephone from Beijing. He refused to give his name.

"Ming Pao," a Hong Kong daily, said more than 10 Chinese were killed and their bodies set on fire.

The police officer said security forces arrested 400-500 people, some of whom were later released. Three cars were set on fire and police fired shots into the air to calm the crowds. "It's been put down," he said.

He said the rioters were Uighurs, Xinjiang's Moslem majority, demanding independence for the region. Clashes are periodically reported in Xinjiang, where the Turkic-speaking Uighurs face an influx of ethnic Chinese.

"There was a protest... It was illegal," said an official with Xinjiang 5 provincial government, who gave his surname, Liu. "Illegal protests are curbed." Liu, reached in Urumqi, Xinjiang's provincial capital, also said calm had been restored in Yining, near the Kazakstan border, 500 km from Urumqi.

Liu said that because of the Chinese New Year holiday he had no more details.

"Ming Pao" quoted an unidentified Chinese man in Yining as saying 1,000 Moslems, mostly aged 17 and 18, beat up, killed and burned their victims before police quashed the violence.

Ismail Cengiz, the secretary general of a pro-independence Uighur group based in Istanbul, Turkey, claimed that 200 Moslem rioters and about 100 Chinese soldiers were killed. The report could not be confirmed.

Modan Mukhlisi, a spokesman for the United National Revolution Front, a Uighur separatist group based in Kazakstan, said that 30 Uighurs died in the riots. He said he did not know further details.

Cengiz, a Uighur, said the riots started when Chinese security forces arrested a group of women reading prayers in a house in Yining on Feb. 4, a Moslem holy night. Rioters then marched on the police station, said Cengiz, of the East Turkestan Immigrants Association.

The Uighurs had their own Republic of East Turkestan from 1944 to 1949. Xinjiang is now one of five autonomous regions of China.

Covering one-sixth of China, Xinjiang has a population of 16.6 million, of whom 38 percent are ethnic Chinese, according to Chinese figures.

China Executes Moslem Rioters

Reuter Report on p.3 of "The Jerusalem Post" of April 27, 1997

Beijing — China executed three people and jailed 27 others for their roles in bloody riots that shook the Moslem region of Xinjiang in February, local officials said yesterday.

The Yili District Intermediate Court had sentenced the men in a public rally Thursday for participating in riots in the far-northwestern town of Yining that killed nine people and injured 198. They were executed the same day.

All of the convicted men were members of the ethnic Uighur minority.

Xinjiang, a vast region that is home to many Turkic-speaking peoples such as the Uighurs, has a long history of ethnic unrest and has recently been rocked by Moslem separatist violence.

The men had been sentenced for the crimes of malicious wounding, arson and hooliganism in the anti-Chinese riots that erupted in Yining on February 5-6.

One man was sentenced to life in prison and 26 were given jail terms ranging from seven to 18 years.

Communist Party officials said that a "handful of serious criminal offenders" had "burnt vehicles and houses and killed public security policemen and innocent people."

"What they did... seriously disturbed and disrupted our political stability and unity," an official said.

Officials said last month they had ended hearings for six men on trial for their part in February's anti-Chinese rioting, which began as a demonstration and turned violent.

Uighur militants say they want to set up their own state of East Turkestan in Xinjiang.

Chinese authorities earlier this month rounded up more than 10 people for allegedly organizing a string of deadly bomb attacks in Xinjiang's capital of Urumqi.

Bombs planted on three buses blew up within minutes of each other in Urumqi on February 25 in an apparently coordinated attack that coincided with the funeral rites in Beijing for paramount leader Den Xiaoping.

The attacks killed nine and wounded 74.

Chinese Police Kill 2 Moslems In Riot Shooting

AP Report on p.5 of *The Jerusalem Post* of April 29, 1997.

Chinese police in a region shaken by separatists killed two people and wounded five when they fired on a crowd of Moslems who surrounded buses taking convicted rioters to jail, an official said yesterday.

The shooting in Yining city, in the northwestern region of Xinjiang, followed a public rally at which three people were sentenced to death and 27 others to prison for involvement in anti-Chinese riots in February.

A crowd of Uighurs, Xinjiang's Moslem majority, surrounded and blocked buses carrying the convicted rioters and ignored police warnings to disperse, said an official at the Communist Party's headquarters for Xinjiang, who gave only his surname, Zang.

"After the sentencing rally, they surrounded the buses," Zang said in a telephone interview from Urumqi, Xinjiang's capital. "We warned them. ... Eventually we opened fire." He said two people were killed and five wounded.

The crowd may have been "emotional because their relations and children had been arrested," Zang said.

The three people sentenced to death at the rally in a sports stadium were executed the same day. The prison terms of the other twenty ranged from seven years to life.

The newspaper "Hong Kong Standard" said the crowd that surrounded the buses numbered 500. But Zang said only several dozen "criminal elements" took part.

He said authorities were investigating whether the trouble was related to Moslem separatists in Xinjiang. Xinjiang's Uighurs and other Moslem ethnic groups have grown increasingly resentful of Chinese rule and settlers in recent years.

The riots in Yining February fifth and sixth, when crowds of young Moslems beat people to death, were among the worst in Xinjiang since the 1949 Communist takeover.

At least ten people were killed and 140 injured, by official count.

Uighurs living in exile in Kazakstan claim to be funneling money and weapons to separatists in Xinjiang. The Uighurs ran their own republic in Xinjiang for five years before 1949.

Kazak police arrested 33 Uighurs yesterday for staging an illegal demonstration outside the Chinese Embassy in Almaty. The demonstrators were protesting the executions in Yining last week.

INDIA

A Dramatic Plea For Understanding From The Hindu Community To The Jewish Community

From a leaflet issued by the Hindu community in America.

The Hindu community has learned much about Jewish history. We have studied the Holocaust, the Inquisition, the persecutions, the expulsions, and the dramatic rebirth of Israel despite seemingly overwhelming odds. Now we ask the Jewish community to learn a little about us and the suffering we have faced at the hands of the Muslims.

The Pagans of Arabia are not there any more to reclaim their Ka'aba. Islam has destroyed them. After that, it has destroyed many more cultures, starting with their places of worship. The Manichaeans, Nestorians and Buddhists of Iran and Central Asia are not there anymore to reclaim their temples and monasteries (and the few Zoroastrians that have survived are too oppressed, too few and too afraid to raise their voice.)

But we have survived, though not unscathed, and we do demand the restoration of our most sacred places. We demand that the Muslim community of India recognize the rights of Hindu society to these three HOLY shrines:

Kashi Vishvanath in Varanasi, Krishna Janmabhoomi in Mathura, and Ram Janmabhoomi in Ayodhya.

Against this perfectly reasonable demand, yet another smear campaign has been unleashed, saying that we preach "revenge". Revenge would mean that we go and destroy the Muslim sacred places in Mecca, Medina, and Jerusalem. We have no intention of doing that. It would also mean wars of conquest, persecution, killing of millions, abducting millions of women and children into slavery, in short, a mirror-image of what the Muslim conquerors and rulers have done to Hindu society. We have no inclination at all to inflict revenge on the Muslim community.

We do not even demand "compensation" or "restitution" and no one has the power to bring the millions of victims of Jihad back to life. The Germans also had no power to bring the victims of Auschwitz back to life. But at least, they have expressed their regrets.

We do not demand the return of the thousands of places of worship that have been forcibly replaced with mosques. All we demand is the return of Three most Holy SACRED PLACES. We merely want these three places back, three age-old sacred places. And we would prefer getting them back from the Muslim community, to getting them back by official decree.

For the Muslim community, this is an excellent opportunity to make up voluntarily for the huge massacres, persecutions, slave-takings, abductions, temple-destructions and swordpoint conversions which its earlier generations inflicted upon Hindu society, as on other non-Muslim communities both in India and elsewhere. Muslims should understand what kind of message they are sending by insisting on continuing the occupation of our sacred places, an occupation which was started by fanatics and mass murderers like Babar and Aurangzeb.

We hope the Jewish community, which wept when its Holy Wall of King Solomon's Temple was in Muslim hands, will support our just demand for the return of our HOLY places of Kashi Vishvanath, Krishna Janmabhoomi and Ram Janmabhoomi.

First Kashmir Local Elections Begin
After 9 Years Of Strife

AP Report in *The Jerusalem Post* of September 8, 1998

Srinagar, India — Squeezed by threats from Moslem rebels and from Indian soldiers, more than half the electorate defied a rebel-called boycott and voted yesterday in the first local election in nine years in strife-wracked Kashmir, election officials said. Three boys were killed in election violence.

Thousands of Kashmiris trekked along mountain trails and highways to vote for the first local election in nine years, but in some places people alleged that Indian soldiers had forced them to vote.

Nearly 300,000 soldiers and policemen fanned out in 26 of the 87 assembly constituency to prevent rebel attacks, and the government said it had arrested 29 people, including three top secessionist leaders who were campaigning for a poll boycott. Voting for the remaining seats will be staggered and completed this month.

Rebels struck at two places, killing three young boys. A 14-year-old was killed in cross-fire when rebels fought a gun battle with soldiers in Lolab, 125 kilometers north of Srinagar. At Tujar Shrief, a village about 55 kilometers northwest of Srinagar, a rocket-propelled-grenade was fired by rebels, killing two boys playing in a schoolyard, officials said.

"Pakistani troops fired across the border in Kargill, forcing authorities to shift two voting stations," Jammu-Kashmir's Chief Election Commissioner Jalil Ahmed Khan told reporters.

India and Pakistan have fought two wars over Kashmir since 1948. But Pakistan's reply to Indian official's charge was not immediately available.

INDONESIA

"In a matter of hours, ten Indonesian churches were destroyed as angry mobs yelled, "Indonesia is Islam, Indonesia is Islam..."

From Voice Of The Martyrs September, 1996 Magazine.

The following materials were received in the VOM office from various sources.

Around 280 churches have been burned, demolished, stoned, attacked and closed since 1991 in Indonesia.

The June 9, 1996 attack in Surabaya, the second largest city in the country was the worst yet as 10 churches were attacked simultaneously by Muslim mobs. The mass media was not able to cover the incident because the government discourages such reporting due to a "political stability" policy. Such a policy also contributes to continuing persecution of churches in Indonesia.

The intense persecution of Indonesian churches marks the rise of fundamentalist Muslims, who are now more equipped as they are educated in Western universities and possess both intellectual capability and rhetorical skills.

Ten Protestant churches were attacked and destroyed in the city of Surabaya in Eastern Java as Christians gathered for Sunday worship services.

According to a report received from a VOM representative in the area more than 5,000 Muslims took part in the riots.

Indonesia has the world's largest Muslim population, with more than 80 percent of its 204 million people claiming to follow Islam. The riots were reportedly led by the Madurese, a large Muslim group.

Chronology of Events on June 9, 1996:

08:00 — Hundreds of shouting people destroyed the Bulak Banteng church building. They used the clurit (a knife with a crescent moon shape) clubs, stones and hammers. As a result of this brutal action two houses and one church apartment were ruined. Several people suffered from this action. A church leader was beaten, kicked, and clubbed while attackers yelled, "Indonesia is Islam. You know that!" This occurred during the Sunday school service.

09:30 — Hundreds of people destroyed the Kristen Kemah Injil Kalvari Church in Bulak Banteng. Evangelist Wesson Solaiman was hit on the back of his head three times. He needed stitches for a 5 cm (about 2 inches) long wound. Several women were indecently handled during the attack.

10:10 — Approximately 1,000 people destroyed the Jatisrono church building. This incident lasted about 30 minutes.

10:30 — The mob destroyed the Pantekosta Tabernakel Church in Wonosari.

10:50 — Bukit Sion church was attacked by about 500 people who marched in with teenagers as their shield, followed by young men and adults. They were followed by bikers and two trucks that were presumed to be used for loading the loot.

11:20 — Firman Hayat church in Jalan Tenggumung was attacked by about 1,500 Madurese after the Sunday service.

11:30 — Station GKJW in Jalan Sidotopo reported that around 500 people came on foot, destroyed the church building with clubs, and beat eight congregation members who had remained in the church. The victims were taken to the hospital.

11:45 — The HKBP church building in Jalan Sidotopo was destroyed by a crowd of about 1,200 people. One of the congregation members was hit on the head.

The Batak Protestant Christian Church, Pogot, wrote:

"Having received the news at 10:45 about the vandalism at Church Cahaya Kasih, one of our congregation members asked for help from the police via a hand phone. Before the police arrived, however, the mob arrived at the Church at 11:45 and suddenly vandalized the church.

*There were around 1,200 vandals. The first group consisted of 300 people in which the majority were children. Ten minutes later the second group, consisting of 400 teenagers arrived. The rest were adults.

"They first threw things at the windows and the church's roof from outside until they were damaged. The second group that arrived forced the gate open and all the vandals came in with wooden clubs and crowbars in their hands. They broke all the window glass and destroyed the doors. They destroyed everything in the church including the congregation's Bibles and song books.

"One of our congregation members tried to stop them by saying, `It is enough, enough, everything has been destroyed.' Because of this he was beaten on his head and attacked by an overwhelming number of vandals."

Anti-Christian Rampage In Indonesia

AP Report in "The Jerusalem Post" of Friday, January 31, 1997

Jakarta — Thousands of Moslems ransacked churches, banks, shops, and cars yesterday after a Chinese Christian trader reportedly insulted Islam by complaining about the loud evening prayers, police and witnesses said.

Police reported no casualties and said the violence was brought under control after three truckloads of troops armed with automatic weapons moved into the town of Rengasdengklok, 50 km east of Jakarta.

Police Sgt. Jumhalim said the unidentified Chinese trader sought police protection after the mob set fire to his home and shop. No one has been arrested, said Jumhalim, who like many Indonesians uses only one name.

Witnesses said thousands of angry Moslems armed with stones and sticks came out of mosques and homes after morning prayers and went on a rampage.

Four churches, dozens of shops, two banks and a Chinese temple were ransacked. The mob also stoned and wrecked 18 cars, setting fire to some of them.

Smoke billowed from one church that was set ablaze, said Joko, a nearby resident. The troops set up road blocks on main streets, warning citizens to stay away from the stricken area, he said.

Joko said the riot was apparently set off by a rumor that a Chinese shopkeeper, a Christian, had complained about the loud prayers at a mosque in the evenings. It was not clear if the trader actually made the remarks.

The ethnic-religious riot is the latest in a series of clashes in the past few months between the two communities.

Ethnic Chinese, mostly Christian traders, are far wealthier than the vast majority of Moslems in Indonesia. About 90 per cent of Indonesia's 200 million people are Islam.

A curfew has been imposed in the area to prevent further outbreaks of violence, Indonesian television reported.

About 40 masked men ransacked a Roman Catholic group's office in a remote Indonesian province on Borneo Island and set ablaze a truck and two motorcycles.

Earlier this month, 5,000 indigenous people called Dayaks, who are mostly Christians, rampaged in the same province, attacking property belonging to Moslem settlers from other parts of Indonesia.

In December, four people were killed and more than 100 buildings burned in Moslem-Christian riots in the West Java town of Tasikmalaya. Five people were killed in October when thousands of Moslems in the East Java town of Situbondo attacked dozens of churches.

Victor Mordecai: Most people do not know or remember that in the 1960's during a period known as the "Time of the Troubles" in Indonesia, the rivers flowed red with the blood of ethnic Chinese people who were branded as communists by the Sukarno regime. Approximately 500,000 ethnic Chinese were killed by their Moslem neighbors. The truth simply is that they were either Christian or Buddhist — most important of all, they were not Moslems and so, they were slated for destruction.

It must be remembered that ethnic Chinese outside of the People's Republic of China are not communists. They are usually Christian or Buddhist business people, financially better off than the rest of the population which is Moslem, and therefore a target for envy and jealousy.

The outrageous part of all of this is that because Indonesia is an oil-producing country, the world will never condemn Indonesia for killing anyone, let alone Chinese, let alone Christians.

The same applies to the Island of East Timor. Colonized by Portugal in the 1500's, the inhabitants of the island speak Portuguese and are Catholic by faith. In 1976, after five centuries of colonial rule, the 1,000,000 inhabitants were granted independence by Portugal and the U.N. Immediately, the Indonesian army invaded East Timor claiming that because it was part of the archipelago of Indonesian islands, East Timor was now conquered for Indonesia and Islam. Over 200,000 Christians were slaughtered defending their homes from the invading Moslem army — a genocide. And the world says nothing.

It could be that because East Timor sits upon some hefty oil reserves underground and under the sea, the world is looking the other way and letting Indonesia usurp and trample upon the rights of the indigenous Christian population.

THE FORMER SOVIET UNION

Tajik Warlord Frees All Hostages

AP report in *The Jerusalem Post* of February 18, 1997

Dushanbe — A Tajik warlord yesterday released all six remaining hostages, five of them U.N. workers, after talks with the nation's president, a U.N. spokesman said.

The citizens of Nigeria, Russia, Switzerland, Tajikistan and Ukraine were freed at 6:15 PM. Moscow time, spokesman Milos Strugar told the ITAR-Tass news agency.

The hostages were released after Tajik President Emomali Rakhmonov ventured into the mountains east of the capital yesterday to negotiate personally with the warlord and convince him to end the two-week-old standoff without bloodshed.

Bakhram Sadirov, who had demanded direct talks with the president, sent two representatives and one of the hostages to meet Rakhmonov in a village near his base about 80 km east of the capital, Dushanbe.

It was unclear whether Sadirov joined the talks. Rakhmonov was taking the former hostages with him back to Dushanbe, ITAR-Tass said.

The warlord's spokesman telephoned Russian news agencies earlier yesterday and promised the hostages would be freed regardless of the outcome of the talks.

A spokesman for the Tajik security ministry in Aushanbe said most of Sadirov's fighters moved deeper into the mountains yesterday in case they should come under attack during or after the hostage releases. He spoke on condition of anonymity.

Sadirov had held as many as 16 hostages since the crisis began Feb. 4, but then released 10. He continued to hold six: two U.N. military observers, three U.N. refugee workers, and Tajikistan's security minister.

The standoff had moved haltingly toward resolution for several days.

Sadirov had demanded the government pick up and deliver 40 of his fighters from bases in Afghanistan. On Saturday, 33 were handed over.

But one of Sadirov's commanders, Said-Murad Kiyamudnov, told the Interfax news agency that the warlord felt betrayed because the government did not return all 40 and seized the ammunition of those it did deliver.

On Sunday, the government tightened its cordon around Sadirov's base and threatened to use force. With the mediation of Russian officials, Sadirov agreed to release five of his remaining 11 hostages — three U.N. workers and two Russian journalists — in return for talks with the president.

Russia has 25,000 troops in Tajikistan, a former Soviet republic, to prop up the hardline government against the mostly Muslim opposition. The troops also guard the country's border with Afghanistan, which Russia sees as a source of drugs, guns and Islamic fundamentalism.

This was Sadirov's second hostage-taking. In December, he seized 23 people, including nine U.N. workers. All were released unharmed.

Islam Sets The Law And Order Vote

Article by Alessandra Stanley in *The New York Times/The Jerusalem Post* edition of Sunday, January 26, 1997.

In the hotly contested Chechen presidential campaign, the backdrop of every campaign poster is Islamic green. All the candidates fervently invoke Allah and Islam in their speeches. But what are they really appealing to? One candidate, Deputy Prime Minister Movladi Udugov, gives the clearest hint: His slogan is "Islamic Order" and it can be found plastered on almost every bullet-scarred wall and bombed-out building in Grozny.

Chechens, who are Muslim by faith and practical by nature, do not share the strict fundamentalism of Iran or Afghanistan. Under Communism, Islam was officially banned, although practiced quietly, as a form of defiance against Soviet colonialism.

But for many voters, who complain of rampant crime and disorder, the notion of Islam as a path to order has had extraordinary appeal in the campaign for tomorrow's election. Secessionist Chechnya has, after all, undergone years of brutal war followed by months of criminal rampages.

"Under Islamic laws, young people will be afraid," Malika Sugaipova, 36, said. "Whether they really pray, or just are more fearful, it will be better." She lives in a neighborhood where most apartment buildings are bullet scarred or bombed out, without running water. She and her neighbors live in fear of marauding criminals and robbers who stalk the area at night.

What appeals most is the draconian reputation of Islamic law — a body of teaching and legal practice generally known as Sharia. In its application, the details of Sharia vary widely from one Islamic land to another. No matter. Here the invocation of it as a slogan seems to be enough.

In September, the acting government led by President Zelimkhan Yandarbiyev, one of several leading candidates, published a criminal code that it said was largely based on Sharia, which directly contradicts Russia's constitution. Among other things, the Chechen code bans alcohol and adultery. People found guilty of adultery are to be punished with 100 lashes. Adultery with a virgin is grounds for death by stoning.

In the first weeks, Chechen officials eagerly carried out show canings, holding public whippings of drunks and other offenders. Sharia is supposed to apply only to Muslims, but Carlotta Gall of "The Moscow Times" saw Chechen fighters soundly beating Russian civilians who had been caught drinking last fall. Such displays mostly petered out after negative reviews in the West.

Still, ever since Chechen rebel fighters finally defeated Russian troops last August, Islam has been at the center of an emerging new Chechen identity. It is not all a matter of Sharia and order. Mr. Udugov, for example, boasts in his official election pamphlet that he has two wives and that his favorite hobby is "Islamic politics."

When the late Dzhokhar Dudayev first seized power in Chechnya and declared independence in 1991, he shrewdly used Islam to bolster national pride. When asked whether he was a practicing Muslim, Mr. Dudayev is said to have replied, "Of course, I pray three times a day." (The Koran calls for believers to pray five times daily.)

But then the business of Islamizing this corner of the Caucasus, some 250 miles from Iran, took a more serious turn. Twenty-one months of brutal war with Russia, which cost tens of thousands of lives, radicalized the society; Chechens rediscovered a stricter Islam both as a solace in suffering and a rallying cry in war.

People who had never in their lives observed the holy month of Ramadan are now fasting. "This is the first time I ever fasted," Tabarek Dejetayeva, 40, explained with a sheepish smile. Her building was repeatedly shelled during the fighting. "The war made me aware of my mortality," she said.

Chechens say a completely Islamic state could not work for them because they have their own strong traditions and national identity. They cite as a prime example "Adat," a word for customary law that refers to the exacting rules of vendetta that have kept rival clans in line for centuries.

The few Westerners still in Chechnya after the murder of six Red Cross workers last month say they rely on the Chechen principle that any harm done to a guest under Chechen's protection has to be punished in kind. "We have armored cars," said Tim Guldimann, who runs the Grozny office of the Organization for

Security and Cooperation in Europe, which is monitoring the elections. "But the Chechen tradition of blood feuds is, to me, more reliable.

All the candidates favor independence. All say Chechnya must become an Islamic state. But the campaign has shed some light on just how radical the Chechen version of Islamic rule is likely to be. The two leading candidates, Shamil Basayev and Aslan Maskhadov, have made it clear that they see Islam as a key part of the Chechen identity, but not as its raison d 'etre.

In the village of Stariye Atagi last week, Mr. Basayev, the rebel commander who led the murderous hostage raid on Budyonnovsk in 1995, stood on the steps of a mosque and told the crowd: "Chechnya is not yet ready for Sharia. We must first educate our children and prepare our society for it."

His chief opponent, Mr. Maskhadov, who was also a war hero, said last week: "I will create a Chechen-Islamic state." His emphasis was on "Chechen."

For the dwindling number of ethnic Russians who remain in Chechnya, however, any heated talk of Islam is frightening. Since the war stopped, attacks on Russians have increased. "What does Islamic Order mean?" Galina Pilipenko, 45, a Russian neighbor of Mrs. Sugaipova, said bitterly, "All that means is that we have to get out of here."

Moslem-Secular Clash In South Russia Leaves At Least One Dead

AP report on p.5 of *The Jerusalem Post* of May 14, 1997

Moscow — At least one man was killed when Moslem villagers in southern Russia clashed with members of a fundamentalist Islamic sect, accusing them of intolerance, a news agency reported yesterday.

More than 600 people were demanding that residents from the puritanical Wahhabi sect leave the village of Chabanmahi in the southern Dagestan region, accusing them of making trouble because of intolerance, the Interfax news agency said.

The Wahhabis locked themselves in a mosque Monday and when a crowd gathered outside there were shots from both sides.

One man was killed, but the report gave no further details.

Russian television also reported from Dagestan that two people were killed and two were wounded in the shooting.

A standoff continued overnight, with the Wahhabis staying inside the mosque and both sides calling for reinforcements from other towns in the area. Interfax said 18 Wahhabis were taken hostage by other villagers yesterday.

Police surrounded the village to prevent the conflict from growing.

Akhmed Tagayev, Dagestan's deputy mufti, said Moslem fundamentalist and breakaway Christian sects should be banned, the ITAR-Tass news agency reported.

"The authorities of Dagestan and Russia have ignored warnings about the threat of proliferation of Islamic fundamentalism," Tagayev said. "We need a law banning the spread of Islamic fundamentalism and of various Christian Orthodox breakaway sects."

Dagestan, a predominantly Moslem republic near the Caspian Sea, is home to people from at least 30 ethnic groups.

Victor Mordecai: While in Moscow in June 1994, 1 was invited to give two interviews on Radio Moscow's "Radio Alef" program, specially aimed at the Jewish public in Russia. My host and interviewer Oleg Gribkov, was shocked to hear me say: "The enemy of Russia is no longer the West. Christian Russia is now the West. The enemy of Russia is and has always been the East of fanatic Islam. He answered me as any good hardline Communist would: "We believe in the fraternity of all the nations." I said to him: "The Church came to Russia in 995AD partly as an answer to the Islamic invasions from the East. Nothing has changed in a thousand years. The rise of fanatic fundamentalist Islam is the threat to Russia. He answered me: "Would you also speak in our churches?"

Chapter Seventeen

The Islamic Genocide In Africa

I believe one of the glaringly unbelievable facts of life when it comes to the media and the one world government is the total ignoring of holocausts throughout the world when the side that is perpetrating the holocaust is Islamic.

I have reviewed many aspects of "Ishmael-Islam's hand is against all his brethren, and all his brethren's hands are against his hand."

Of course, for me, my greatest motivation is to defend my home, my family, my country Israel, and my people, the Jewish people. Through my travels, I have learned that the Christians are my people as well, and indeed the Moslems put their finger on it in the Koran. The Jews and the Christians are one people, the People of the Book. We Jews are the root. The Christians are grafted in as the branch. But we are one in the eyes of the God of Abraham, Isaac and Jacob.

However, I must widen the scope of my attention. Without going into ideological or theological differences with other religious groups such as Hindus or Buddhists, I do believe that we are all children of God and that God mourns for all his children who are tortured, killed or enslaved. At the same time, the virtual future of mankind, of civilization, of this planet is hanging in the balance because of the weapons of mass destruction being hoarded for future use by those who believe in Allah the war god. These weapons could be used indiscriminately against Jew, Christian,

Hindu, Buddhist, or against anyone, for that matter, including Moslems with whom fanatic Islam has a grudge.

At the same time, having been raised in the post-WWII, post Holocaust period, I am particularly sensitive to genocides whether they be against the Armenians by the Turks, the Jews, the Chinese in Indonesia, the people of East Timor, or anywhere else for that matter.

But the most glaring modern holocaust, I believe, is that of the blacks of Sudan. There are differing estimates as to exactly how many people have died. But we know poison gas has been provided by Iran and Iraq to the Islamic government of Sudan in its civil war with the Christians and animists of the south, an area sitting atop the greatest as of yet untapped petroleum reserves in the world.

For the sake of mammon and petroleum, millions of blacks have been slaughtered, enslaved and exiled by the Sudanese Moslems of the north, and the world virtually maintains a radio, TV and news blackout. The Islamic "Final Solution" to the black problem in southern Sudan is the eradication of all non- Moslems estimated to be between 6 to 8 million in the south of Sudan. After this holocaust is completed, God forbid, then the Moslems of the north will exploit the rich oil reserves. One of the purposes of this book is to provide an alternative news source to my readers.

God will then judge all of us afterward for exactly what we did, could have done, and did not do to save our black brothers in sisters in distress from this holocaust.

On March 26th, 1996, I spoke in Springdale, Arkansas, at a "Blow the Shofar in Zion" — Israel Prayer Conference a meeting of Christian intercessors and missionaries from all over the U.S. and all over the world.

After I discussed the confirmed atrocities against Christians in the Sudan by the Moslem fundamentalist government, especially the confirmed use of poison gas and other chemical and biological agents, provided by Iran, Pastor Steve Wolcott approached me. He congratulated me that finally someone was speaking out about the use of poison agents by Moslems against Christians.

Steven Wolcott served as a missionary in refugee camps in the north of Zaire. There are an estimated 500,000 south Sudanese refugees who have escaped the horrors of the Islamic attacks out of the north. He continued saying that all of northern Zaire was now sick from these poisons blown by northerly winds across the border from southern Sudan, just thirty miles away. Pastor Wolcott heard the artillery bombardments across the border just to the north.

Everyone in these refugee camps as well as Zairean civilians, not only Sudanese refugees, he said, were afflicted with this strange form of dysentery, one of the manifestations of the Gulf War Syndrome.

(It took the U.S. Administration in Washington thirty years to admit the existence of Agent Orange. I wonder how long it will take them to admit Gulf War Syndrome.)

The following are a collection of articles from the press which I hope will shed light on the plight of the blacks of Sudan.

Sudanese Dissidents Form Army To Topple Islamic Government

AP report by Salah Nasrawi in *The Jerusalem Post* of Wednesday, October 16, 1996.

Sudanese dissident groups have agreed to create a new military force to try to topple the Islamic-oriented regime in Khartoum, an opposition leader said Monday.

Farouq Abu Issa said the Sudanese National Democratic Alliance decided to launch the militia at a meeting of leaders of its factions over the weekend in the Eritrean capital Asmara.

The alliance was formed by several opposition groups and the southern rebel Sudan People's Liberation Army last year to try to oust the Sudanese government backed by the Islamic National Front of Hassan Turabi.

"All our guns have now been put together to get rid of the oppressive regime of the Islamic Front," Abu Issa told the Associated Press.

The SPLA has been fighting the Sudanese government since 1983 in an effort to win more autonomy from the Moslem-dominated regime, in Khartoum, for the Christians and animists in the country's south. More than 1.3 million have died in the fighting and resultant famines.

Abu Issa said a strategy was worked out for attacks by the new military force to spur a national uprising that will eventually topple the government, which is headed by President Lt.-Gen. Omar el-Bashir. Under this strategy, Abu Issa said, the SPLA will step up attacks on the Sudanese army in the south while the new force concentrates attacks on army garrisons and positions along the eastern border with Eritrea.

Abu Issa, who lives in exile in Cairo and took part in the Asmara meeting, said the new militia was being formed from officers and troops who deserted the government forces and joined the opposition.

Last month, the Sudanese government said it arrested a number of military officers and civilians in connection with a plot to blow up installations in Port Sudan on the Red Sea. At the time, the alliance claimed that its guerrillas attacked an army position in the area, which is close to Eritrea.

Sudan Mobilizes After Rebel Attacks

AP report on p.4 of *The Jerusalem Post* on January 14, 1997.

Khartoum — Sudanese President Omar el-Bashir yesterday called for a mobilization of the army and civilian militia after rebel forces attacked towns on the Sudan-Ethiopia border.

A statement issued by the palace early in the morning said the forces must "defend... the homeland and deter the enemies of Islam and humanity."

The statement used the phrase "jihad."

Sudan's state-run radio and television were carrying only patriotic music yesterday, and several demonstrations were held in the capital in support of el-Bashir's call. Several hundred people were at each rally.

The mobilization came after rebels of John Garang's Sudan People's Liberation Army on Sunday attacked the Sudanese towns of Kurmuk and Zasan near the Ethiopian border, apparently wresting control from the Sudanese army.

The two towns are about 600 km southeast of the Sudanese capital Khartoum.

A statement issued early yesterday by the Sudanese armed forces' general command accused Ethiopia of fighting with the Sudanese opposition.

A dispatch from Egypt's Middle East News Agency said the fighting for the towns Sunday involved "different kinds of artillery" fired from inside Ethiopian territory and lasted for six hours, died down then resumed for another four hours.

There were no immediate reports of casualties from the remote region.

The Sudanese rebels apparently managed to occupy a large swath around the border towns in Blue Nile state, MENA said.

Sudan has an active military force of about 89,000 and paramilitary units known as the Popular Defense Force of about 15,000 men. The militia's reserve is about 60,000 strong.

The Sudan people's Liberation Army has been fighting since 1983 to try to win autonomy for the South's Christians and animists from the Islamic North. More than 1.3 million people have died in the fighting and resulting famines.

El-Bashir, who took power in a military coup in 1989, has vowed to end the uprising. He has made inroads into Garang's following by offering peace agreements to some of Garang's commanders and promising to enact a new constitution that would give the Southerners exemptions from Islamic law.

Sudan has increasingly accused neighboring countries of intervention on behalf of the rebels in Sudan.

Relations between Sudan and Ethiopia have soured since Ethiopia and Egypt accused Sudan of involvement in an attempt on the life of Egyptian President Hosni Mubarak in June 1995 in the Ethiopian capital Addis Ababa. Sudan has denied it.

"Sorrow and Shame: Brutal North African Slave Trade Ignored and Denied"

By Samuel Cotton
Article in *The City Sun*
March 22-March 28, 1995 Edition

On March 4, Black Africans journeyed from all over the United States to meet at Columbia University. Mauritanians and Senegalese from Washington, along with Ugandans and Sudanese from as far away as Ohio, would spend two days discussing slavery - the beast that continues to bite deep into African flesh.

They would go into grapple with the enigma of receiving virtually no support on the issue of chattel slavery from African American spiritual and political leaders.

Many of the Africans are Christians who have been murderously persecuted by the expansionist Islamic fundamentalist governments of Mauritania and the Sudan. The problem - they will not submit to a process of Islamization which demands that they renounce their Christian faith. Yet these Africans are refused an audience with Black Christian ministers, who prefer in some cases to wine and dine with the Arab enslavers.

Others are Black Muslims from Mauritania who are dumbfounded and disgusted by the fact that the prominent Black Muslim leader, Louis Farrakhan, continues to visit and have good relations with the Sudan, which enslaves Black Muslims and Christians alike. They are disillusioned by Black leaders with African names, who live in houses filled with African statues and walk the streets in full African regalia, but will not raise one voice against slavery.

One African stated that "African Americans have been at the forefront of the international campaign against Apartheid. Yet as an African working in the field of human rights in Africa, I am constantly struck, and saddened, by the extent to which a combination of factors have discouraged the majority of Black Americans from speaking out about human rights abuses in sub-Saharan Africa," said Rakiya Omaar, a Somali, in *The Washington Post.* "Each year, hundreds of Black Americans visit the famous island of Goree in Senegal, from which many of their ancestors began the painful voyage to enslavement. Yet, just a short distance north of Goree are villages and refugee camps providing sanctuary to thousands of Blacks who ran away to escape slavery in Mauritania, some of them as recently as three months ago."

Why don't African Americans speak out about chattel slavery in the sub-Sahara? Why does Jesse Jackson's office refuse to give a statement?

The African Anti Slavery Group has repeatedly, over the past months, mailed documentation and faxed material to the office of Jesse Jackson, but follow-up calls to his aide, Lisa Gibson, failed to yield a response. The author faxed documentation to the Rainbow Coalition on March 9, 1995, at the request of aide Jeff Griffith. The fax was received, and Griffith said that "Jesse Jackson is busy with affirmative action, and like anybody else, Jesse gets tied up and can only speak on one issue at a time. Right now, slavery is not on his agenda." This writer was told, however, to call the following day for a statement.

Sadly, Griffith met an untimely death and all the material was allegedly lost. His superior, Stephanie Gadlin, requested that this writer fax the material again and call later for a statement. Gadlin felt that the slavery issue would be good for Jackson to have on his agenda, since he is scheduled to go to the Middle East. No statement was issued.

Two years ago, on July 15, 1993, white Congressman Frank Wolf wrote a letter to Benjamin Chavis, who, at the time, was serving as the NAACP executive director. "Most recently, I received a copy of a very disturbing State Department cable containing reliable information that in the Sudan, human rights abuses such as kidnapping, slavery and the export of women and children from Southern and central Sudan are escalating dramatically, despite the denials and rhetoric from Sudanese government officials ... I hope that you will speak out against the continuing cruelty which has caused the people of Sudan so much pain and suffering. The efforts of the NAACP could be the difference between life and death for millions of people."

Chavis did not respond, and Rep. White wrote again to him on Aug. 19, 1993. "Since I last wrote you, thousands more in southern Sudan have died.

"Please let me know if the NAACP is willing to step forward. Please let me know if you will personally become involved. This is not an easy task, but the combined efforts of many Americans - could result in saving the lives of tens of thousands of innocent people."

There would be no response to this letter or to a similar plea to Randall Robinson, executive director of TransAfrica, on Aug. 19, 1993.

The weight of the evidence indicates that white political leaders and activists are the only ones working to stop the slave trade, and that Black leaders are not displaying any real interest in stopping the buying and selling of Black Africans. This slave trade is common knowledge in Congressional circles and, shamefully, Black leaders have not even attempted to educate the African American public on the issue - an issue which lies at the very root of the Black experience in America.

Are Black Americans simply playing at being Africans with no real love or attachment to Africa and African people? Could it be that African Americans are in love with a fantasy of Africa and do not possess any real understanding of African realities and world views? These questions require critical thinking that will move African Americans past the kente cloth and fashion, to an examination of whether or not there is a relationship between themselves and the African. The presence in the United States of the Mauritanians and the Sudanese refugees can be a springboard for the exploration of African realities.

The African and the Arab

For African Americans to address the contemporary slave trade and offer support, they must first resolve the philosophical question of form versus content: The outward display of Africanisms, i.e., dress, language and rhetoric, versus the possession of a feeling of solidarity with Africans and an African view of the world.

Both Africans and African Americans acknowledge a common place of origin and both have served as human fodder for the Arab slave trade. However, the Black American appears to have forgiven the Arabs for their participation in the slave trade, while they continue to hold the feet of white Americans and Jews to the fire for their participation.

Black spiritual and political leaders travel to Islamic fundamentalist countries where they have ties and friendships, and sources report that Arab money funds a number of the pet projects of some Black politicians and religious leaders.

In view of the above, when the Mauritanians and Sudanese request help from African Americans, will there be enough people in the Black community to offer support? Or will Black Americans have to effect a major paradigm shift to give such aid? The answer lies in an examination of the African world's view of the Arab and the problems that that view poses for the African American.

An African Perspective

"The African never wanted anything to do with the Arab, because he is a slave trader and we have never forgiven him for the slave trade," said Benedict Lagu, the soft-spoken and friendly son of the former vice president of the Republic of Sudan (1982 to 1985).

"The Arab will always try to enslave people because it is in his culture to enslave people. The Arab is an expansionist, he will never be satisfied with just the north of Sudan. In reality, he will not be satisfied until the whole world worships Islam. This is the view of the whole Arab world, they are all fighting against southern Sudan, they are all pouring money into Sudan, Iran, Iraq, Syria, Libya and Egypt - all of the Arab countries are of one mind. They all support Sudan so that it can crush the south. They want to enslave the entire south and use its resources. Through the south of Sudan they can move into all of Africa. It is the gateway."

Simon Deng, the secretary to the minister of information for the Southern Sudanese Community in America added, "To the Arab, the African is born to be his slave. It does not matter that some have the same skin color as you, color is not the issue here, they consider themselves Arabs. The issue is the mind and the belief of the people and this is a problem that involves two things - race and religion.

"They consider all the Southern Sudanese as slaves. When they look at you they say 'abit,' which means 'slave,' because if you are non-Muslim and Black you are fit to be a slave. Arabs are not considered part of Africa. Egypt is not Africa because it is the mother of the Arabs."

Deng's perspectives, the enmity that exists between the Arab and the Black African, and the belief systems that say Black Africans are inferior and born to serve the Arab, appear to be supported by the historical narrative.

Historically, we know that Arabs, English, Portuguese, Dutch, Spanish, Africans, Catholics and Jews, at one time or another, participated in the slave trade. Native Americans also played a part.

"All of the five civilized Indian nations were Black Slaveowners and slave traders" says Clause Anderson, the author of *Black Labor, White Wealth.* "Worse, all of these Indian Nations supported and fought on the side of the South in the Civil War, in fear of losing their Black slaves."

These are historical realities that are part of the African past and cannot be changed. However, the saga of the Arab slave trader and the relationship with the Black African transcends time. The Arab Muslims were "One of the first and oldest religious enslavers of Black Africans," says Anderson. "They began regular military invasions into East and West Africa around A.D. 700. By A.D. 1000, Muslims routinely combined their commercial trade with spreading the Islamic faith in Black African communities. Medieval Muslims considered Black Africans to be primitive and especially suited for enslavement.

"Muslims from the Middle East have enslaved and sold into North African slave markets no less than one million Black Africans every 100 years, for the past 1,000 years," states David Brian Davis, in *Slavery And Human Progress.* This practice represents no less than 10 million Blacks enslaved and exploited by one group alone. Ironically, most Black African countries converted to the Islamic faith during the 14th century. The Arabs' continuous enslavement of Blacks, therefore, must be driven by factors other than Blacks' religious faith."

What are these factors? Well, as in the case of present-day Mauritanians and Sudanese, enslavement is not for the advancement of Islam. This we know, because the law of Islam says that slaves taken in a holy war are to be released after conversion. However, this does not occur in Mauritania or the Sudan, because after the slaves convert, the Black Muslims remain enslaved. Ergo, the enslavement of Black Africans, is the manifestation of an ancient racial belief system, the belief that the Black African is born to be the slave of the Arab.

"Since color was [and is] the decisive factor in slavery, it was important to know who was and was not a member of the Black race. Moors were not classified as members of the Black race. In northwest Africa, the offspring of Blacks, white Berbers and Arabs became known as Moors ... Few identified with West African Blacks, who lived south of the Sahara," states Anderson. "However, the few Moors who were Black, with the aid of some Islamic converts, pushed the doors to West Africa's natural and human capital wide open...

"With the Black Moors and Islamic converts, the Arabs began their penetration of Africa. Often they exerted religious pressure and continually fostered holy wars that weakened the great West African empires," posits Claude Anderson.

"Arabs labeled Black Americans pagans, then pressured them to disavow their own West African culture and practice of ancestor worship and to accept instead, Arabic culture based in the Islamic religion. This cultural and religious conversion undermined Blacks' African heritage and broad sense of a Black community. Moreover, the religious conversion to the Islamic faith gave Arabs nearly unrestricted access to West African societies and wealth."

This Arab approach to Africa and Black Africans continues to this day and it is against this paradigm that the Mauritanians and the Sudanese struggle.

The Arab and the African American

Benedict Lagu's statement that the African never wanted anything to do with the Arab requires further explanation. There were Africans who wanted relationships with the Arabs. They were Black leaders - the African tribal chiefs.

"West African tribal chiefs had a long history of exchanging slaves with Arab traders. Eventually, they expanded the practice to European traders," explains Anderson. "...The Arab and European traders became convinced that, if tribal chiefs could procure slaves, the trade would be profitable and they had no reason to expect reprisal from any Black nations. A massive slave trading operation developed, and according to an article in *The Washington Post*, the Arabs were still engaged in the slave trading of Blacks in 1993."

Working from the centuries-old paradigm that Blacks are primitive buffoons who will sell their people for a few trinkets while they extract the real gold from the situation; Arab expansionists manipulate some leaders in the African American community with great faculty.

A case in point: A Sudanese scholar, Dr. Augustine A. Lado, is an assistant professor in the department of management and labor relations at Cleveland State University. Lado is also the president of Pax Sudani, an organization of African Sudanese and human rights activists committed to exposing and campaigning against slavery and other gruesome atrocities perpetrated against Africans in modern-day Sudan.

In Africa, Lado routinely risked his life by resisting Arabization and Islamization. In this country, he began seeking the help of Christian churches in Cleveland.

"I contacted the Good Shepherd Baptist Church in Cleveland and requested to speak there on a Wednesday night to explain to them what Christians are experiencing in the Sudan. When we arrived, they were not ready for us. The church officials were absent, and we were given the cold shoulder - we eventually left," explained Lado.

"Then shortly after that, it came to my attention that a Rev. Sterling Glover, pastor of the Emmanuel Baptist church and chairman of the Cleveland Cuyahoga County Port Authority, had invited a Sudanese Delegation. It was headed by Dr. Ali Al-Hajj (minister of the Bureau of Federal Government) and Minister Mirghani Mohamed Salih (deputy chief of mission) of the Sudanese Embassy in Washington.

The meeting was to establish a trade alliance with the Cleveland business community and the African American business community. Lado recalled that when Pax Sudani threatened to picket the luncheon, three members of the organization were invited to speak. However, they were denied access on arrival.

Again, there would be no connection between the African Christians and the African American Christian ministers. However, the relationship between Dr. Ali Al-Hajj and Rev. Glover was solid and intact.

The *Plains Dealer*, Cleveland's largest newspaper, on Thursday, Dec. 15, 1994, commented on the Black Christian Minister's relationship with the Sudan. "The Greater Cleveland International Trade Alliance is hosting a lunch at the Ritz-Carlton Hotel today. Those who were planning to go to the meeting should consider a few well-known facts about the country they are courting," stated the editorial. "Sudan's ruling regime came into power in 1989 after overthrowing the democratically elected government. It has sought to impose strict Islamic law on all Sudanese, regardless of their religion... The Sudanese government has targeted not only Christians and animists, but other Muslims who do not adhere to its strict edicts... Human rights organizations have reported government involvement in massacres, kidnappings, and in transporting and selling its captives, including children, into slavery." Rev. Glover responded in the article by saying that he "knew all about the accusations against the Sudan before his first trip there. He maintains that none of the atrocity charges against the government have ever been proven. A cease-fire has ended the warfare and elections have occurred. I know that my efforts are legitimate and right," reports *The Plains Dealer.*

Rev. Glover's responses are the same erroneous excuses that many African American leaders give for ignoring the Black African slave and jumping into bed with the Arab slavers.

A journalist watching these events stated, "It seems as if Glover hasn't been keeping up. Almost as quickly as the warring sides agreed to a cease-fire, they broke it. If elections were held, it's hard to believe that a regime that has toiled so hard to suppress its opponents would suddenly embrace free and fair elections."

Glover has been to the Sudan three times, two paid trips by the Sudanese government and one trip paid for by city tax dollars. Dr. Lado accessed the public records, showing the expenses for the third trip. Glover stayed in the air-conditioned Hilton during his trip and the Sudanese government convinced him that there is no slave trade.

The results of playing the statesman are tragic. Glover returned to the United States and discredited the Sudanese human rights activists in Cleveland by stating that there are no atrocities or slavery. This resulted in further alienation of the Africans from the Black Christian community. Again, the Sudanese Islamic fundamentalists had squelched an anti- slavery movement in Cleveland, and were free to continue raping, pillaging and enslaving Black Africans without protests from Black America.

This tactic is common knowledge among Middle Eastern minorities suffering pressure from Islamic fundamentalists. "The

Leadership Committee For A Free Middle East, a coalition of non-Arab, non-Muslim captive nationalities in the Middle East and North Africa, is well aware of the situation in both Mauritania and the Sudan, says Najib Khuri, a Lebanese Christian. Particularly in the Sudan, there has been a concerted effort to suppress the facts concerning the existence of chattel slavery.

"It is the most embarrassing dark little secret in the Arab world, and its exposure in the West, particularly to the African American community, would have a devastating impact on the oil-financed Arabist agenda. A major part of that agenda is to enlist, through deception and manipulation, African American support in its efforts to both Arabize and Islamize Africa and the entire Middle East."

As the *Cleveland Plains Dealer* put it, it may be working in some quarters. Black leaders appear to be giving that support by their silence and ineptitude.

Before the Black religious and secular community discredits the Mauritanians and the Sudanese, however, they should consider a couple of important points. Black leaders are not trained to find slavery in countries with deceitful governments. In addition, Black ministers, even if they were sincere, do not understand how modern chattel slavery operates in countries with demographics like Mauritania and the Sudan (the largest country in Africa). Leaders like Rev. Glover are over their heads in this game and are betraying hundreds of thousands of Africans languishing in slavery.

Demographics And The Modern-Day Slave Trade

By Samuel Cotton
Article in *The City Sun*
March 29-April 4, 1995 Edition

Our update on today's North African slave trade continues this week with professionals who know how to find evidence of the slave trade. Gaspar Biro, a specially appointed United Nations human rights monitor, stated: "Abduction of children, as well as of women... is routinely practiced ...Women and children are kept in special camps where people from the north or from abroad come to purchase them for money or goods such as camels. Young girls and women are purchased for housekeepers and, in some cases, wives. The boys are reportedly kept as servants." Why did Biro find what Rev. Sterling Glover, pastor of the Emmanuel Baptist Church and chairman of the Cleveland Cuyahoga County Port Authority missed? The reason - he is a trained and experienced special investigator for the United Nations and was not in the Sudan for a dinner date. Biro lived amidst the repressive regime of the late Rumanian dictator Nicolae Ceausecu and knows how governments hide oppression.

"I lived always with one foot in prison. I know well how totalitarian governments operate, how they think they can hide things and what they try to do," says Biro. "I think perhaps the Sudanese overlooked that possibility when they let me in the country." (*The Washington Post*, 3/26/94).

Mauritania: Where Slavery Is A Way of Life

In Mauritania, the modern-day slave trade is a cautious and sophisticated one. Even if one is serious about finding the slave markets, the task is difficult for a number of reasons. Interviews conducted with African Americans indicate that when they think of slave markets, they think of stable markets such as one might have found in South Carolina in the 1700s - opening each day and closing each day at a certain hour. Very rarely in North Africa are there open slave markets. Slave markets in Mauritania are usually highly mobile, situational, and discussions around the buying and selling of slaves are coded.

Slavery has been a way of life in Mauritania for many centuries. "There are tens of thousands of Black slaves who remain the property of their master, subject entirely to his will, working long hours for no remuneration, with no access to education and no freedom to marry or to associate freely with other Blacks," says *Africa Watch*. "They escape servitude not by exercising their 'legal' rights, but mainly through escape."

It is important for skeptics to do the math. This slave trade predates the 1400s and continued until "...July 5, 1980, [when] the government of President Mohamed Khouna Ould Haidallah passed a decree abolishing slavery for the third time in Mauritania's history," states *Africa Watch.* "The abolition was essentially a public-relations exercise prompted by external considerations.

"It was never intended as a well-thought-out policy aimed at eradicating the age-old practice of slavery."

This need to declare that they are abolishing slavery at three different times should tell African American leaders, who are resistant to this information, that slavery existed until recently and still exists.

In fact, the group El Hor, which was developed to advance the interests of haratines (former slaves) and slaves, brought things to a head in Mauritania. It was "the controversial sale of a slave woman, Mbarka, in Atar in February, 1980 [that] brought the brewing crisis to a head," states *Africa Watch.* "There was nothing uncommon about such sales. What distinguished this case was that a well-educated haratine, Lt. Barak Ould Barek, wanted to marry the slave in question. As she was apparently particularly beautiful, her master decided he could sell her for a great deal of money on the open market.

"At the marketplace, two beydanes (meaning "white" in Hassaniya, an Arabic dialect) fought over her and the case came to attract national attention. ...This led to organized demonstrations in Nouakchott, Rosso, Nouadhibou and other towns. ...These activities led to government suppression and torture. El Hor still exists today, but does not constitute a significant political force...active members do not dare meet openly or discuss their affairs publicly for fear of violent reprisals. If slavery has 'ended,' it is difficult to understand why an organization whose objectives are to improve the life of former slaves [and slaves] should be forced into secrecy."

These historical events led to a change in how the slave trade is conducted. "Slaves are still bought and sold but with a difference, that is, without the publicity that was previously considered so distasteful," Diop, a Black health worker exiled in 1989, said to *Africa Watch.* "Nowadays, beydane tribes make discreet arrangements among themselves. A slave is given in exchange for something else."

Moustapha, 48, a recently escaped slave, was interviewed by *Africa Watch,* in the River Senegal Valley, on June 1, 1990. "It's only the semantics that have changed," he said. "People hesitate a little more now in using the word 'slave,' except in anger or as an insult.

Depending on the region, different euphemisms exist, especially in the cities. Sometimes you hear 'my student.' Every Mauritanian knows when the word is being used to describe a slave and when it refers to a student in school.

"Then there are the 'presents.' I recall the case of a young woman who had a child. The child, who was eight months old, was given to a cousin of the master, as a 'present' - for life. It was agreed not to transfer the child to his new owner until the mother had stopped breast-feeding him. Others say my 'domestic' - that is, domestics who work 24 hours a day for no pay, who have no rights at all. The master's family treats them as they have always treated their slaves, and they still think of themselves as slaves, because no one has told them anything different."

These are the difficulties in finding the slave trade in Mauritania. This is why you will hear North Africans telling disbelieving African Americans, "Come with me and I will show you how it is done. I will take you to where it is happening. Tell the government to let me take you where I want to take you," says Sabit Alley, the area coordinator for the Southern Sudanese Community in America. "I will prove it to you, if the Sudanese government will let us move through the Sudan without interference."

Sudan's Twin Ravages: Famine and the Sword

Finding the slave trade in the Sudan, the largest country in Africa, presents a different set of problems. Analysis would have to be conducted in a war zone, amidst heavy fighting between the Arab north and the Black south. It is in this atmosphere of death and war, far removed from the air-conditioned rooms of the Hilton Hotel, that the trained observer must hunt the slave trade.

Through the smoke of battle, one can see that over five million South Sudanese, mostly Christians, have been driven from their homes. Another two million lie dead from the twin ravages of famine and the sword.

Unlike some African American leaders who spend their time fraternizing and dining at the table of the Sudanese government, a white congressman, U.S. Rep. Frank R. Wolf of Virginia's 10th district, descended into the hellish atmosphere of the South Sudan to examine the plight of the Black Africans. As a result of this trip,

Rep. Wolf wrote the former executive director of the NAACP, Benjamin Chavis, a letter on July 15, 1993, and stated: "I visited southern Sudan in February of this year, my third trip to Sudan since 1988. The conditions I witnessed on this recent trip - the starvation, the disease, the indiscriminate bombing by government forces, the utter hopelessness - were more distressing that anything I have seen in Ethiopia, in Somalia, or anywhere else in the world. As many as 500,000 people have died in the past decade. Right now, four million human beings risk death in Sudan.

"Operating beyond the reaches of the international community, the government has had a free hand to wage what is widely considered a genocidal war against the non-Islamic Southerners," reports The *Bay State Banner.*

The enslavement of Southerners is an important part of the north's repression, according to Sudan expert Robert Collins. "It's like the Wild West," he said, describing the process by which Southerners are enslaved. "You ride out there with your friends, you shoot up a village and take prisoners. ...Women and children are enslaved and men who are not able to escape are generally shot," Collins said.

Darius Hakim, a Catholic priest and Latuho tribesman whose tribe sits on the border of Uganda and the Sudan, reported the statements of a Sudanese who risked his life to bring attention to this plight.

"Capturing and trafficking in children is still flourishing and particularly active in Southern Kordofan and Darfur.

"It is caused by the mass displacement of people, uprooted from their land, in the course of armed clashes and the ethnic cleansing, and is favored by the nature of the soil, with vast savannas and bushlands, where one can roam for days, without meeting or being met by anybody.

"This is the land of the Rizeigat, Massiria, and Baggara Arab tribal groups... They have answered with enthusiasm and religious fervor to the call to jihad, the holy war, which gives them full freedom in dealing with the unbeliever - but mostly, if not only, attracted by their want of possessing weapon, of robbing and plundering, and of satisfying their basest instincts. All women, girls and children are there, unprotected, to be feasted upon... The time of the long lines of enchained slaves marching north is over. Now truckloads of children are seen moving in the same, traditional direction."

The attacking of Black African villages in the south, bulldozing the villages to the ground, setting thousands of men, women and children adrift in the countryside, and killing, raping, and enslaving them at will is the leit-motif of the slave trade. The very nature of this type of activity causes slave markets to appear and disappear. Transactions take place quietly among relatives when the Arab militia returns home with their war booty of slaves.

This is the rugged and bloody path that African American leaders must follow if they are serious about hunting the elusive slave trade and returning home with a clear conscience. This is the path the African American community must demand their leaders follow before they accept their reports and turn their backs on Africans.

The Slavery Issue: A Crisis In Black Leadership

By Samuel Cotton
Article in *The City Sun*
April 5-April 11, 1995 Edition

The issue of chattel slavery, and the systematic rape and murder of an African people is being increasingly heard in the dialogue of the Black community. Such dialogue, however, only indicates a potential or a resistance movement on the slavery issue and not a predictor.

How the African American community addresses or does not address, engages or does not engage this issue, will define us as a people to this nation and to the world. It will explain if the strident Black voices of social protest heard frequently in the national discourse are the products of a broad moral vision or simply the whimpering of self-interest - whether the gnashing of our teeth over social injustice is just an empty sound emanating from a people whose practice of morality is clearly selective.

Those in the Black community who claim identification with Africa will be unable to rise to this historic occasion without the ability to access and process accurate information. It would also be beneficial if the Black community had leadership on the issue of slavery. The sad truth is that it does not. African American leaders are hiding under their beds until this gunfight over the question of slavery is over.

This disgraceful, cowardly and self-serving behavior also holds true in Africa. "Why haven't African regional or continental organizations exposed and attacked slavery?" is the trenchant rejoinder from William Pleasant of *The Daily Challenge,* in the March 30th edition of that paper. Pleasant presses the issue by stating that "It would stand to reason that the Organization of African Unity (OAU) would lead the charge against such a barbaric practice in its own backyard. But the OAU has remained silent."

Pleasant astutely observed that, "In the 1980s Black politicians, activists, and celebrities tripped over each other to get photographed being arrested at South Africa's Washington, D.C. embassy. It became a chic activity. Apartheid in South Africa had to go, and it did, no small thanks to the grassroots Black community in this country."

Since African American leaders will not join this issue until it becomes popular, the work of educating the grassroots Black community falls to the Black press. The problem with the Black press is that it is also suspect.

"At this moment, a group of Black American journalists are touring Sudan as guests of the regime, the Muslim Arab clique responsible for the slaughter of hundreds of thousands of their own people, particularly non-Muslims and Blacks. The Nation of Islam's Minister Akbar Muhammad is acting as the leader of the press junket designed to counter Samuel Cotton's charges," says Pleasant (*The Daily Challenge* 3/30), who has experienced a number of these staged events in African countries.

"No doubt, these Black American pundits will return to write and broadcast glowing reports on the Sudan. That's what journalists do if they ever want to get invited to the Sudan again." Pleasant's perspective is corroborated by another Black journalist, Keith Richberg:

"Are you Black first, or a journalist first? The question succinctly sums up the dilemma facing almost every Black journalist working for the 'mainstream' (read: white) press. Are you supposed to report and write accurately, and critically, about what you see and hear? Or are you supposed to be pushing some kind of black agenda, protecting Black American leaders from tough scrutiny, treating Black people and Black issues in a different way." (*Washington Post Magazine*, 3/26)

There are real pressures and dangers for Black journalists speaking the truth, especially for any Black writer who eschews committing intellectual incest with Black readers. Keith raises serious questions, and "Many of those questions were at the heart of the debate stirred up a decade ago by my *Post* colleague, Milton Coleman, when he reported remarks of Jesse Jackson referring to Jews as 'Hymie.' Coleman was accused of using material that was off the record; more troubling, he was accused of betraying his race. For being a hard-nosed journalist, he suffered the wrath of much of the Black community, and even had to endure veiled threats from Louis Farrakhan's henchmen."

Things Go Better with Junket

Is it betraying African Americans to tell them the truth? "Last March in the Sudanese capital of Khartoum, I ran into a large group of Black Americans who were also staying at the Khartoum Hilton," says Keith. "They were there on some kind of fact-finding trip, and being given VIP treatment by the Sudanese regime. Some of the men went all-out and dressed the part, donning long white Sudanese robes and turbans. Several of the women in the group covered themselves in Muslim wrap.

"The U.S. Ambassador in Khartoum had the group over to his house, and the next day, the government-controlled newspaper ran a front-page story on how the group berated the ambassador over U.S. policy toward Sudan. Apparently, some members of the group told the ambassador that it was unfair to label the Khartoum regime as a sponsor of terrorists and one of the world's most violent, repressive governments.

"'After all,'" they said, 'they themselves had been granted nothing but courtesy, and they had found the dusty streets of the capital safer than most crime-ridden American cities." I was nearly shaking with rage. Couldn't they see they were being used, manipulated by one of the world's most oppressive regimes? Human Rights Watch/Africa - hardly a water carrier for U.S. policy - had recently labeled Khartoum's human rights record as 'abysmal,' and reported that 'all forms of political opposition remain banned both legally and through systematic terror.' And here were these Black Americans, these willing tools, heaping praise on an unsavory clique of ruling thugs."

Press junkets to the Sudan are just that - tools used to obfuscate the issues and provide information tailored to soothe consciences hungry for an excuse not to enter this difficult struggle.

Current News Perspectives

For the African American community to give birth to resistance, all information must be disabused to that Black Americans, regardless of whether they are Muslim or Christian, Republican or Democrat, can make intelligent and conscience-grounded decisions on the slavery question.

Slavery is an irrefutable fact, corroborated by numerous sources. A yearlong investigation by *Newsweek* magazine found that slavery of Black African Muslims has existed and continues to exist in the Islamic Republic of Mauritania. Eyewitness accounts, testimony by slaves, pictures and documentation abounds on this subject. Slavery is a fact in the Sudan and just as in Mauritania, it is racial in nature. Frank Kiehne, Congressman Donald Payne's foreign affairs advisor, stated, "We're convinced that slavery still exists in Mauritania.

"We know that slavery exists in the Sudan but it's pretty hard to pin down, because it's mainly in the south and it's hard to get in and out of there."

The Sudanese and the Mauritanians are not against the Arab as a man, nor against Islam as a religion. Mauritanians are struggling against being enslaved, because of their Black skin by Arabs who worship Allah as they do. Mohamed Nasir Athie, a Black African Muslim, exemplifies the pain of that type of struggle. While other Black African Muslims lost their faith and stopped praying to Allah because of the pain they experience when Beydanes (white Muslims) enslave, rape and kill their people, Mohamed continues to praise Allah. Mohamed does not view the enslavers of Mauritania and Sudan as true representatives of Islam, and therefore, refuses to allow their actions to destroy his relationship with Islam.

The South Sudanese are against slavery, Arabization and Islamization. This is a struggle against oppression, not against a religious paradigm. Arabization is the policy of trying to systematically and forcefully convert people by teaching them the Arabic language and culture and discouraging them from using their indigenous languages and practicing original traditions.

Islamization is the forceful conversion of non-Muslims into Muslims. These twin policies are carried out with deadly force by the Islamic extremists, and not just in North African countries.

The Middle East is comprised not just of Arabs and Jews; it has many minorities who are also suffering intensely from the twin policies of Arabization and Islamization. These minorities know of the enslavement of Black Africans and support their struggle.

"The Copts of Egypt, the Assyrians of Iraq, the Lebanese Christians, and last, but most significantly, the African Sudanese, all represent non-Arab/non-Muslim, primarily Christian communities in the Middle East region... and have experienced centuries of oppression at the hands of the Arabs," says Najib Khuri. "These captive nationalities have struggled to maintain their ethnic and religious identities against incredible odds.

"For decades, the Christian peoples of this region have looked to the United Nations, the West and the European Christian church for help in stemming the tide of Arabization and Islamization. They have experienced nothing but treachery and betrayal, primarily because of the incredible amounts of money generated by the oil-rich Arab states, which has been used to bribe the international community into a hypocritical posture of silence concerning the oppression of the non-Arab nationalities all over the Middle East region. Billions of dollars have been spent, not only to oppress these peoples, but to crush their identities, to deny their very existence to the world."

Consequently, the Mauritanians and the Sudanese are circling wagons with the other minorities in the Middle East. Africans find in this arrangement mutual protection and support against the twin policies of Arabization and Islamization and centuries of slavery.

Progress Despite Opposition

Despite setbacks, Black Africans are making progress, and it appears that a modern-day grassroots abolitionist movement to fight the enslavement of Africans is being born.

Rep. Eleanor Holmes Norton, Washington D.C.'s Delegate to Congress, who is the first Black official to speak up against the continued enslavement of Blacks in North Africa, joined with Reps. Barney Frank (D-Mass.) and Frank Torricelli (D-NJ). They have co-sponsored Resolution #49, requiring the United States to act against human bondage. House Resolution #49 would make the eradication of slavery an "important goal for the U.S. Government in all of its activities."

It directs the Secretary of State to include in the State Department's annual human rights report, "a full report on slavery where it exists throughout the world." It requires that the United States, in cooperation with regional organizations and the United Nations, "draw up a multinational plan to put an end to slavery where it exists throughout the world."

Commenting on the House Resolution, Eleanor Holmes Norton (D-Washington, D.C.), told AASG, "Our own history commands that the U.S. lead the way to the worldwide eradication of slavery. Beginning with the inclusion of a report on slavery in the Secretary of State's annual human rights report, the U.S. is in a strong position to work with other nations to completely eliminate slavery before the year 2000."

Though this statement is encouraging, Norton's statements are nonspecific and do not condemn Mauritania or the Sudan. Hopefully, in the future, when this is popular, she will take a firm stand on the African issue.

Another courageous African American is television journalist Tony Brown. Last December, *Tony Brown's Journal,* PBS's highly respected Black-oriented news show, aired an exposé of the slave trade in North Africa. Entitled, "Today's Slave Trade," the program featured AASG's executive director, Mohamed Athie, and research director, Dr. Charles Jacobs.

Athie and Jacobs exhibited color photos of Blacks serving their masters in Mauritania, and explained the inner workings of the slave business. Reached for comment, Tony Brown told AASG, "This is a most incredible story that needs to be told. That Blacks are in bondage, still serving masters in 1995, is stunning. I am glad that my show helped get out the facts. There was a considerable response to the program and I commend Mohamed Athie and Charles Jacobs for their work."

With the support of the Student Chapter of the National Association of Black Social Workers (NABSW) at Columbia University, the AASG was able to hold a successful meeting with the Sudanese and the Mauritanians on March 4 and 5. Officials from the South Sudanese Community in America, Pax Sudani, and the Committee for Human Rights in Mauritania agreed for the first time to work together to place the issue of human bondage on the American public agenda.

The Mauritanians and Sudanese also planned for an AASG Conference on "Modern Day Slavery," to be hosted by the NABSW at Columbia University in May. The meeting will feature human rights experts and activists from Mauritania and Sudan, as well as journalists who have witnessed slavery. AASG will also invite three U.S. Congress persons who co-sponsored House Resolution #49, requiring the United States to act against slaving nations: Barney Frank (D-Mass.), Eleanor Holmes Norton (D-Washington, D.C.), and Frank Torricelli (D-NJ). The May Conference on Modern Day Slavery" is open to the public. For more information, call (617) 278-4324.

In a joint statement, Mohamed Athie, AASG's executive director and former diplomat at the Mauritanian Embassy in Washington, and Simon Deng, Information Secretary of the South Sudanese Community in America, declared, "We two peoples have formed a bond. Alone, each of us has failed to mobilize American public opinion regarding the horrors perpetrated against our peoples. But now united and focused on a demand to abolish the scourge of slavery in our lands - a human abuse long thought dead - we will not fail to elicit broad public support, and hopefully, U.S. government action."

Chapter Eighteen

Farrakhan's Swamp Of Hatred

by David Tell, for the Editors
Article in *The Weekly Standard*
October 23rd, 1995

All good men despise him, but the Honorable Minister Louis Farrakhan, peerless master of demagoguery's magic arts, has already defeated them. And they do not know it. A week ago Sunday, ABC's Sam Donaldson asked the cleric about President Clinton's reluctance to endorse the Nation of Islam-sponsored "Million Man March." But the purpose of his march is to "organize black men" for self-improvement, community development, job creation, and crime reduction, Farrakhan responded, all crinkly smile and soft voice of wounded innocence. "What intelligent person wouldn't want to embrace that kind of idea?"

He has a point. It's hard to find such an intelligent person just now. Thank you, Minister Farrakhan. Roll credits.

The rhetoric of embarrassment that governs American race relations has already made its half-hearted, half-witted accommodation to Farrakhan's latest, and so far greatest provocation. The dupes and fanatics who yoke themselves in his Nation's bow-tie uniform will be a small fraction of the massed crowd on the Mall. For almost all the rest of us, left and right, black and white, the consensus judgement on the march is this: message good, messenger — in varying degrees — bad. All we are allowed to disagree about is whether and how thoroughly the latter damages the former. Farrakhan is, after all, the nation's leading anti-Semite. Does it matter?

Sure, it matters. Opponents of the march have the better of this oddly muted debate. There would be no "million men" without Farrakhan, and there would be no Farrakhan without anti-Semitism. At his first Lincoln Memorial appearance, during the August 1983 March on Washington II, Farrakhan departed from his long-established, sordid script to offer unmodulated praise of Martin Luther King, Jr. and to decry "these artificial barriers that divide us as a people" into opposed creeds and races. He was warmly received by the audience. But he was completely ignored by the media.

It was not until the following year that Farrakhan became famous, as an unignorable surrogate speaker in Jesse Jackson's presidential campaign. You remember: He called Judaism a "gutter religion" and issued death threats against Washington Post reporter Milton Coleman, who had dared to report Rev. Jackson's "Hymietown" remark, and New York City Clerk David Dinkins, who had dared to criticize him. We would never have heard of Farrakhan otherwise. And deprived of that negative celebrity, won by violating basic cultural taboos on a national stage, he would, by his own standards, hardly exist at all. That's what it means to be a demagogue.

The Anti-Defamation League expresses its understandable, necessary concern about "the most mainstream event led by an anti-Semite in recent American history." The ADL also proclaims its confidence that the "vast majority" of march participants will not "subscribe" to Farrakhan's bigotry. That last part is too generous. How many marchers will there be this week who do not know that Farrakhan is a Jew-hater? By responding to his call, by listening to his appeal, by joining him, they will be accepting a tacit, charter subscription to anti-Semitism. All of them.

But what if, just for the sake of argument, Farrakhan weren't an anti-Semite? ADL spokesmen say they "understand and support" the black directed goals of the Million Man March. The American Jewish Congress says it supports those goals "enthusiastically." The White House, three days before the March, amended its position to "let's see if we can't build on the positive." Allowing for differences of tone and vigor, that's what everybody says. Unmistakably implying in the process that but for the Jew stuff, Farrakhanism is basically harmless.

Shame. Farrakhan's anti-Semitism wounds and infuriates. But it is not by any means the worst thing about him. He poses no serious threat to Jews, or to white Americans generally. Louis Farrakhan does pose a threat, however, a direct and grave one, entirely removed from the question of anti-Semitism, to black Americans. Doesn't that matter? Or hasn't anyone noticed.

To begin with, the man is a charlatan of classical proportion. For decades now he has preached a gospel of black economic self-determination, urging his followers to withdraw their commerce from the larger society, to spend and sell only among their own. Forget the stupid theory involved and consider Farrakhan's practices. With a $5 million interest-free loan from Moammar Gadhafi in 1985, Farrakhan launched something called POWER, Inc., which he promised to turn into a "billion-dollar corporate entity" by 1990. Its retail enterprises would create jobs and investment capital benefiting millions of blacks — if, that is, they each scraped together $20 a month to purchase POWER's first product line, soaps and shampoos.

A comprehensive investigative series earlier this year by William Gaines and David Jackson of the Chicago Tribune proves, predictably, that POWER is a fraud. And that Farrakhan, who claims that he "owns nothing" is a thief. Nation of Islam-affiliated companies are saddled with debt, unpaid bills, and hundreds of thousands of dollars in tax delinquencies. Their assets are personally and directly controlled — in clear violation of federal law — by Nation officials, most of whom are members of Farrakhan's immediate family. POWER pays their heating bills.

And unsuspecting black people, most of them poor, pay for all the rest. Donors to the Nation's "No. 2 Poor Treasury" get a T-shirt. Farrakhan gets the money. His name is on the bank account, which has bought him a 77 acre rural retreat and a Land Rover. He also owns two stately homes in Chicago, a Mercedes, a Lexus, innumerable imported shoes and suits, and God knows what else.

This is not "harmless". And neither is the truest deepest goal of Farrakhan's march. He — the presumption! — asks black men to "atone" for their crimes to self and family, and to give up their dependence on a corrupt greater America, and ostensibly unobjectionable, even conservative, summons that has muzzled the march's would-be critics. But he is asking these black men to atone as Black Men, not as individuals, for sins he has elsewhere and exhaustively ascribed solely to the conspiracies of White Men. And it is not the subordinate material connection that blacks now have to whites that Farrakhan seeks to erase, as his march manifesto makes clear in its complaints against pending federal budget cuts. It is their psychological connection with America he wants to sever. He wants black men to withdraw into hatred. And dehumanize themselves.

Louis Farrakhan, the messenger, is appalling. But even had he never once in his life uttered the word Jew, his message — and this march — would be worse still.

Last year at Howard University, Colin Powell told an assembly of students that "African Americans have come too far, and have too far yet to go, to take a detour into the swamp of hatred." There is "danger in the message of hatred," he warned, "however cleverly the message is packaged, or entertainingly it is presented." This year, this month, by contrast, Mr. Powell says through his spokeswoman that while he can't attend the Million Man March (scheduling conflict, you understand), he "supports its purpose."

Its "purpose" is to identify and legitimize a "swamp of hatred" as the proper home for 12 percent of our citizens. Americans — black Americans especially — deserve better than the puling response Farrakhan's march has earned so far.

"Inside The March: Farrakhan Is King"

By Matt Labash
Article in *The Weekly Standard*
October 23rd, 1995

Amidst metal chairs and rec-center acoustics in a frat house basement along a roughneck patch of northeast D.C., an alliance of Washington-area groups called the Youth Organizers Committee is about to announce its solidarity with Louis Farrakhan's Million Man March — his invitation for black men to "straighten their backs" and pledge their troths to family and community.

The organizers, from groups with freshly minted, oddly con-jugated monikers such as "Cease Fire Don't Smoke the Brothers," are skull-capped and kufi'ed. Even the Baptists look fairly serious about not getting out-Islam'ed in front of the media assemblage, and greet recurrent As-Salaam-Alaikums with right-back-at-you Alaikum-Salaams. They assume their places on the stage in wrist-clamped Panther stances, making sure their faces broadcast the proper radical menace.

Brother Ronald Moten of the aforementioned "Cease Fire" eventually gets down to business: "Any black man who speaks out against the Million Man March, I don't care if you're Christian, Muslim, whoever — we gonna start stepping to you," he says. "We're not with no more Uncle Toms and we're getting tired of those who cannot be behind the brothers on the street, and the brothers in prison have been neglected too long." Moten knows a thing or two about the latter brothers — he spent the last four years with them for selling drugs.

Next up is Malik Zulu Shabazz, founder of Unity Nation. Shabazz is traveling solo today, without the African Warrior Staff he often trots out when he wishes to put the fear of Allah into the hearts of onlookers. Citing an experience Farrakhan claims to have had where he was beamed about a spacecraft and told by the Hon-orable Elijah Muhammad, founder of the Nation of Islam, that Ronald Reagan was plotting genocide for the black community, Shabazz bore witness:

"We stand today by clear and convincing evidence, by the drugs being poured into the community, by the men being locked up, by the lack of education and destruction of the inner cities, that there is a war being planned against black youth. And before the United Snakes government is allowed to fulfill this death plot against the black family and particularly the black man... the black man is ready to rise up and take his place."

Malik'll do just fine as one of Farrakhan's young ambassa-dors. For it is this very mix of metronomical oratory, scorched-earth paranoia, and penchant for Caucasian genocidal punchlines that has made Farrakhan the preeminent leader in the black commu-nity today. The Million Man March is his power play, the way he intends to prove to traditional black leadership and to the world of white devilry that he is the man to see. Considering that the march has no clear message and no real agenda, it's fair to say that the only real message, the only real agenda, is Louis Farrakhan.

The articulated plan is as follows: One million black men (no women invited except Maya Angelou, Rosa Parks, and the widows of slain civil-rights leaders, including one whose demise Farrakhan is long rumored to have played a part in) are to descend on the Mall in Washington. Numbers are hard to come by especially from the Nation, but the one million thing sets the bar a bit high, considering one-fifteenth of all black men in America will have to show. Along with ousted NAACP leader Ben chavis, his co-director, Farrakhan has deemed this "a holy day of atonement," lifting irony-free the name of the holiest day in the faith he so ecumenically described as a "gutter religion." A flier back in March urged African-American males to "realize our political strength, recognize our economic power, mobilize the men in our communities in unity" by coming to the march.

Farrakhan's aims reveal a gaping moral abyss in the world of black leadership. Where once Medgar Evers urged economic boycotts in Jackson, Mississippi, with a clear-cut goal of racial integration, Farrakhan is urging all non-attending blacks to stay home from work and school and make sure to keep all their money away from Mister Charlie: "Since so many of you love to be all white, then be all white, it's all right. America must taste how it feels when her ex-slave is not in her midst."

Conflicting messages abound. Farrakhan recently stated: "We have looked for too long for the government to solve our problems," while comrade Chavis insisted, "We are not letting the government off the hook." Even the march's name, as the Washington Times noted, seems prone to schizophrenia: "Million Man March" or "Day of Atonement and Reconciliation" or "Day of Absence" or "Day of Positive Action."

But it's not as if the garbled Farrakhan message gets in the way of his popularity. He derives his appeal less from moral authority and clear thinking than from tapping pure, unfettered rage. As the University of Chicago's National Black Politics Study revealed in 1993-94, 69 percent of blacks surveyed thought Farrakhan represented a positive viewpoint as opposed to being a dangerous extremist — this on the heels of the publicity crush surrounding the 1993 Kean College speech delivered by his associate Khallid

Muhammad, who gained headlines for his pithy characterization of Jews: "Why do you not understand my speech, Jew? Even because you cannot hear my word. You are of your father, the Devil." Muhammad later got a standing ovation at Howard University, the black school in Washington where most recently law students burst in hysterical cheers upon hearing of O.J. Simpson's release.

Those Howard students are not exactly vagrants and junkies, a fact that offers a glimpse into Farrakhan's remarkable popularity among upper-echelon blacks. And where African-American politicians are concerned, Farrakhan has successfully mau-maued the mau-mauers. The Congressional Black Caucus, under Kweisi Mfume's leadership, struck a "covenant" in the fall of 1993 with Farrakhan, patching up relations further legitimizing him despite his frequent anabases into bogs of lunacy.

It's not as if the black congressmen are strangers themselves to some of his more radical agenda items, such as reparations — the idea that white America should pay the descendants of slaves for the indenture of their ancestors. Caucus members have proposed reparations bills over the years; even in a hostile Republican climate, Rep. Earl Hilliard of Alabama piped up this past July, "I believe in reparations to truly make the playing field level."

Still, why the blind acquiescence to Farrakhan? After all, the CBC is made up of people who have garnered tens of thousands of votes at the ballot box and who have therefore laid fair claim to leadership. First, if you are a black politician, you don't want ideas like "We will tar and feather them, we will hang them from the highest limb, we will chop off their heads and roll them down the street" — spoken by somebody who means it, somebody with followers — gaining a foothold among the constituents back home in the district.

New York Republican Rep. Peter King has battled Farrakhan for two years over the estimated $15 million the Nation of Islam has earned from federal contracts. "The problem is that too many of the black leaders are reluctant to take Farrakhan on," King says, recounting a bipartisan press conference attacking Farrakhan in which he deliberately tried to include local ministers. "We must have several hundred black churches, and friends of mine came back and said the pastors, quite frankly, were afraid to come because Farrakhan has such strong support among their congregations."

Which buttresses the dirty little secret of black politics — that surrogate anti-Semitic buckshot never hurt anyone's street credentials. The truth is, Farrakhan can fill the Washington Convention Center a lot faster than say, Maryland Rep. Albert Wynn, whose very name causes most African Americans across the country to say, "Who?" And the Anti-Defamation League, the Jewish group that is one of his most vocal opponents, doesn't carry much weight with Maxine Waters's South Central L.A. district. Figures obtained by the Center for Responsive Politics show that in the 1993-94 cycle, pro-Israel PACs gave only $58,350 to the entire Black Caucus, while Farrakhan's lecture fees can top $20,000 in an inner-city theater. Historically, Jewish money has fallen on black politicians like manna, but no longer. Thus, Farrakhan goes unchallenged by petrified legislators who have already lost a lot with his ascension to power, and must be fearful of losing more.

There has been a schism, however in what once looked to be a unified clergy front that could have given Farrakhan the religious cover he needs. He suffered a very public rebuff by the two million-member Progressive National Baptist Convention and the 8.2 million-member National Baptist Convention headed by Henry Lyons. Jesse Jackson said publicly that Lyons supported the march, and Lyons, Jackson's former campaign manager, responded by calling his assertion "an absolute lie."

The Rev. Bennett Smith of the Progressive National Baptist Convention also declined saying, "We have difficulty marching under the banner of any other name than Jesus Christ. But this is a march originated and promoted by the Nation of Islam.

And though the buzzword "ecumenical" began to circulate as fast as Jesse Jackson could square up to a microphone, it would appear from Farrakhan's original tenets that he too might be reluctant to endorse another's banner. He may be prone to torch one if it gets in the way, as an article in the March 29 issue of his sect's newspaper, the Final Call, put it: "In this day and time, opposition to the establishment of Islam will be totally and completely destroyed."

The march even seems to be dedicated to advancing what Nation of Islamites call the Muslim Program (a program that would not make much sense to the 600 million people around the world who practice Islam in the traditional sense). When Farrakhan began heavily promoting the Million Man March last December, the Final Call reported that Arif Muhammad, the nation's mid-Atlantic minister and march coordinator, said "march plans are evolving but will emphasize points contained in the Muslim Program which range from social and economic justice to land and reparations."

Another article in the same issue said, "Minister Louis Farrakhan has stressed that the march will be unlike any other because it will bring Black men to the fore and put the 'Muslim Program', a wide-ranging plan for independence and self-determination, to America's leaders.

A close look at the Program would be enough to give pause to Smith or anyone else with even a soupcon of prudence. The highlights are laid out in every issue of the Final Call. Under a "What the Muslims Want" headline, they state: "We want our people in America whose parents or grandparents were descendants from slaves to be allowed to establish a separate state or territory of their own — either on this continent or elsewhere. We believe that our former slave masters are obligated to provide such land and that the areas must be fertile and minerally rich."

As if signing away the Great Basin isn't penance enough, here's the rider: "We believe that our former slave masters are obligated to maintain and supply our needs in this separate territory for the next 20 to 25 years."

And this: "We want freedom for all believers of Islam now held in federal prisons. We want freedom for all Black men and women now under death sentences. We want the government of the United States to exempt our people from ALL taxation as long as we are deprived of equal justice under the laws of the land."

Lest anyone think Farrakhan's ambitions are getting in the way of the old inflammatory rhetoric, there is only a slight difference between now and the greatest hits of yesteryear. Remember 1985's "It is an act of mercy to white people that we end your world" or 1988's "The Jews cannot defeat me, so I will grind them and crush them into little bits"? Well, these days his strains are a bit muted, lacking perhaps the old red-meat pithiness, but just as hateful nevertheless, with conspiratorial flow charts connecting all heinous acts to whichever Jewish financier comes to mind.

Even in a forum as mainstream as *This Week With David Brinkley*, Farrakhan offered only the most limp-wristed deflection when Sam Donaldson asked about the meaning of his comment, "Little Jews died while big Jews made money in World War II. Little Jews were being turned into soap, while big Jews washed themselves in it."

"That's an allegorical thing," Farrakhan said.

And will anyone buck up while Farrakhan surveys his troops in his mack-daddy imported silks, and realize that they are legitimizing the Tom Metzger, the George Lincoln Rockwell, the Adolf Hitler of the Maryam Mosque? Rep. Peter King says it looks doubtful: "That's why I'm critical of the Black leadership, because it's very easy when people are in poverty, are living in dire circumstances, to fall prey to demagogues and that's what Farrakhan obviously is. And that's when it's most incumbent upon responsible leaders to step in say, this (is) not the way to go — this guy is dangerous, this guy is wrong, this guy is evil. But they seem afraid to do it."

Gaddafi, Farrakhan Seek To Influence U.S. Election

Dateline, Cairo January 26, 1996, News Services

Tripoli, Libya — Libyan dictator Moammar Gaddafi this week pledged $1 billion to influence American minorities in this year's presidential election.

The pledge was made in the course of a visit to Libya by Nation of Islam leader Louis Farrakhan, according to JANA, the Libyan government news agency.

JANA reported that the two agreed to "mobilize the oppressed minorities" — particularly blacks, Muslims and Native Americans "to play a significant role in American political life."

"Our confrontation with America used to be like confronting a fortress from outside," JANA quoted Gaddafi as saying. "Today we have found a loophole to enter the fortress and to confront it from within."

According to JANA, Farrakhan replied, "I have met my brother, Col. Moammar Gaddafi, for the sake of unifying Arabs, Muslims, blacks and oppressed communities in America to play a strong, significant role not only in the American elections, but in American foreign policy."

After visiting the ruins of Gaddafi's house that was destroyed in an American air raid on Tripoli in 1986, which came in retaliation for Libya's alleged involvement in a bombing at a German nightclub frequented by U.S. Marines, Farrakhan wrote in the visitors' book "I implore God to punish our enemies hundreds of times, just as they did to us and against you," JANA said.

Chapter Nineteen

Testimony Of A Martyr — Rashad Khalifa

May 7, 1996

One of the unusual phenomena that has accompanied me during the year and a half as I published the first four printings of this book has been the remarkable outpouring of testimonies by Jews and Christians who hear my message and feel compelled to relate similar experiences and revelations.

On March 17th, 1996, I appeared on a Christian radio program in Kansas City, Kansas. My interviewer mentioned that I would be speaking at a church that night in Lee's Summit, Missouri. The phone rang, and a gentleman asked exactly where so that he could attend.

After the church service that night, the gentleman approached me and invited me to lunch the next day. At lunch, he told me that his name was Charles Sands II and that he had lived for a number of years in Tucson, Arizona. He related to me the unbelievable story of a good man, a Moslem man of God who had been murdered by fellow Moslems because of his beliefs! Since I had planned to drive across the country with a stop in Phoenix, I decided to investigate this matter.

I first called the Arizona Daily Star. They confirmed they had a whole file on Rashad Khalifa, the murdered Moslem. They photocopied 26 pages of material spanning eighteen years. According to the Arizona Daily Star of Saturday, July 8th, 1978, Khalifa was born in 1936 in Tanta, Egypt and came to Tucson in 1958 to study at the University of Arizona. He received his doctorate in biochemistry from the University of California where he taught for two years before spending six years in industrial research.

In 1976, he served as science adviser to President Muammar Qaddafi of Libya, and in 1978 served as a technical expert for the United Nations Industrial Development Organization.

Khalifa was married to Stephanie, a native Tucsonan, and their two children are a son named Sammy and a daughter named Zeinab.

Khalifa taught Arabic at the mosque located on 739 E. 6th Street in Tucson. He related in the 1978 article that a 1976 discovery by computer scientists offered the world tangible proof that the Koran is divine scripture. In addition, he said, the Koran was a pioneering document in guaranteeing women equal rights.

In inheritance matters the text grants women "a determinate share" of material goods, he said. It permits women to divorce men, and it guarantees alimony payments to women who are divorced.

Then on Saturday, February 5th, 1983, another article appeared in the Arizona Daily Star by a reporter, Judith P. Smith:

"At the beginning of 29 of the 114 chapters of the Koran, the Moslem holy scriptures, letters appear. They appear to be abbreviations, but their meaning has remained unknown for 1,400 years.

Now, Rashad Khalifa, the imam or minister of the Mosque of Tucson, believes he has cracked the mysterious code.

The letters, Khalifa said, are part of a mathematical formula proving that the Koran is divine scripture and that it has been perfectly preserved.

The key to the formula is the number 19, which means "God is One," Khalifa said.

He explained that before the invention of numbers, people used the alphabet to express numbers. Using this system, Khalifa assigned a numerical value of one to ten to the first ten letters in the Arabic alphabet, then added up the numbers represented by the letters in the Arabic word for one.

The four characters, with their values of six, one, eight and four, equal 19, which symbolizes the message of the Koran, Khalifa said.

"The theme of Koran is that we shall worship one God, the one God alone, and never idolize anyone or anything else. The whole message of Koran centers around the one God, and it was discovered that 19 equals one."

Khalifa confirmed his theory about the number 19 after he completed a computer analysis of the Koran, word by word, over a ten year period, and saw consistent numerical patterns in the words and letters.

He found, for example, that the opening statement of the Koran, which says "In the name of God, most gracious, most merciful," in English, has 19 letters in the Arabic language.

Also, that the first word in the opening statement occurs in the Koran 19 times; the second word, "Allah" in Arabic, occurs 2,698 times, or a multiple of 19 (19 x 142); the third word, "Rahman," occurs 57 times, or 19 x 3, and the fourth word, "Rahim," is mentioned 114 times or 19 x 6.

Khalifa's analysis of the puzzling lettered chapters (some start with just the letter "Q," and others have up to five letters before the main text) yielded even more multiples of 19:

In both chapters 42 and 50, which are each titled "Q," for example, there are 57 Q's or 19 x 3.

These two chapters, which have 57 Q's each contain a total of 114 Q's which equals the number of chapters in the Koran. (Khalifa used the traditional Moslem spelling of Quran for the scriptures, which is important because the Q is one of the keys to the mathematical formula.)

Chapter 68 is initialed with the letter "N", and there are 133 N's, or 19 x 7.

Khalifa has written a book about these and his many other examples called: "Quran: Visual Presentation of the Miracle." He also finished a book for skeptics, in which he showed the location of all the key letters in the Arabic version of the Koran so doubters can count for themselves. The book is available from Islamic Productions, 739 E. Sixth St., Tucson 85719.

Khalifa's computer project grew out of his other work with the Koran, a translation that he says is the first by someone whose mother tongue is Arabic.

Khalifa, a chemist who heads the pesticide reside section of the state chemist's office, began his translation work more than a decade ago when he was living in St. Louis. "I decided I would not move from one verse until I understood it perfectly," he said. "I worked on the first chapter for a week, and the second, which begins with the letters "ALM", for four years. I looked up all the books and found that no one knew what the letters meant."

"I then started with the shorter verses of the chapter to see if there was a consistent pattern of the use of the letters ALM, and then programmed the computer to count the letters. I was curious about them, like an average Moslem," he said.

But what he found almost knocked his socks off. "The mathematical relationship of all these letters proves that the Koran cannot be human made," he said. "This is the first physical evidence for God, and it may take several generations to be appreciated. This marks a new era in religion. You don't need to have faith anymore."

The completeness of the mathematical code also proves, Khalifa said, that the Koran is the inspired word of God. "God pledges, in Chapter 15, that he will keep every letter: 'Surely we sent down this message, and surely, we will preserve it.' The whole system collapses if one word is changed."

Khalifa also has studied the possibility that another book like the Koran, with its exacting numerical code, could be written.

"The Koran is the highest standard in literary excellence," he said. "The odds are one in 63 octillion that another book could be written like this."

Khalifa said there are many skeptics about his work, and he believes Satan is trying to block any news about the code because of its "scientific proof" that God exists.

There is no "central office" in the Moslem faith to promote his work, so he is relying on word of mouth to publicize it.

The Koran, he said, is similar to the Bible in some parts, and he and other Moslems believe it was sent by God through Mohammed during the period 610 AD to 632 AD as a "final edition" of the Bible.

"We believe that the source of the Bible and Koran is the same. The Koran came down at a stage of human development where the message was finalized."

The Koran "puts everything in perspective — who we are, where we are going and why we are here," Khalifa said.

Much like the Bible, it has rules for living, a description of the time when the world will end, information about heaven and hell, and stories of people like Moses and Abraham.

"It answers our most burning questions," Khalifa said.

The third and final article prior to the murder of Rashad Khalifa appeared in the Arizona Daily Star on Tuesday, February 21st, 1989, with the famous Salman Rushdie affair:

"2 City Moslems Say Order To Kill Rushdie Is Wrong"

"Islam is a 'peaceful religion,' and Ayatollah Ruhollah Khomeini has violated its basic tenets by commanding Moslems to kill the author of a controversial book, two Tucson Islamic leaders said yesterday.

But one of the leaders said author Salman Rushdie's novel, "The Satanic Verses," should be banned by the U.S. Government.

"Khomeini and people like him are more guilty than Rushdie," said Imam Rashad Khalifa, spiritual leader of the Mosque of Tucson, 739 E. Sixth St.

"The Koran (Moslem holy scriptures) guarantees freedom of expression," Khalifa said, "At no place in the Koran does it advocate killing a person for his beliefs.

"What you're hearing from Khomeini and others is the noisy minority. Moderate Moslems are absolutely opposed to killing."

Fundamentalist Moslems around the world have protested "The Satanic Verses" since it was published in England last year.

They maintain the fictional work blasphemes their religion by portraying the prophet Mohammed's wives as prostitutes and by suggesting that Mohammed wrote the Koran, rather than receiving it from God.

Last week, Iranian spiritual leader Khomeini proclaimed that Rushdie, a 41-year-old Indian-born British writer, and his publishers "are hereby sentenced to death."

"I call on all zealous Moslems to execute them quickly, wherever they find them, so that no one will dare to insult Islamic sanctity," Khomeini said, according to a Tehran Radio broadcast.

Iranian leaders have offered a bounty of $5.2 million for Rushdie's death.

Rushdie issued an apology Saturday for causing distress to Moslems. But Iranian officials reportedly said that the apology was not sufficient to cancel the death sentence.

Imam Muhammad Ishaq Qureshi, spiritual leader of the Yousuf Mosque at 250 W. Speedway, said that "Islam is not spread by the sword. It is a peaceful religion.

"We do not agree with the action of Ayatollah Khomeini," said Qureshi, 55, who is a native of Pakistan. "We do not like violence. He (Rushdie) should not be killed."

Qureshi emphasized, however, that Rushdie's novel "hurts the feelings of every Moslem" — and he said the U.S. Government should ban the book.

"We condemn that book very strongly," he said. "It lies about the holy prophet. He is our dear prophet, and we love him and respect him very much.

"We recommend that the book should be banned by the government in this country because it hurts the hearts of more than a billion Moslems (worldwide)."

Khalifa, 53, a chemist who came to Tucson from his native Egypt in 1959 to work at the University of Arizona, displayed a copy of Rushdie's book and said he has read it.

"I wasn't offended by it," he said.

"I thought the man was an extraordinarily gifted novelist and very knowledgeable of Islamic history," Khalifa said. "He uses language novelists use. He was doing his job as a novelist.

"Those up against the book did not read the book," he continued. "The closest it got to insulting the prophet is that prostitutes were named after the prophet's wives. It's bad taste — but nothing else."

Khalifa estimated there are about 1,000 Moslems in Tucson. He said there are three mosques in the city — the Mosque of Tucson, Yousuf Mosque and the Islamic Center, 1627 E. First St.

Efforts to reach an Islamic Center spokesman were unsuccessful yesterday.

Khalifa said it's likely that some Tucson Moslems would support Khomeini's call for the death of Rushdie.

"But the moderates outnumber the others here, hopefully," he said.

He said the best response to Khomeini's actions would be a "unified international censure of that kind of behavior. It would be great if the U.N. did something to guarantee the freedom of expression of any writer in the world."

Khalifa said he expects Rushdie to survive despite Khomeini's call for his execution. "I don't think anything will happen to him," he said.

On January 31st, 1990, Khalifa was found murdered in his mosque.

The following are a series of articles or parts of articles from the Arizona Daily Star which paint a horrifying picture of what is in store for America.

Thursday, February 1st, 1990:

"An internationally renowned and controversial Islamic leader was killed early yesterday morning in a Tucson mosque.

Imam Rashad Khalifa, 54, the founder and spiritual leader of the Masjid, or Mosque of Tucson, 739 E. Sixth St., was found "in a kitchen area" by the mosque's secretary, authorities said.

Officials said Khalifa had received death threats because of his interpretation of the Koran, the sacred book of Moslems.

Khalifa, according to friends and associates, caused anger and hatred in the Islamic community because of his interpretation of the scriptures.

And a police homicide sergeant said there is a possibility his death may be connected to political or religious problems.

FBI Involvement

The FBI was called in to help the Tucson Police Department because of the possibility Khalifa was slain because of political or religious beliefs.

Police responded to the mosque at 5:45 a.m. after a report of a shooting authorities said.

Police would not confirm if Khalifa, who once was a science adviser to Libyan leader Col. Moammar Qaddafi, was shot, or, say what type of wounds Khalifa had suffered.

Number Of Avenues

"There is a possibility that motives (for the slaying) may include political and religious problems," said homicide Sgt. Charles Armijo of the Tucson Police Department.

"There are a number of avenues we're pursuing," Armijo said. "We are not limiting ourselves to any one specific lead or area at this point."

FBI Special Agent Larry Bagley, supervisor of the Tucson office, said agents will coordinate out-of-state leads and that the agency has offered police its laboratory services.

"Khalifa is a moderate Moslem who's made interpretations of the Koran that has angered many Middle Eastern Moslems," said a law enforcement official who asked not to be identified.

"He's been a high-profile person who has received death threats in the past," the official said.

Khalifa, an imam, or spiritual leader of the mosque, made a computer analysis of the Koran and wrote books about his findings, friends and associates said.

Edip Yuksel, who was an assistant to Khalifa, said Khalifa arrived at the mosque at about 2 or 3 a.m. every day to work on his religious writings and translations of the Koran.

He said Khalifa, who founded the mosque, was well-known among Moslems because of a computer analysis of the Koran that showed a mathematical formula that Khalifa said proved the Koran is divine scripture.

Khalifa, who wrote books about his finding, also published a translation of the Koran in which he omitted two satanic verses, said a friend of Khalifa's who asked not to be identified.

Khalifa accused other Moslems of following a satanic Koran, an accusation that caused anger toward Khalifa and hatred of him, said the friend.

Khalifa also claimed to be a messenger of God, and mainstream Moslems believe that Mohammed was the last messenger, the friend said.

Khalifa continually preached that Moslems should not idolize Mohammed, Jesus Christ or saints, rather they should only worship God, said Yuksel.

Yuksel said Khalifa was "controversial from Turkey to Morocco and from Saudi Arabia to Iran."

Yukself said he was "90 percent sure" that Khalifa's slaying was the work of a religious fanatic.

"I can't believe that it would be so soon," Yuksel said. "He received a death threat a few days ago," Yuksel said of Khalifa. He did not release further information on the threat, but said police knew about it. Police would not talk about the threat.

Anned Betteridge, a University of Arizona Middle Eastern studies professor, said Khalifa wasn't a mainstream Moslem.

"He did not recognize sectarian differences. He felt that all Moslems are Moslems," said Betteridge, executive secretary of the Middle East Association of North America.

"We're all sorry about his death," Yuksel said. "We believe in the resurrection. We believe he went to heaven."

Khalifa, in 1976 was a science adviser to Muammar Qaddafi, and later was imprisoned by the Libyan leader said Yuksel. Yuksel said some of Khalifa's friends were executed and that Khalifa was released from prison.

The next day, February 2nd, 1990, the Arizona Daily Star gave the following report:

"A homicide detective said yesterday that police are "leaning toward the possibility" that the slaying of Islamic leader Rashad Khalifa was a religious assassination.

Khalifa, founder and spiritual leader of the Masjid, or Mosque, of Tucson was stabbed numerous times, and a .22 caliber gun was found under his body Wednesday, officials said.

"We're leaning toward the possibility that it may have been a religious assassination," said homicide Sgt. Charles Armijo.

Yesterday afternoon, followers hugged each other and expressed their sorrow near where Khalifa's body was found in the mosque. Followers gathered to pray.

Before the prayers began, Abdullah Arik, assistant to Khalifa, said Khalifa began receiving threats more than 20 years ago when he began preaching that people must worship God and not Mohammed, Jesus Christ, or saints. Khalifa accused other Moslems of following a satanic Koran, an accusation that directed anger and hatred at him, said a friend.

Arik said the FBI contacted the Tucson Police Department about three days before the killing about a murder plot. Arik said the plot to kill Khalifa originated in Salt Lake City and that he believed someone was arrested. He said police warned Khalifa about the plot.

Armijo denied that police told Khalifa about a plot.

Yesterday, FBI Special Agent James Screen, of Salt Lake City, and officers of other law enforcement agencies there denied knowing about a plot to kill Khalifa.

A law enforcement official, who did not want to be identified, said that several years ago, a plot to kill Khalifa was discovered. But the plot did not originate in Salt Lake City, the official added.

The official said that "some other agencies" knew about the plot, and that the Tucson Police Department was given the information.

"It may or may not be related to what happened now," the official said. "We will be looking into it."

FBI Special Agent Larry Bagley said FBI agents will conduct out-of-state interviews on the case for the Tucson Police Department. He would not comment further.

Tucson police Lt. Anthony Daykin, community services division commander, said police are working with the FBI in gathering "intelligence on reports of (death) threats."

He said because of the possible international implications the investigation will take some time.

A month after the assassination, on March 4th, 1990 the *Arizona Daily Star* provided the following report:

Death Of A 'Messenger'—Friends And Foes Say Khalifa Was Killed Because Of His Teachings

Rashad Khalifa knew he would die soon, say his followers.

Khalifa's followers — there are an estimated 50 in Tucson, perhaps several thousand worldwide — say their leader knew why, and how, and perhaps even when, he would die. It was ordained, they say, by Allah.

And they proclaim Rashad Khalifa as Allah's messenger. They say God tells them so in the Koran, the holy book of Islam.

Khalifa's detractors — and there are many throughout the Moslem world— say he was a supreme egoist, a misguided soul who preached a silly, invented message to inflate his self-worth...

Khalifa's basic tenet was that the Koran is the only book Moslems need follow.

Anyone who properly worships the God of Abraham, be he Jew or Christian or Moslem, is blessed within the eyes of Islam, according to Khalifa's writings.

This view attracted the venom of major Islamic religious and political leaders, supporters and critics alike say.

"Rashad taught that America is blessed above all other countries, even those in the Middle East," recalled his follower Muhtesen Erisen, a local businessman. "He taught that the greatest gift of God is freedom. Because the leaders of the Middle East have taken from their people the right of free thought, thus they will face the fiercest of retribution."

The fact that Khalifa was stabbed to death in his mosque proves his death was part of Allah's plan, Khalifa's followers say.

Several important imams have been stabbed to death in their mosques, they point out, since Islam was founded by the Prophet Mohammed, who died in AD 632.

In his March 1990 newsletter, published in January (seven months before Iraq's invasion of Kuwait — Victor Mordecai's interjection)— evidence, some of his followers say, that Khalifa knew his end was near — he detailed precisely how he believed Allah would punish the Middle East for failing to heed God's message.

Khalifa included a story from the Arizona Daily Star outlining a University of Arizona space scientist's theories about a massive comet or asteroid strike generally believed to have devastated the Earth 65 million years ago.

Khalifa predicted another such cataclysm would befall the Earth this year, with Allah directing the main impact to occur in the Middle East.

Khalifa's newsletter, in the style of many such Islamic publications, are full of dramatic pronouncements of doom for Middle Eastern political and religious leaders.

While Khalifa was a tenaciously devout Moslem, according to his followers, he did not accept Islamic traditions and doctrines common in his Egyptian homeland and throughout the Middle East.

Because these all-but-inviolate traditions are handed down from father to son in the Islamic world, Khalifa apparently felt it necessary at some point in his spiritual development to renounce his father, according to one follower. "He referred to his father as his ex-father."

Computer Study Of Koran

Khalifa's initial notoriety was due to the fact that between 1968 and 1981, using a computer to study the original Arabic Koran, he developed what he maintained was cold, clear mathematical proof that the scriptures were written by God.

According to critics and supporters, the discovery at first was well accepted throughout the Moslem world, where it was taught briefly in some religious universities. It even merited a passing mention in that bastion of logical Western thinking, Scientific American. However, with the publication of his second major work, "Koran, Hadith, and Islam," in 1982, Khalifa became more controversial among Moslem faithful.

Khalifa strongly rejected "hadith," generally defined as that body of Moslem writing that details the early practices of the Prophet Mohammed. He wrote and published a book slamming hadith.

The book was "slanderous," according to Ihsan Bagby, acting secretary general of the Islamic Society of North America, which claims about 50,000 members in the U.S. and Canada.

Slanderous Beliefs

"Khalifa denigrated the prophet, and he denigrated the beliefs of Moslems in general," Bagby said, adding such an act alone "would have been enough to endanger his life from somebody fanatical enough to respond to his slanderous beliefs."

"Most hadiths of Mohammed are nothing but fabrications," a Khalifa follower said. "They purport to tell us how Mohammed entered his house, how he slept in bed, whether on the right side or the left, even how often he slept with his wife. And Rashad pointed out that the Koran had nothing to do with these fabrications. He pointed out that Mohammed himself said there is only one book, and that is the Koran."

Hadith arose, the follower said, because various political and religious leaders within Islam sought to carve out personal power bases.

"Look at what Moslems do now," he said. "The whole religion is different than what Mohammed taught. Look at Khomeini in Iran — people falling all over his body. The Koran teaches the body isn't important."

If his attack on hadith earned him enemies in high places, Khalifa's subsequent attempts to prove mathematically that two of the Koranic verses were "satanic," or not authored by God, earned him even more condemnation.

"The verses were added within probably 40 years of Mohammed's death," a follower said. "Real Moslems knew these two verses were questionable, but the majority did not know. Rashad wrote a story about it.

It angered the fanatics and threatened their imams with loss of face, he said.

Working For Israelis

"In Egypt someone wrote Rashad is working for the Israelis," he said. "They arrested some of his followers in Egypt."

The final straw, according to Bagby, came about one and a half years ago, when Khalifa claimed in his newsletter to be a messenger of God mentioned in the Koran.

"This enraged many people," Bagby said. "None of us have any sympathy for what he was doing. Recently he even claimed to have ascended into heaven and to have walked in heaven. Obviously somebody took it in his own hands to stop him."

Khalifa's followers say the Koran defines a messenger as one who comes after a great prophet, such as Moses, Jesus or Mohammed. A prophet gives his people a book containing God's word, they say, while a messenger merely purifies that message, blowing away the impurities put there over the centuries by impure human beings.

Translated Koran

Khalifa, they add, never made up things, but based all that he said on the Koran alone. He was the first native speaker of Arabic — the language in which the Koran was written — to translate the book into English, his followers add. They praise the work for its clarity and simplicity. Critics say they haven't read it.

Who was Rashad Khalifa?

"He was very gentle, most kind, super-good to children, super-nice to his wife," Erisen said. "He was kind to everybody, kind to strangers. Words cannot describe his kindness. He had no ego."

The record shows Khalifa was born in a small village in Egypt.

As he was later to reject hadith, he reportedly rejected the teaching of his father, whom followers have heard him describe as a Sufi master. Sufism, the mystical form of Islam, teaches that ultimately there is no reality but God.

After coming to the U.S. in 1959, Khalifa received a doctorate in biochemistry from the University of California at Riverside in 1961 and married Phoenix native, Stephanie E. Hoefle, in Tucson in January 1963. Khalifa's followers say she is not Moslem — a fact that Moslem critics seized upon as evidence that he did not properly observe the religion.

In 1976, Khalifa served as a science adviser to Libyan strong man Col. Moammar Qaddafi, whose government imprisoned Khalifa briefly.

Khalifa's "Dark Side"

More recently, Khalifa was involved in a dispute that some say shows he had a dark side.

Linda Abib, a 27-year-old mother, said she thought Khalifa was a kind and considerate man when she and her husband began renting one of his apartments next to the mosque in 1988.

But she and her 3-year-old son recently left Khalifa's sect and went into hiding.

Abib won a court order of protection from her husband, but said in a recent interview that she fears "not only a violent husband, but a violent religious cult. That's what he (Khalifa) was running."

His followers deny the accusation. Their religion is one of peace and love, they maintain.

Abib said Khalifa endorsed the beating of disobedient wives — something Khalifa's followers deny. (Interjection by Victor Mordecai: In verse 34 of Sura IV of the Koran entitled "Women" men are commanded to beat disobedient wives. See page viii in Introduction to this book.)

Concluding this article, Erisen said: "They think they killed him, but they were only messing with his body. They did the same thing to Jesus. They thought they were crucifying Jesus, but his soul was with God."

Second Article From *The Arizona Daily Star*, 4 March 1990

LONE ASSASSIN — KILLING WASN'T THE WORK OF ANY GROUP, ISLAMIC SCHOLAR SAYS

It is doubtful that any organized Islamic faction such as the shadowy Moslem Brotherhood was responsible for Rashad Khalifa's murder, a leading Islamic scholar says.

Secretive, and organized by "cells" so its ultimate leaders are protected, it was the Moslem Brotherhood that engineered the 1981 assassination of Egyptian President Anwar Sadat for his peace-making overtures to Israel, according to some authorities.

The Brotherhood was formed in Egypt in the 1920's and has an estimated 1,000 members in the U.S..

But Mohammed T. Mehdi, spokesman for the National Council on Islamic Affairs, based in New York City, says he believes Khalifa's murder was more than likely the act of an individual.

"The stupid person who did this will give him (Khalifa) more credit," Mehdi says. "Over time he could become a martyr, even if he was not able to obtain any meaningful standing within the Islamic world during his lifetime."

Mehdi has written extensively about Sirhan Sirhan, the Palestinian born assassin of Robert Kennedy. He recently completed a book attacking the Ayatollah Ruhollah Khomeini's call for the death of "Satanic Verses" author Salman Rushdie.

Mehdi says Moslems should have ignored Rushdie, Khalifa and other critics of Islam.

Death sentences and assassinations give undue publicity to their victims' views, says Mehdi, who describes himself as a moderate Moslem troubled by the intolerance and fanaticism that has gripped the Middle East.

Although Khalifa's murder may have been horrible — and rendered even more repulsive because it occurred on American soil, where freedom of speech and religion are guaranteed to all under the First Amendment to the U.S. Constitution — Mehdi pleads for understanding on the part of Tucsonians in particular and Christian Americans in general.

"Intolerance and violence have played their part in Christianity, too," Mehdi points out.

He notes that such deplorable behavior did not begin to abate in the West until well after Europe entered its modern era with the Renaissance, 400 years ago. Mehdi marks the start of Arab modernism with World War I.

"American Moslems are the most fortunate Moslems in the world, because here we have the freedom to think, to reevaluate our traditions and to judge their validity," Mehdi says. "And when we put our act together, Moslems here can lead Moslems in the old country into the 21st century."

Third Article In *The Arizona Daily Star* Dated March 4th, 1990

"MATHEMATICAL STUDY USED TO SHOW 'MIRACLE OF THE KORAN'"

Rashad Khalifa preached what he called the "miracle of the Koran," which he maintained, is evident in the first verse of the scripture holy to Moslems.

Khalifa applied the rigors of computer analysis to the Koran to discover his "miracle."

He maintained that the first verse contains exactly 19 letters in Arabic, the language in which the Koran was written 1,400 years ago and is still spoken today...

He said he believed God placed the 19 based code in the Koran not only to reveal His presence, but to thwart those who would add unauthorized verses. Khalifa claimed to have found two such verses both, he said, erroneously glorifying Mohammed, Islam's prophet, rather than God alone.

Police Seek Leads In Khalifa Murder Case
Wednesday, June 20, 1990

Tucson Police are seeking information on the murder of a 54-year-old Moslem religious leader here January 31st.

A secretary going to early morning prayers discovered the bloody body of Rashad Khalifa in the kitchen area of his mosque. A handgun, which Khalifa carried for protection, was found under his body.

It appeared he had been stabbed to death, investigators said at the time.

Tucson police and the FBI have not eliminated other possibilities, but they say it is most likely Khalifa was murdered because of his religious beliefs. He was the leader of a religious group with an estimated 50 followers in Tucson and perhaps several thousand worldwide, authorities said.

Khalifa's followers said he preached ideas distasteful to fundamentalist Moslems, such as that a Jew who worships his God correctly is a righteous person according to the Koran, the holy book of Islam.

They said Khalifa also believed that the Koran contained a "satanic verse," which he said was put there by clerics intent on glorifying Mohammed, the prophet of Islam, at the expense of God who, Khalifa maintained, should be humankind's sole object of veneration.

Tucson Mosque Slaying May Be Linked To Sect
The Arizona Daily Star, **Monday, October 12, 1992**

Colorado authorities are investigating a possible link between an Islamic fundamentalist sect and the slaying of an internationally renowned Islamic leader here more than two years ago.

Officers raided a 101-acre compound owned by the sect in Colorado last week, seizing attack weapons. In other raids, four men were arrested.

The compound had been used for military training, an investigator said.

Law enforcement authorities say they may have evidence that could implicate members of the FUQRA sect in the January 31st, 1990, stabbing death of the controversial leader Rashad Khalifa, the Rocky Mountain News reported yesterday.

"We have been aware of the possibility of the FUQRA involvement in the homicide shortly after the incident," said homicide Sgt. Charles Armijo of the Tucson Police Department.

"We are currently unaware of what's happened in Colorado, although we have been working with the FBI since the homicide occurred," he said.

"We will be in contact with the FBI and Colorado authorities to see what they have retrieved and what information they have implicating FUQRA in the homicide," he added.

"We are not aware of any FUQRA activity in this state apart from one incident with Khalifa," he said.

Armijo confirmed that not much is known about the group, whose members law enforcement authorities have tied to terrorist activities.

Joe Reyes, head of the FBI's Tucson office, said yesterday that he is unable to comment on the Colorado investigation or give any details of the case.

Sheriff George Chavez of Chaffee County, Colorado, said the group apparently is made up of Black Muslims who were all born in the U.S..

Chavez added that other law enforcement officials said some of FUQRA's activities may be bankrolled by people in Pakistan and Afghanistan.

The organization was said to be responsible for a 1983 bombing of a Portland, Ore., hotel owned by followers of Indian guru Bhagwan Shree Rajneesh. A man with ties to FUQRA was convicted in the case, according to a Rocky Mountain News article.

The raid at the compound last Thursday occurred after a year long investigation into the bilking of $355,000 from the state worker's compensation fund, Chavez said, noting that the FBI had initially contacted Colorado officials about a possible problem with FUQRA.

He said five men were indicted on federal racketeering charges related to the bilking. They are Chris Childs, James D. Williams, Vicente Rafael Pierre, James L. Upshur and Edward Ivan McGhee, he said.

Four are in custody, and authorities are searching for the fifth, Chavez said.

They were arrested during raids at homes in Colorado Springs and a home in Lycoming County, Pennsylvania, Chavez said.

No ages or hometowns of the men were available yesterday.

About 60 federal, state and local law enforcement authorities took part in the raid at the compound, which is near Trout Creek Pass, a rugged and remote area in the Pike National Forest.

The compound is near the town of Buena Vista, about 70 miles west of Colorado Springs.

Police seized attack weapons, including AK-47s, M-16s, and M-14s, at the compound. Officers also found 21 children and three adults there.

The land was purchased by the sect, which had been at the compound for four years, said Chavez. He said his officers had been watching the compound for about two years.

"We've been monitoring them and have been concerned about stolen weapons and ammunition. Our main concern is the safety and security of our county," Chavez said.

He said investigators gathered information that about 30 people, both men and women, underwent military training at the compound, including the handling of weapons and hand-to-hand combat.

He said the children attended school on the compound, which also has a chapel, a mobile home and two houses.

The root word of FUQRA, according to the Arabic dictionary, means a "military unit or established unit deployed to terrorize or frighten people," said Abdullah Arik, who was Khalifa's assistant and who became the mosque's director after Khalifa's death.

Worshipers at Khalifa's mosque have tried to carry on normally since his death, but even two years later, death threats are still left on the mosque's answering machine, Arik said.

Seven Charged In Conspiracy
To Murder Tucson Islamic Leader

The Arizona Daily Star — Sunday, April 11th, 1993

Seven Islamic fundamentalists are charged with conspiracy to murder a renowned Islamic leader killed in Tucson, but authorities still don't know the identity of the cleric's slayer.

Rashad Khalifa, 54, the founder and spiritual leader of the Masjid of Tucson, was killed three years ago but the case remains unsolved, said Tucson Police homicide Sgt. Charles Armijo.

Seven members of the FUQRA sect from Colorado were charged in the murder conspiracy in February, Armijo said.

Members of FUQRA, a group of Black Muslims who were born in the U.S., have been tied to terrorist activities, law enforcement authorities say.

On Feb. 19, Colorado authorities charged James D. Williams and Edward N.L. Flinton with conspiracy to murder, accusing them of masterminding the plot to kill Khalifa, said Assistant State Attorney General Doug Wamsley in Denver.

Five others — Chris Childs, Curtis Baylor, Vicente Rafael Pierre, James L. Upshur and Edward Ivan McGhee — also were charged with conspiracy to murder because they knew about the plot, Wamsley said.

Flinton, Baylor and Childs remain fugitives, he said. Williams was released two weeks ago on a $35,000 bond from the El Paso County Jail in Colorado Springs, and the other three remain in jail, authorities said.

In 1989, Colorado Springs police uncovered the murder plot when they searched a storage locker in a burglary investigation. Also found in the locker were 40 pounds of explosives, said Wamsley. He said authorities told Khalifa of the plot.

Four months later, the mosque's secretary found Khalifa dead in the kitchen of the building shortly before 6:00 a.m.

Wamsley said investigators found "surveillance notes of the mosques," including details about when worshipers arrived and left. Even noted were the police patrols in the area, which were believed to be more frequent because the mosque was near the University of Arizona, he said.

Photographs of the mosque and Khalifa's followers also were found, Wamsley said. He said notes outlining the methods of murder were recovered.

The preferred method was to stab Khalifa, Wamsley said. The second choice was strangulation, the third was death by poison and the fourth was to shoot Khalifa with a silenced .22 caliber gun, he said.

Included in the notes were what to do if worshipers entered the mosque, Wamsley said. "They were to be herded off into a room and told the mosque was being robbed, and then the people were to be killed," he said.

"Fortunately, no one came in (at the time of the murder)," Wamsley said.

Follower Abdullah Arik, who was an assistant to Rashad Khalifa, said last week that he had no idea who infiltrated the mosque years ago to spy on the congregation and gather information that the killer or killers used.

"We welcome everybody with good thoughts and those who want to worship God," Arik said.

SUSPECT IN TUCSON MUSLIM LEADER'S SLAYING JUMPS BAIL

Scripps Howard News Service—Colorado Springs, Colorado

Friday, February 25, 1994

Authorities expressed little hope yesterday of soon finding an extremist who vanished before his scheduled sentencing for fraud and terrorism.

James Williams, 41, a leader of the Colorado Springs cell of the extremist group FUQRA, jumped his $50,000 bail and failed to appear before District Judge Michael Heydt Wednesday for a prison sentence of up to 96 years on four felony charges.

Assistant Attorney General Doug Wamsley confided that authorities have no idea were Williams might be and have had little success finding other FUQRA members who have gone into hiding.

"I'm confident there are other FUQRA groups throughout the country, and I'm just as confident that if he (Williams) sought their help, he would receive it," Wamsley said.

Despite his convictions and a record of travel outside the country, Williams was allowed by Heydt to remain free on $50,000 bond until his sentencing.

Williams had even traveled at least once to Pakistan.

My readers will excuse me for including so many articles from the Arizona Daily Star and have shown great patience in reading this all.

Please allow me to relate a story I have heard numerous times from many Jews who originate from Islamic lands.

The question is asked: "Who wrote the Koran?" There is a Jewish tradition that says that the Bedouin Mohammedans were illiterate and needed someone literate, a man of God, to write them a holy book. And so, the story goes, they kidnapped a great rabbi of Babylon, where the Talmud was concurrently being compiled.

This rabbi was placed in a deep pit and commanded by the successors of Mohammed to write them a holy book, or else he would be executed. They promised to free him upon completion of the book.

And so the rabbi, an expert in the legalisms and gematrias of Talmudic Judaism set to work to put together a book for these Mohammedans, after which he would be set free. However, when the book was completed, instead of receiving his freedom, the Mohammedan leaders commanded the women of the tribe to throw stones into the pit because there was a devil in the pit. So they double-crossed the rabbi and killed him in spite of their promise.

The Jewish traditional story continues that the rabbi, who wrote the Koran under great duress, obviously, and wanting to remain loyal to God, placed all kinds of loopholes that would make any sophisticated reader of the Koran find inconsistencies and satanic verses just as Rashad Khalifa did. However, for 1400 years, and until the invention of the computer, there was no one interested enough or sophisticated enough to reveal the great fraud known as the Koran.

Rashad Khalifa died a martyr even though for the wrong reasons. The letters "ALM" which appear at the beginnings of many of the Koran's chapters, and which no Moslems understand, are purported to be abbreviations for Alif, Lam, Mim in Arabic, or Alef, Lamed, Mem in Hebrew. Jewish tradition has it that the rabbi included these abbreviations to mean Ani Lo Ma'amin, which translated means: "I don't believe," something kidnapped people try to weave in to their messages when their captors force them to make statements contrary to the truth.

As for Khalifa's being overwhelmed with the repetition of the number 19 in many sequences, this expertise in numbers is a tradition in rabbinical circles. Any rabbi worth his salt can put together acrostics and other texts full of numerical coincidences. The Jewish prayers said thrice daily, include a special Amidah prayer comprised of 19 benedictions. The Moslems believe in the lunar year; the Christians in the solar year. The Jews believe in the solar-lunar cycle of 19 years.

Khalifa says that the rules of 19 are broken when the two satanic verses are included, so the Koran was touched by man at some stage, and even Khalifa said that the whole book collapses when tampered with. And so he was assassinated, probably by Black Muslims, taking their orders from one or more Islamic powers in the Middle East. Remember, that in Addenda I, Qaddafi pledges one billion dollars to Louis Farrakhan. Is it not logical that the latter would provide foot soldiers to the former so that he could confront the fortress of America from within?

Is it not satanic that the Koran commands Moslem Believers not to take a Jew or a Christian for a friend? (Sura V) Is it not satanic for the Koran to command: "Thou shall not kill any man whom God has not deemed that you should kill, except for a just cause!" Are the Koran believing Moslems so unsophisticated as to swallow this hook, line and sinker?

Is it not satanic for men to be commanded to beat their women if they fear disobedience?

Is it not satanic for the Hadith to call for the total annihilation of all the Jews on judgment day, especially because the Messiah is a Jew?

If the Koran is a rabbinic fabrication, what does that make Islam, which is based on the Koran?

There is only one book, and that is the Bible. There is only one God, the God of Abraham, Isaac and Jacob, and not the moon god of Allah. This is what the final battle and the day of judgement will be all about.

Conclusions

In writing this book, I have utilized forty-eight years of life experiences, including twenty-seven years of shared insights with my Egyptian-born wife, five years of translating from Islamic texts and press, five years of intensive M.A. theological studies involving Judaism, Christianity and Islam, and finally, forty-eight years of finally coming to appreciate the greatness of western civilization and democracy in general, and the United States of America in particular.

Much is at stake during the coming years. People think that with the demise of Nazism and Communism, all is well. I believe the greatest challenge is yet to come. Again, just as individual Germans are not to be blamed for the terrible deeds of Adolf Hitler, nor are Russians to be blamed for the excesses of Communism, so too are individual Moslems in their vast majority not to be blamed for the demonic and evil strategies of radical fanatic Islam — whether it be based in Iran, Iraq, Afghanistan, Pakistan, Syria, Sudan, Libya or anywhere else for that matter.

My belief is that the greatest enemy of all of us is ignorance. If Christians, Jews, and Moslems would all try to work together in brotherhood, study together, pray together and reason together, maybe things would be different. However, unlike in Christianity and Judaism, where there are differences of opinion even among the more devout, in radical Islam there can be no toleration of the infidel. The term "infidel" includes Moslems who are not loyal and obedient to the most radical and hateful Islamic extremists and willing to be used as tools by these extremists.

Steven Emerson shows explicit videotapes of people such as Sheikh Faez Azzam, who says: "Allah's religion, may He be praised, must offer scalps; must offer martyrs; blood must flow; there must be widows; there must be orphans; hands and limbs must be cut; limbs and blood must be spread everywhere so that Allah's religion may stand on its feet." (From a speech given in Atlanta 1990 from Emerson's film documentary "Jihad in America").

The vast majority of Moslems in the U.S. as well as throughout the world do not subscribe to such statements. However, due to Iran's global aims that the 21st century will be the century of Islam, more and more Moslems are joining or are being forced to join this Jihad in America, as well as Jihad in Israel, as well as Jihad worldwide.

This problem will not go away by itself, but will only grow if left untreated. It is incumbent on humanity to wake up to this global threat in order to save what we all cherish: our freedom and our civilization.

Since the initial writing of this book in the summer of 1994, several new factors came into play which have a direct bearing on the overall thrust of what I perceive as being the radical Islamic threat to the U.S., to Israel, and to the whole world, including the vast majority of Moslems who are not a part of the radical-fanatic fringe.

In the last week of July, 1994, I received a parcel containing various Israeli newspapers of that same month which had accumulated at my home in Jerusalem.

In the July 15 edition of *The Jerusalem Post*, on an inside page there appeared a small report taken off the international wire service about big time counterfeiting of U.S. dollars by both Iran and its erstwhile enemy, Iraq. It appears that senior officials at the Department of the Treasury in Washington had been bribed by the Iranians and had sold to the Iranians all the equipment, techniques, chemicals, and paper to print the perfect counterfeit $100.00 bill.

Since the Iranians had plenty of income from oil, they did not need counterfeit dollars. The purpose of the illegal printing was solely to sabotage the economy of the "Great Satan," the U.S.A.

On the other hand, Iraq, suffering from the economic embargo placed on it by the world community, did need dollars, and so the report continues, the Iranians advised the Iraqis about whom to bribe in Washington, and so now the Iraqis, too, are in the big-time counterfeiting business — the more the merrier, — also for the dollars, also to do in the "Great Satan".

Then, on July 22, another small report appeared again in Israel's English language newspaper, *The Jerusalem Post*, again off international wire service to the effect that President Clinton had just signed an order calling for the preparation of a new U.S. currency which would replace the present U.S. banknotes. The portraits of the presidents would be 50% larger, and holograms would be included to make counterfeiting more difficult. The report stated that this currency would replace the old currency by 1996. And now, the $100 notes have indeed been replaced.

On July 29, 1994, a week later, on the way to LaGuardia Airport to catch a flight to Orlando, I stopped off at a local newspaper stand to pick up the Friday editions in Hebrew of the Israeli newspapers Yediot Ahronot and Ma'ariv. On the second page of the second section of Yediot Ahronot appeared a small article about a sting operation of the FBI which was reported to have taken place in Orlando, Florida, just a few days before. It seems an Iranian national and a British national were caught by the FBI trying to acquire sixty Stinger anti-aircraft missiles.

Now, a few things bothered me about this piece of information. Firstly, it is a known fact that about 300 Stinger missiles are still unaccounted for from the Afghanistan War.

For all those who may not know or who do not remember the Afghanistan War, it was a war in which the Soviet Union more or less was trying to ensure that Afghanistan, which was not part of the Soviet bloc would now become such a part. The U.S. and the West, of course, as part of this cold-war scenario supported the Mujahideen Islamic rebels in their battle to expel the Russians from Afghanistan.

The purpose of this book is not to relate the history of the Afghanistan war or even a small part, but merely to say that the Stinger missile was what wreaked havoc on Soviet air communications and supplies in that mountainous country, and in the end made the Russians realize how costly and hopeless their expedition had become. From the top line MI-24 helicopters to the heavy Antonov transports, no Soviet aircraft was immune to the Stinger missiles.

The bottom line was, the Russians pulled out of Afghanistan and 300 Stinger missiles remained in the hands of the various fighting factions in that land. I vaguely remember an article which appeared a few years ago in some newspaper, probably *The Jerusalem Post,* about a fierce competition between the CIA and the Iranian SAVAK to buy up these 300 Stinger missiles, but considering the objective and subjective conditions in the field, the Iranians were most likely to get their hands first on these Stingers.

And so, returning to Orlando, we see the long Iranian hand trying to acquire more Stinger missiles. The question is, why?

As I spoke in an Orlando church later that week, I asked congregants and visitors who had come to hear me speak, exactly that question. I spoke about the counterfeiting of U.S. dollars as a way to destroy the economy of the "Great Satan" as the U.S. is called by Iran. But another way to destroy the American economy is by paralyzing national and international civil aviation.

Indeed, if the Stinger could chase the Russians out of Afghanistan, so too could the Stinger make the takeoff or landing of a jumbo civilian aircraft impossible — of any jumbo, of any airline, of any country.

And if the Iranians are actively acquiring U.S. made Stingers, how much easier would it be for them to acquire Russian made SAMs or Strellas?

If the deaths of 100 Argentinian Jews in the bombing of the Jewish Center in Buenos Aires in the summer of 1994 was a terrible shocker, then how much more so would the deaths of 450 innocent passengers in an American airline at any airport of the world?

A Jewish gentleman who had come to the church to hear me that night got up and was very visibly upset. He said to me that his Congressman, Representative Bill McCollum of the Orlando district, had said the very same things about counterfeit dollars and about Stinger missiles being a danger to civil aviation, but he had said these things four years before — in 1990!

The Jewish man said that people could not believe Rep. McCollum, who, by the way, was/is at the forefront of the Congressional Task Force Against Terrorism. People thought four years ago that such reports were fanciful, to say the least.

Now, four years later, I was repeating the very same things that Rep. McCollum said. The rhetorical question this Jewish man asked then was that if this was the case, wasn't anything being done? Secondly, if this was the case, didn't the people have a right to know? My answer was: well, thank CNN for O.J. Simpson, because that's all you will get in your news. There is a conspiracy of silence by the media in all matters concerning Iran or Islam. By the way, one pastor who heard me that night in church had heard something on a local Christian radio station about the FBI sting operation. Nobody else, though, had heard a thing.

In November, 1994, on a new lecture circuit, I visited and spoke in a wonderful church in Brownsville, Texas. After I had spoken, the pastor and his wife and a few wonderful couples took me out to a local restaurant for dinner. One of the ladies then revealed a startling tidbit of information for me: her son had been a green beret and before, during, and after Operation Desert Shield and Desert Storm, her son's unit had contingency plans for a terrorist infiltration into the U.S. from across the border in the Mexican regions straddling the border — especially in the vicinity of the city of Matamoros, just across from Brownsville. The expected terrorist infiltration was not of Mexicans, but of Islamic radical terrorists taking advantage of the lax entry and exit rules into and out of the United States.

By the way, just an update, when I visited this same church again in August 1997, I thanked the congregation for providing me with the above tidbit of information. After I spoke, three congregants came up to me and provided me with three more testimonies:

The first testimony was of a deputy sheriff who was on patrol with his sheriff at 4:00 AM sometime during Israel's Peace in the Galilee Operation in Lebanon (1982-83). The police officer said they received an urgent call for assistance from another squad car on patrol not far away. When the sheriff and deputy arrived at the scene, they found a pickup truck heavily loaded and sagging virtually to the ground. After the six illegal infiltrators, who were wet from having swum across the Rio Grande River at Boca Chica, were handcuffed, the local policemen unloaded the pickup and found dozens of assault rifles, "plastique" dynamite, and other weapons. These were not Mexicans or Latins, but Islamic terrorists. The

ATF was immediately called in, swooped up the suspects and their vehicle to Houston and promptly shredded the local law enforcements reports. The local policeman said the ATF told him "This never happened. Forget it." And he did until he heard me speak at the church.

The second testimony was of a health inspection official. She said they had just had a seminar on the need to look out for anthrax, botulism and bubonic plague as well as a list of another twenty unpleasant maladies. When she said to the directors of this seminar that all these things had been eradicated in Texas decades ago, they answered her: "Well, look for it now. It's back." It's just that she did not know the reason why these plagues were back. After my speech at the church, she knew why.

The third testimony involved the Casa Romero detention facility for illegal aliens entering the U.S.. Many of the detainees there are Moslems — again, not Mexicans or Latin Americans.

In October 1994, an Israeli correspondent, Sarah Friedman, wrote in the Hebrew daily "Maariv" about the ease with which Islamic militants cross the borders between Argentina, Brazil and Paraguay. A pattern of the international implications of the Islamic conspiracy was becoming clearer.

Further, to what I discussed in Chapter VII, about the hit squads sent by Iran into Europe and South America, now there are entire regions in Latin America — from the tip of Argentina to the south to Mexico in the north, in which Moslems are free to roam totally free of surveillance and to deal with the enemies of Islam in any way they deem fit.

According to the article, "Four Days in the City of Terror," by Sarah Friedman, in Ma'ariv of October 7, 1994, there are three cities: Ciudad del Este in Paraguay, Foz Do Iguacu in Brazil, and Puerto Iguazu in Northern Argentina. These three cities form a triangle, commonly known as the terror triangle. Sarah Friedman spent four days in this "Hezbollahland." Thousands of Shiite Moslems originally from Lebanon and Syria now live in this region. They have terrorist training bases, weapons of all kinds, and yes, of course, drugs. Money from this region flows to Lebanon and Iran, and evidently to those responsible for the terrible blast which claimed 100 lives at the Jewish Community Center in Buenos Aires.

But I think the most interesting part of the article was when Sarah Friedman went into a gun shop in Ciudad del Este, Paraguay, and placed an order with a $150.00 down payment for assorted guns, ammunition and other accessories, and without a flinch, the gun shop owner gave her a receipt and promised her delivery within two weeks. One can buy literally anything in this triangle of terror from guns, to RPGs to dynamite. The armies and police forces of Argentina, Brazil and Paraguay, for reasons known to them, have decided not to interfere or intervene in any way in this loose and open border area of contraband and smugglers.

From my own personal knowledge, I can relate an experience my sister-in-law told me about her period as an emissary in Maracaibo, Venezuela a few years ago. She and her husband drove up to the Colombian border in an area known as Guajira, and found everyone there to be dressed up in typical Arabic dress (head to toe robe known as the galabiyah). Since my sister-in-law knows Arabic, she addressed the men she saw in Arabic, and they offered to sell her car across the border as contraband, would pay her dearly for the car, and then she could claim insurance back in Venezuela. Other illicit offers, including drugs, were made.

On my lecture circuit to Colorado Springs in September 1995, I spoke at a small home bible meeting, attended primarily by Hispanic Americans. When I discussed the Islamic threat to Latin America, one of the young ladies told me about her father who is a congressional deputy from the island of San Andreas in Colombia.

She told me that several attempts had been made on her father's life by Moslem militants. It transpires that the island, a tourist attraction, has been taken over by an "invasion" of Moslems from the Middle East who have bought up much of the real estate, especially the hotels, have fired the Christian employees and replaced them with "imported" Moslems from the Middle East who work in their place.

The lady's father is trying to defend the interests of the natives who are Colombian and Christian from the Islamic invasion of the island. Suffice it to say, the Colombian government in Bogota is closely following developments on the island of San Andreas.

Again, the purpose of this book is not to catalog terrorist smugglers or invaders in South America, merely to show that there is a problem of unsealed borders, no surveillance, and complete freedom to move about, to deal in contraband merchandise, drugs, or even arms. (By the way, an article to this effect appeared in The New York Times International edition of January 11, 1995).

I have even received reports that the Chiapas Indians, who were in rebellion against the central government in Mexico City, were receiving their arms from the Moslems — another sign that the Moslem radicals will look for diverse ways of destabilizing the U.S., Mexico, or any other "western" or "Christian" country. It was even a consideration that by the Moslems sabotaging the stability of the Mexican economy, and its currency, the peso, this would add to the woes of the U.S. economy which is a guarantor of the Mexican economy. Happily for the West, Mexico overcame its monetary problems in 1995-6 with the aid of the U.S..

In November 1994, a month after Sarah Friedman's Ma'ariv article appeared, there was a screening nationwide in the U.S., as well as worldwide (in Israel) of "Jihad in America," a documentary program by Steven Emerson, formerly of CNN. Though I saw it in San Antonio, Texas, I know from the churches in the Rio Grande Valley that it was not shown in the valley. Similarly, it was not shown in the Orlando-Titusville area of Florida, nor was it shown in the Williamsport area of Pennsylvania, nor in Tulsa, Oklahoma, all areas where I have spent much time.

It was surprising to me how many people there were in San Antonio and New York, where the program was aired, who did not see it. This movie should be aired again and again and again, until all Americans see it. It should be shown in schools, churches, synagogues, and yes, even in mosques.

Personally, I believe that Steven Emerson, whose life is now threatened by the Islamic fanatics, deserves the Congressional Medal of Honor for this film. Though I am sure he had much assistance from the CIA and FBI, as well as other official agencies in obtaining secret videotapes exposing what radical Moslems in America have planned for "The Great Satan" America, Steven Emerson remains "politically incorrect" because the "powers that be" in America do not want to run afoul of Islam in any form or the petrodollar. In fact, Steven Emerson chose to leave CNN because CNN wanted to control the editorial content of the film and Steven Emerson wanted to maintain his academic integrity.

In April 1995, a terrible bomb went off in Oklahoma City at the Murrah Federal building killing either 168 or 169 people. (The difference in the count depends on how you count a spare leg that did not belong to any of the other bodies and was probably that of the suicide bomber — John Doe II.)

By the way, in Emerson's Jihad in America videotape, FBI investigations had revealed that, in addition to blowing up the twin towers of the World Trade Center in New York City, in February 1993, fanatic Islamic long-term plans called for the blowing up of more tall, important buildings throughout the U.S.. Listen to what they're saying!

But in spite of this, with the conviction of Timothy McVeigh, the judge considered the involvement of "international" (read: Islamic) terrorists as "wild imagination." (Don't confuse me with the facts, my mind is made up!)

Here are some facts about the Oklahoma City bombing:

1. Warnings had been received from the Middle East prior to the bombing. (From article by Haim Shibi — "Yediot Ahronot" Israeli Hebrew daily page 2 — April 20th, 1995)

2. The fertilizer salesman sold the fertilizers that were used in the bombmakings to three Middle Eastern Moslem men. The fertilizers were packed in 80-100 lb. reinforced paper bags to increase the concussion effect of the bomb. They paid cash for the fertilizers. (CBS news report Friday morning April 20th, 1995)

3. The three middle eastern men were seen escaping from the scene of the blast in a brown Chevrolet and that this vehicle was later found abandoned at Dallas-Ft. Worth Airport. (From Haim Shibi's article in above question #1.)

4. The three middle eastern men were reported by CNN to have traveled on the highway in convoy with McVeigh when he was pulled aside by the highway patrol. (CNN Public Service announcement on behalf of the FBI a few months after the blast.)

5. Radio Teheran Iran reported immediately after the blast that it was "an internal American affair"? How did the Iranians know this so soon after the blast?

So the judge said that international terrorism was wild imagination. You be the judge.

As for TWA 800, theories abound about vapors and fumes in the gas tank causing an explosion, thus dismissing the theory of a missile.

1. **How did hundreds of eye witnesses see a missile going up to his the plane?**
2. **Why did the Air France flight just behind TWA 800 veer off precipitously to evade the missile?**
3. **Why did laboratories in Washington DC admit to explosive chemical residues on the wing between engines #3 and #4?**
4. **Why did the report from the laboratory say that the metallic configuration of the wing had been altered... that the melting of the metal could only have happened from explosive chemicals... that a gas tank explosion could not have generated a heat high enough to melt the metal of the wing?**
5. **There were at least two military pilots who saw a missile, probably a Soviet SAM, going up and hitting TWA 800?**
6. **Saddam Hussein promised the world a big surprise on Iraq's National Day — the same day TWA 800 was downed.**
7. **Retired Air Force General Parton was interviewed at 6-8 PM on September 18th, 1997 KTOK Radio and said that the evidence clearly showed that TWA 800 was brought down by a Soviet type missile. Thereby eliminating the possibility of it having been a friendly fire missile.**
8. **The NTSB video animation shows the airplane continuing to ascend and then plummeting straight down. Satellite imagery shows TWA 800 spiralling down as if the wing had been shot off.**
9. **So I ask you, my reader, who would fire a Soviet made missile at an American airliner?**

Again, is this a case of wild imagination or is a cover-up going on? Again, in Steven Emerson's "Jihad in America" the FBI reveals in November 1994 that fanatic Islamic plans included the shooting down or blowing up of U.S. aircraft. Ramzi Youssef, the mastermind behind the World Trade Center bombing also made ten bombs to blow up U.S. aircraft in the Far East. That is how he was apprehended.

Shouldn't Americans be warned? Does the people have the right to know or not to know?

In Hosea 4:6 it says: My people are destroyed for lack of knowledge:

I feel it is my duty to share that knowledge.

In November 1996, a report to the Congress of the United States of America was prepared by the Anti-Terrorism Task Force on Unconventional Warfare about an imminent war in the Middle East. Yet most Americans and even Israelis know nothing about such a war. (www. cmep.com - congressional report)

My fear is that when all this comes about, it will involve not only a war against Israel, but a war against America as well. Perhaps, the American economy, perhaps the world economy will crash with the international war of terrorism that will be waged by fanatic Islam.

In Ezekiel 33:6 it says: But if the watchman see the sword come, and blow not the trumpet, and the people be not warned; if the sword come, and take any person from among them, he is taken away in his iniquity; but his blood will I require at the watchman's hand.

This is why, with all the risk involved, I have written this book. Fanatic Islam is a global threat, and God will judge all of us and have mercy on us.

Victor Mordecai

Addenda

Throughout the writing of this book in its five editions, I have always tried to avoid dealing with Saddam Hussein in a frontal or confrontational manner. Firstly, I thought that he was not going to last. Secondly, this book deals with the phenomenon of fanatic Islam which will seem to last for quite a while, so my hopes were "ignore him, he will sooner or later disappear — deal with principles not individuals. Keep the book evergreen."

However, firstly, Saddam Hussein has not and probably will not be going away at his own free will in the near future, and secondly, this barbarian leader's behavior is in principle systematic to fanatic Islam, and perfectly in keeping with the whole Islamic world overview. With the latest information I have received, if anything, Saddam Hussein personifies fanatic Islam as a global threat. I am indeed keeping the book evergreen.

At this late date in December 1997, the whole Islamic world is solidly opposed to any kind of political or military action against Iraq be it from the U.S. or the West. The window of opportunity is now slammed shut to act against Saddam. The entire Islamic world empathizes and sympathizes with someone who is directly responsible for the deaths of one million Moslems in the Iran-Iraq war of 1980-88 and the additional deaths of, according to Saddam's own calculations one a half million Iraqis as a result of Desert Shield, Desert Storm and the resulting U.N. sanctions imposed on Iraq. Of course, the Iraqi regime blames the U.S. and the American people for these deaths even though they resulted from the actions of this war criminal Saddam Hussein.

The reason for including this addenda in the book is because Saddam has been actively pursuing revenge against the U.S. and will not cease. This is a threat to the American people, to the Jewish people (this includes the Christians who are considered Jews in the eyes of Islam) worldwide including Israel, and finally a threat to the world with the use of weapons of mass destruction.

Indeed U.S. Secretary of Defense William Cohen went on record on all major U.S. television and radio stations the first week of December 1997 explaining how Saddam Hussein had enough biological and chemical weapons to wipe out the entire human race. Secretary of Defense Cohen added that 28 major U.S. cities were known to be targeted for "nationalist and religious" terrorist attack in which these same weapons of mass destruction would be used.

Throughout my book, I discussed such terrorist actions as the counterfeiting of the U.S. dollar, the bombing of the twin towers of the World Trade Center in New York City, the bombing of the Murrah Federal Building in Oklahoma City, the downing of TWA 800, Ramzi Yusef's preparation of 12 bombs to blow up U.S. civilian airliners in the Far East as well as the hit teams deployed throughout the U.S. just waiting for orders to attack. Even though there are such hit teams in the U.S. and worldwide from Islamic countries other than Iraq, particularly from Iran, Syria, Lebanon, Sudan, the Palestinians and over 300 Fuqra Black Muslim hit teams, a pattern seems to be becoming clearer and clearer that Iraq is in the forefront — the vanguard of this international terrorism. What is sure, is that the common enemy of all these Islamic global terrorists are the Judeo-Christians whether they be in the U.S., Israel or worldwide. This week's pan-Islamic conference shows all the Islamic countries supporting Iraq against American western "aggression."

It was Saddam Hussein against the U.S. Now, Saddam has succeeded in turning the confrontation into pan-Islam against the U.S. Saddam has galvanized all the Islamic countries to confront the U.S. No more is there this much touted "Arab-American" alliance against Iraq as existed until September 29th, 1997. I am deeply disturbed that the U.S. Administration blames Israeli Prime Minister Benjamin Netanyahu for being an "obstacle" to this purported Arab-American alliance because of Israeli "intransigence" over the price Israel must pay the Palestinians for the U.S. to have an alliance with the Arabs against Saddam Hussein — an alliance that will never be. It is not because of Israel but because the U.S. squandered every opportunity it had to remove Saddam Hussein from power for either its self-serving purposes or because of superficiality, shallowness, and ineptness in knowledge of the realities of the Middle East.

I will never forget how Israel destroyed Iraq's OSIRAK nuclear reactor in 1981. Israeli military assessments at the time pointed to Iraq's plan to put together an invincible strategic machine that would inevitably allow Iraq to dominate if not gobble up Kuwait, the Gulf States, Saudi Arabia, Jordan and maybe even Syria. Of course, Saddam Hussein promised to erase Israel from the map. He saw himself and still sees himself as the reincarnation of Saladin, the Moslem hero who expunged the Christian crusaders from the Middle East 700 years ago.

Let us not forget that in 1981, Saddam was in the throes of a war he started with neighboring Iran. Israel surgically took out this reactor just before it went "on line" incurring the wrath of all the world. President Reagan was furious with Israel. But I think President Bush was thankful (in retrospect, of course) that Desert Shield and Desert Storm did not have to contend with an atomically weaponed Iraq. Israel paid the price for doing the world a great service.

In 1986, U.S. Naval Intelligence had some very alarming information about Iraqi development of biological and chemical weapons with which it was planning to "erase" Israel from the map. When U.S. Naval Intelligence refused to share this information with Israeli intelligence, a young naval intelligence officer asked his superiors about this. The answer of his superiors was; "We'll pick up the Jews off the beaches of Tel-Aviv." This young officer was later arrested for providing this same information to Israel that had been promised by the U.S. to Israel in an intelligence sharing agreement the U.S. had signed with Israel but that the U.S. was not keeping. This young officer's name is Jonathan Pollard. He is still incarcerated in December 1997 for keeping America's word to Israel.

In April 1990, Saddam Hussein announced he was ready now with enough biological and chemical weapons to erase half of Israel off the map. Again, as mentioned earlier in the book, Egyptian President Hosni Mubarak signed an agreement with Saddam Hussein, that Egypt would attack Israel two weeks after Iraq did, but Iraq miscalculated, and mistakenly attacked Kuwait causing Egypt great damages thereby negating or disrupting this Iraqi-

Egyptian alliance to attack Israel. God Almighty worked wondrously to harden Pharoah's heart thus deflecting Satan's wrath away from Israel.

When "Stormin' Norman" Schwartzkopf was somewhere on the road to Baghdad, President George Bush ordered him to halt, to about-face and leave Saddam in power. Big, big mistake. Here Saddam was teetering on the brink of the precipice. His cruel, inhuman regime could have been replaced. The U.S., the U.N., the world could have imposed from above a democratic, humane system in Iraq. The Iraqi people could have been saved over one million people dying from food and medicine sanctions imposed by the U.N. ad infinitum. Dear reader, don't think for a moment, that the Iraqi leadership will not hold the American people responsible for this. Vengeance was planned with the attempted assassination of President Bush when he visited Kuwait just after Desert Storm. The toppling of the twin trade towers in New York was intended to kill 20,000 Americans, thus dwarfing the Japanese attack on Pearl Harbor. Iraqi agent Ramzi Yusef prepared bombs to blow up 12 civilian American airliners in the Far East. One bomb succeeded in going off on a Manila — Tokyo bound flight. One passenger was sucked out of the plane and fell thousands of feet to his death.

As mentioned earlier in the book, Iraq has been following Iran's lead in counterfeiting U.S. dollar banknotes in order to destroy the economy of the "Great Satan" Christian USA.

Again, I was hoping not to have to use some newspaper articles from the Jerusalem Post Israeli English language daily, but considering what I will be quoting from in articles spanning the months February to August 1995, all I can say is "deja vu."

February 15th, 1995—page 1. MOSLEM EXTREMISTS TARGET WALL ST.

Marilyn Henry — New York

Wall Street is bracing for a possible terror attack after police said that they had received "uncomfortably credible" reports that Moslem extremists planned to strike at American capitalism, "Newsday" reported yesterday.

Law enforcement sources said they had received tips about a possible attack, although it was not clear what kind of attack was likely. Law enforcement officials were not sure what the target would be.

"From the language that was used, we think that a stock exchange is the likely target," sources told Newsday. The timing was to occur before the end of Ramadan.

Officials said the attack was to protest the trial of Sheik Omar Abdel-Rahman and 10 others charged with conspiracy in the February 1983 World Trade Center bombing.

Victor Mordecai: The World Trade Center bombing was masterminded by Ramzi Yusef, an Iraqi agent. Hence the Iraqi connection to a possible attack on Wall Street. On February 15th, this article appeared. There was no attack on Wall Street because security was beefed up. However, two months later on April 19th, the Murrah Federal Building was blown up in Oklahoma City.

The next article is on page 3 of the August 14th Jerusalem Post.

"NEW YORK AIRPORTS ON TERROR ALERT" by Marilyn Henry, New York

New York area airports are on the highest state of alert since the Gulf War after the report of a possible "suicide massacre" from Islamic fundamentalists.

The heightened security over the weekend is in addition to measures that went into effect at Kennedy, LaGuardia and Newark airports earlier in the week,

Kennedy, the main international hub was a specific target for terrorists, Newsday reported yesterday. The FBI received intelligence reports that Hamas and Hizbullah (Hamas is Palestinian and Hizbullah is Lebanese) were planning a strike, possibly a "suicide massacre," at the airport, the newspaper said, quoting unnamed law-enforcement officials.

The security precautions were taken in light of several events: the arrest of Mousa Abu Marzook, who is facing extradition to Israel on charges that he is linked to Hamas' terror activities (Israel dropped its extradition request. Abu Marzook was freed and traveled to Jordan where he is now Hamas leader in Jordan.); the current conspiracy trial of Sheikh Omar Abdul Rahman and nine others in a related terror case.

Finally, a week later on August 21, 1995, the Jerusalem Post carried this headline on its first page:

'SADDAM PLANNED TO INVADE KUWAIT, SAUDI ARABIA THIS MONTH'

Dateline Amman; Jordan — Top-ranking Iraqi defector Lt. Gen. Hussein Kamel Majid said yesterday his flight from Iraq had foiled plans by Saddam Hussein to invade Kuwait and Saudi Arabia this month.

He also described Saddam's son Uday, a rising power in Baghdad as "crazy and whimsical" and predicted that the regime would be toppled soon in a coup or revolution.

"The latest movement of a large number of troops toward Basra was aimed at entering Kuwait. All army units were informed to enter Kuwait and the eastern parts of Saudi Arabia," said Hussein Kamel, Saddam's son-in-law. "The move was reversed after... our departure."

His revelation appeared to confirm U.S. reports of "unusual" Iraqi troop movements.

The U.S. has reinforced its military presence in the Gulf to thwart potential Iraqi threat to Kuwait and Jordan.

Meanwhile, Rolf Ekeus, head of the U.N. Special Commission in charge of disarming Iraq, said Baghdad had handed over important data on its weapons programs after "a new turn" in relations with U.N. disarmament officials.

Victor Mordecai adds: The new turn in relations was probably in response to all the information Hussein Kamel Majid revealed with his defection to the west.

The three above articles are from 1995. And now again, in 1997, we see Saddam rearing his ugly head again. It is kind of like a person sick with a bacterial infection going to the doctor, getting a prescription of antibiotics and then taking just enough antibiotics to get rid of most of the symptoms, but not all of them. Then, as expected, the infection returns with a vengeance because the patient has not gone all the way to defeat the sickness. A newer more powerful antibiotic is prescribed, but then, again, the patient stops short of finishing off the sickness. In the final analysis, the bacteria develops enough resistance to be immune to any type of antibiotics. In this case, America is the patient and Saddam Hussein the bacteria. The patient dies.

The present constellation of political powers is lined up solidly now against the U.S. The U.S. could have finished off Saddam Hussein in 1991 when Schwartzkopf was on the outskirts of Baghdad. The Kurds of the north and Shiites of the south were betrayed by a fickle U.S. State Department and abandoned to their cruel fates at the hand of Saddam Hussein after the U.S. initially mobilized them. These potential allies will never again trust any U.S. administration. Hussein Kamel Majid and his brother were basically ignored by the U.S. after their debriefing with U.S. intelligence. It was because of these two brothers that the U.N. knew Iraq was hiding information about its massive program to produce weapons of mass destruction. As a result of their testimonies, Iraq all of a sudden "started to cooperate" and come clean. Because the west turned their backs on the Majid brothers, they returned to Iraq to be slaughtered by Saddam Hussein. The U.S. has basically blown every opportunity it had to depose Saddam Hussein. In the past, it was the Iraqi people who paid with tremendous suffering for America's failure to remove this mad tyrant. But now the turn of the U.S. and the world will come to pay for the negligence and ineptness which allowed Saddam Hussein to remain in power.

History repeats itself. Hitler could have been destroyed after his beer hall putsch of 1923. He could have been eliminated in 1933 as he assumed power. He could have been subdued by a forceful and wise leadership of England, France and the U.S. in the 1930's. Instead, his strategic agenda, as written in "Mein Kampf" were basically ignored. The world paid for this with World War II and the deaths of over 60 million people of all nations. And my people paid a third of our total population — or six million.

Today, I fear that more people may die than in World War II in what could be World War III. Iraqi as well as Islamic agents from all over the world are now pre-positioned throughout the U.S. and the world ready to carry out all kinds of mischief when orders are received from Baghdad, Damascus, Teheran, etc.

The day before TWA 800 came down, Saddam Hussein made a speech before his national assembly: "Tomorrow is Iraq's National Day and we will give the world a big surprise." (Dr. Laurie Mylroie, Washington, D.C.)

My conclusion here is not a happy one. Saddam's strategic goals were and remain to build up his war machine so that he can dominate and conquer the Middle East like the great conquering Saladin of the 13th century. Nothing in his thinking has changed since 1981. The only thing that has changed is that now, after the deaths of over two million Iraqis, America is in checkmate with Islamic terrorists on American soil. With the downing of U.S. aircraft, the blowing up of key buildings in the U.S., the attacking of America's oil sources in the Persian gulf by Iraqi weapons of mass destruction, the spreading of biological and chemical weapons will come the fall of Wall Street, the American economy, the dollar and what is perceived in the Islamic world as America the Great Christian Satan. And on the flag of Iraq is inscribed "Allah Akbar" or Allah is Greater (than the God of Abraham, Isaac and Jacob).

This is a terrible global problem that has nothing to do with Israel or Prime Minister Benjamin Netanyahu, and yet both are scapegoated for American incompetence and self-serving prostration to the petrodollar or "mammon". It is ironic that in spite of the hundreds of millions of dollars Yasser Arafat and the Palestinians have received in U.S. grants, they were and remain Saddam Hussein's, greatest and most enthusiastic supporters. Yet never a word in Washington or the media against them. Only Israel bears the onus. The blame for the present situation lies firmly in Washington, D.C., the White House and the State Department as well as other capitals worldwide.

I am not optimistic as to what man's wisdom can do. My faith is in what the Lord, God of Israel will do to defeat the Satan of Saddam Hussein and fanatic Islam. Still, we will all be judged by God for what we did or did not do to fight His battle. Those of us who believe in the God of Abraham, Isaac and Jacob must make our stand together at this time. We must not remain complacent. The future of humanity and civilization are hanging in the balance.

APPENDIX

Missionary Steve Wolcott confirms appearance of dysentery and other "Gulf War Syndrome" type afflictions in northern Zaire

On March 26th, 1996, I spoke in Springdale, Arkansas, at a "Blow the Shofar in Zion—Israel Prayer Conference." It was a meeting of intercessors and missionaries from all over the U.S. and the world.

After I discussed the confirmed atrocities against Christians in the Sudan by the Moslem fundamentalist government, especially the use of poison gas and other chemical and biological agents, provided by Iran, Pastor Steve Wolcott approached me. He congratulated me that finally someone was speaking out about the use of poison agents by Moslems against Christians. He continued saying that all of northern Zaire was now sick from these poisons blown by northerly winds across the border from southern Sudan, just thirty miles away. Everyone, not only Sudanese refugees, he said, was afflicted with this strange form of dysentery, one of the manifestations of the Gulf War Syndrome.

It took the U.S. Administration in Washington thirty years to admit the existence of Agent Orange. I wonder how long it will take them to admit the truth about Gulf War Syndrome.

Direct inquiries to:

**Victor Mordecai
P.O. Box 18209
Jerusalem, Israel 91181
Fax: 011 972 2 629 0574 Ext. 7157**

**For reordering this book in the U.S.
1-800-540-0828**

**www.vicmord.com
e-mail: vicmord2001@yahoo**